D0786939

The **Politically Incorrect Guide**™ to

SOCIALISM

The Politically Incorrect Guide™ to
SOCIALISM

Kevin D. Williamson

Since 1947
REGNERY
PUBLISHING, INC.
An Eagle Publishing Company • Washington, DC

Copyright © 2011 by Kevin D. Williamson

All rights reserved. No part of this publication may be reproduced or transmitted in any form or by any means electronic or mechanical, including photocopy, recording, or any information storage and retrieval system now known or to be invented, without permission in writing from the publisher, except by a reviewer who wishes to quote brief passages in connection with a review written for inclusion in a magazine, newspaper, or broadcast.

Cataloging-in-Publication data on file with the Library of Congress

ISBN 978-1-59698-649-7

Published in the United States by
Regnery Publishing, Inc.
One Massachusetts Avenue, NW
Washington, DC 20001
www.regnery.com

Manufactured in the United States of America

10   9   8   7   6   5   4   3   2   1

Books are available in quantity for promotional or premium use. Write to Director of Special Sales, Regnery Publishing, Inc., One Massachusetts Avenue NW, Washington, DC 20001, for information on discounts and terms or call (202) 216-0600.

Distributed to the trade by:
Perseus Distribution
387 Park Avenue South
New York, NY 10016

For Sara H. Duncan

CONTENTS

Chapter One

FRESH FRUIT FOR
ROTTING VEGETABLES

"The problem with capitalism is *capitalists*.
The problem with socialism is *socialism*."

—Willi Schlamm, Austrian ex-socialist

In March 2010, North Korean president Kim Jong Il finished up a pet project of his: resolving economic difficulties resulting from his regime's failed attempts at currency reform. He accomplished this by abducting and torturing several high-ranking members of his Korean Workers Party, who were beaten so badly that they could not open their eyes or speak as they were lashed to a post on the firing range at a military school in Pyongyang. Just as well for them; there was nothing to see except gun barrels, and nothing they might have said would have made much difference. Each was shot nine times for the crime of committing "treason against the people" in the course of enacting "unrealistic" currency reforms. Hundreds more elite party officials were dismissed, very likely to be sent to labor camps along with their families.

This was not Kim's first purge. In 1992, anticipating his assumption of power from his ailing father, Kim had organized the execution of twenty army officers and the expulsion of about 300 others. Hundreds more military officers were killed in a 1995 purge when Kim came to formal power. During the famine of 1995–98, which had been preceded by an intense propaganda campaign celebrating the healthful effects of subsisting on

Guess What?

★ Socialists and communists themselves acknowledge that socialism is not separate from communism

★ It is risk aversion, not revolutionary fervor, that drives socialism

★ State control is more important to the socialist than egalitarianism

one or two meals a day, millions of North Koreans died of starvation due to the disastrous policies associated with Kim's "Juche Idea" school of economics. According to the view from Pyongyang, the official state ideology—which goes by the irony-proof name "kimilsungism"—cannot fail, it can only be failed. So in reaction to the famine, the secretary of agriculture was denounced as an American spy and summarily executed, and thousands more officials were put to death, sent to camps, or otherwise disposed of. Kim's political-economic misadventure left as much as 12 percent of his country's population dead, and many more would have died had the famine not been alleviated by massive food aid from the hated capitalists in the United States of America.

If North Korea's experience is extreme, it is not alien to that of other similar nations, including those with more democratic systems than North Korea's.

Family Traditions

"I was shocked when I heard my uncle, Soo Jo, was looking for me. I didn't expect him to be alive."

Kim Jong Il, President, North Korea, *Chosun Ilbo*

A few months after Kim's 2010 purge, Venezuela was engulfed in political scandal as its state-run groceries ran out of essential foodstuffs such as milk and flour, while huge stockpiles of food were left to rot in government warehouses. A disastrous blend of corruption and incompetence, as fundamental a part of Venezuela's system as red flags and workers' slogans, had cost the hungry poor of that country as much as 75,000 tons of food—perhaps as much as one-fifth of the total annual imports of PDVAL, the main state-run enterprise tasked with distributing subsidized food to Venezuela's thousands of Soviet-style groceries. A former president of PDVAL's board of directors, all of whom were hand-picked by Chávez and his advisers, was duly arrested and charged with corruption, while Chávez protected a close adviser also implicated in the case.

Why the food was left to rot was a mystery; the most likely explanation is that PDVAL's political overseers, who fund their operations with revenues from Venezuela's state-run petroleum operations, were receiving kickbacks from the overseas suppliers and had never intended to distribute the food, which was stumbled upon by authorities working on an unrelated investigation. They had, the theory goes, simply placed the orders, collected their under-the-table commissions, and left the food to spoil, there being no further profit in actually distributing it.

Hungry for Change

"'The private sector seeks profit, and the government seeks the people's well-being,' [Venezuelan food minister Felix] Osorio told *National Geographic News* during a recent visit to the Pinto Salinas Mega Mercal. 'The free market doesn't call the shots—regulation does.'

"So sporadic shortages of basic foodstuffs have become routine for many of the country's citizens.

"...When food shortages became critical in Venezuela last year, for instance, Helen Mercado and Luis Boada visited store after store searching for milk for their three-year-old son. But many times the young couple had to settle for liquid yogurt, which is more widely available because it is unregulated."

National Geographic, July 2008

Chávez's response to the scandal was unequivocal. "We won't rest," he thundered. "We will get to the bottom of this case. But this will not divert us from our route toward our main goal—socialism!"[1]

Venezuela's experience is not entirely alien to the United States, either. And it is worth keeping in mind, for context, that Americans are only a few generations removed from the experience of real hunger. That has not stopped the U.S. government from adopting socialist policies that keep food off of Americans' dinner tables. Consider this report from Ann Crittenden, writing in the *New York Times* in 1981: "From afar, it looks like a red haze on the horizon. But...it [later] becomes clear that what lies in the distance is actually mounds of oranges. Stretching in all directions are millions and millions of navel oranges...all abandoned to rot under the California sun. The oranges have been dumped under what is known as a Federal marketing order."[2] In a later report, "Forbidden Fruit," Doug Foster wrote, "Oranges are left rotting so as to keep prices high for farmers and to keep consumers from buying oranges at lower prices. Does the government know what it is doing? Does it care? The response of USDA bureaucrat Ben Darling is, 'Oranges are not an essential food. People don't need oranges. They can take vitamins.'"[3]

There is a long history of such strange activity in the United States. John Steinbeck reported from a similar scene during the Depression: "The works of the roots of the vines, of the trees, must be destroyed to keep up the price, and this is the saddest, bitterest thing of all. Carloads of oranges dumped on the ground .... A million people hungry, needing the fruit—and kerosene sprayed over the golden mountains. There is a crime here that goes beyond denunciation."[4] But unlike the rotting food in Venezuela, the spoiled provisions in the United States—oranges, corn, silos full of grain—were not a crime; they were the intended result of public policy enacted during the New Deal and carried out through the Reagan era.

What Socialism Is, and What Socialism Isn't

"Socialism" is a word that means many things to many people, and socialism has taken many forms in the world. Socialism applies, with equal accuracy, to the totalitarian regimes of Kim Il-Jong, Joseph Stalin, and Fidel Castro, the authoritarian but nominally democratic government of Hugo Chávez, and the social democracies of Sweden and India. Some countries practice totalitarian socialism, in which all aspects of life are brought under political discipline; this is generally what we mean by the word communism, regardless of whether that political discipline is overseen by an organization calling itself the Communist Party.

Socialism's apologists insist socialism and communism are utterly different and non-comparable things; authoritarian apples and democratic oranges. This is entirely untrue; for that we have the socialists' own word and the communists' testaments as well. The most hardcore communists in the modern era—the rulers of Soviet Russia, Red China, and North Korea—routinely refer to their systems as "socialism," and especially, as "scientific socialism," the grand old Marxist term. Today's socialists, in unguarded moments (and often when speaking among themselves) acknowledge that socialism is socialism is socialism, and that while the question of form is not negligible (life under Stalin was immeasurably worse than life in the socialist England of the 1970s), it is a question of variation within a species, not variation between species. In a 2010 symposium in the socialist journal *Dissent*, Michael Walzer wrote,

> "Which socialism?" In the not-so-distant past, when Norberto Bobbio, the Italian political theorist, first asked this question, it was (or so it looks today) relatively easy to answer. There were only two choices: the version of socialism that prevailed in what we might think of as the Long East, which stretched from North Korea across the Soviet Union all the way to

Albania, and the version that prevailed in the Short West, from the Bonn republic to the British Isles.[5]

Some countries practice limited socialism within the context of an otherwise liberal democracy, with the pre-Thatcher United Kingdom being a typical example. And other countries have what civics textbooks sometimes call "mixed economies," with broadly liberal free-enterprise systems existing alongside state-owned or state-managed industries. Some nations are almost entirely dependent on a single socialized industry, such as the Arab oil emirates and their state-owned petroleum corporations. In many Western European social democracies, the healthcare systems and some heavy industries are socialist enterprises. In the United States, education, agriculture, and healthcare are to varying degrees operated by the state or subjected to socialist central planning through regimes of regulation, subsidies, and redistribution. This book will argue that it is possible to examine socialism both within fully socialist systems and within the socialized sectors of mixed economies, and that socialism, in all those contexts, exhibits consistent characteristics.

What are those characteristics? How can programs as different as North Korea's collective farms, Venezuela's state-run groceries, India's state-managed enterprises, and American public schools all be categorized as part of the same kind of system? And if the definition of *socialism* is that flexible, how can it mean anything at all?

To answer these questions, we must ask another: what is socialism? It's often difficult to get an honest or rational answer to that question.

A Communist Finds Religion

"If you understood what communism was, you would hope—you would pray on your knees—that one day we would become communist."

Jane Fonda, University of Michigan speech, 1970

Idealistic socialists in the West usually will tell you that "socialism" is anything other than what actual socialist governments have achieved in the real world. What is important to keep in mind is that socialism is not a particular set of political conditions, but a specific kind of economic arrangement. Socialism is not identical with left-wing politics, and social-ism is not confined to the Left. The various kinds of political systems that have arisen from socialist economies, from Soviet authoritarianism to India's "license raj," are in no small part responses to the inadequacies and contradictions inherent in socialist systems of production and distribu-tion—systems that seek to ignore or to subvert the laws of economics.

But the laws of economics can no more be set aside than can the laws of physics or biology. The political responses to the economic contradic-tions of socialism inevitably are conditioned by the culture in which the socialist system is operating. Cuban socialism was never going to look like the socialism of India, the socialism of Sweden, or the socialism of the U.S. public-school sector. But with a little work and the proper criti-cal approach, it is possible to distinguish, for example, which qualities of Indian socialism are *Indian* and which are *socialist*, which features of U.S. public-school systems inhere in our national culture and which derive from its socialist nature.

To do that, we will need a better working definition of socialism. Our model of socialism will have two main parts: 1. the public provision of non-public goods, and 2. economic central planning.

Socialism means, among other things, using political agencies to pro-vide goods and services that otherwise would be provided privately in the marketplace. In its most extreme form, socialism means government direction of the economy as a whole. Socialism in its milder expressions takes the form of nationalized industries (the Chilean copper-mining industry under Allende, Pakistan's petrochemical sector and heavy industries under Bhutto), government ownership or direction of firms (Alfa Romeo under Mussolini, the Japan National Railway), direct government provision of goods and services (the British Health Service), or government management of nominally private marketplace activities (farm subsidies in France, Fannie Mae in the United States).

A slightly more technical definition of socialism is this: *the public provision of non-public goods.* "Public goods" is a loose phrase, of course, and it means different things to different people.[6] For the purposes of this discussion, the expression will be used in its technical economic sense: "public goods" does not mean things that are good for the public or things that the public wants, but goods that by their nature cannot be easily provided by the free market, goods such as national defense, law enforcement, and certain kinds of public services.

Every government undertaking engaged in the public provision of non-public goods is an instance of socialism, at least at a trivial level. But socialism of that sort probably is better described as "welfare statism."[7] As a practical matter, all modern governments engage in some public provision of non-public goods, and, therefore, engage in what we might call low-level socialism, or *ad hoc* socialism. That does not mean that every government is, in a meaningful sense, socialist, or that it would make sense to describe every government that runs a public school or a state highway as socialist. There are questions of degree, and questions of judgment, and the answers to those questions will vary from case to case.

This Truth Is Self-Evident

"A government can't control the economy without controlling people. And [America's Founding Fathers] knew when a government sets out to do that, it must use force and coercion to achieve its purpose."

Ronald Reagan, "A Time for Choosing," 1964

So what distinguishes a garden-variety welfare state from a system that well and truly deserves to be identified as *socialist*? Beyond the public provision of non-public goods, a second factor—economic central planning—will be crucial to identifying and understanding what differentiates real socialism from the normal mishmash of welfare-state policies typically found in Western liberal democracies and affiliated forms of government.

What is important to realize is this: socialism, as we will be discussing it, is not entirely synonymous with welfare-statism. Socialism is not simply about the redistribution of wealth or income through taxes and government-assistance programs. Socialism is often described as a system that makes charity compulsory, but it is much more (and, at the same time, rather less) than that. Socialism means central planning. A food-stamp program is welfare; government-run farms and grocery stores are socialism. A government housing subsidy is welfare; government-run housing projects are socialism. A school voucher is welfare; a government-run school system is socialism.

Every advanced society engages in some form of charity, and, in practically every advanced society, some of that charitable activity is routed through the mechanism of the government. There are many reasons for that, including popular psychology and self-interest, but the reasons do not, for the most part, include efficiency or the ability to effectively serve the needs of the poor and vulnerable. One of the reasons for using the state in this manner is that government provision of services is thought to guarantee at least a minimal level of services. In reality it does no such thing, but it does create at least the illusion of a "social safety net." And that feeling of security, even though it is only tenuously based in reality, is politically valuable.

One of the real emotional fault lines running through all politics in advanced societies is the question of risk aversion. Small business owners, entrepreneurs, self-employed people, professional investors, and innovators are less risk averse than is the general population—almost by definition. Highly risk-averse people do not start businesses; instead, they tend to go to work for well-established businesses or, in many cases, for the government, particularly in education. They tend to work in and trust large institutions. That risk-averse population is the natural political home of socialism in the developed world, and particularly in the United States and the other English-speaking countries.

Highly risk-averse people are willing to trade some amount of efficiency, innovation, and progress for security. For instance, risk-averse Americans prefer the guaranteed low returns of the Social Security system (which in fact are, for most black men and for other shorter-lived Americans, guaranteed *losses*) to the higher returns and manageable risk of private savings and investments. They prefer the guaranteed mediocrity of the government school system to the possibility that a largely privatized system would poorly serve some students. In the recent debate over American healthcare reform, many of the better-informed and intelligent progressives understood that greater government management of the healthcare system would lead to losses in efficiency, innovation, and quality, but were willing to accept that trade-off in exchange for guaranteed access to care, even if that care is of diminished quality.

But you will practically never meet an entrepreneur who believes that Social Security is a better way to organize Americans' retirements than private investment accounts. Likewise, you will practically never meet a public-school teacher who believes otherwise. That is the covert psychology of socialism in advanced societies.

Unlike in nineteenth-century Europe or twentieth-century Asia, it is not revolutionary fervor that undergirds the movement toward socialism in the advanced world—in fact, it is its opposite: risk aversion. The Achilles' heel of socialism is that political organization of a given activity does not in fact eliminate risk, or even reduce it in a reliable and predictable way. As of this writing, the U.S. Social Security system is many trillions of dollars short of having the funds it needs to actually pay the benefits it has supposedly guaranteed, and it is almost certain that some combination of higher taxes, means testing, and benefits reduction will result in millions of Americans' failing to receive the benefits they were promised. In other words, the government guarantee of benefits is no guarantee at all.

Similarly, the failing government-school system does not guarantee that poor and minority students will escape the crippling, lifetime burden of receiving a shoddy education at exorbitant expense, but the opposite—it guarantees that the great majority of them are deprived of the educational opportunities enjoyed by the white middle class. (And they *will* pay a higher price for their "free public education," too: federal tax

Keeping Hope Alive

"Through its own internal feuding…the SP [Socialist Party] exhausted itself forever and further reduced labor radicalism in New York to the position of marginality and insignificance from which it has never recovered. The story is a sad but also a chastening one for those who, more than half a century after socialism's decline, still wish to change America. Radicals have often succumbed to the devastating bane of sectarianism; it is easier, after all, to fight one's fellows than it is to battle an entrenched and powerful foe. Yet if the history of Local New York shows anything, it is that American radicals cannot afford to become their own worst enemies. In unity lies their only hope."

Princeton undergraduate thesis by Elena Kagan, U.S. Supreme Court Justice appointed by President Obama, *New Yorker*, June 4, 2010

policy lavishly subsidizes homeownership for middle-class Americans, offsetting the modest property-tax bills that accompany it. Conversely, the poor tend to live in rental housing, struggling to pay rents inflated by the higher real rates of taxation levied on apartments and other commercial real estate.)

Socialist central planning always works best for the class that produces the central planners, who can see to it that their own interests are relatively well served, which is why in the United States socialism is a phenomenon of the middle class, not the working class. It is, contrary to the Hollywood version of American politics, also a corporate phenomenon; Big Business is a reliable friend of central-planning regimes, because large enterprises believe, correctly, that they will be able to use the planning apparatus to serve their own interests, for instance, by using heavy regulatory burdens to prevent new competitors from entering their markets.

And yet socialism retains a certain allure, even though in the United States and some other countries it usually is forced to go by another name—liberalism, progressivism, "putting people over profits," etc.

The Plan: The Alpha and Omega of Socialism

Beyond risk aversion, another main source of ideological sustenance for socialism, rarely spoken of in public, also is psychological: using the apparatus of the state to enforce charity gives one the delectable satisfaction derived from the exercise of virtue—with none of its costs. This is why socialists make so much of their commitment to the poor—a theoretical commitment whose practical fruits are hardly anywhere to be seen in the socialist regimes with which the world has documentable experience. It is also why socialists intentionally conflate socialism with welfare-statism and simple charitable impulses. Socialism, the writer and publisher Roger Kimball notes in *The New Criterion*,

> is optimism translated into a political program. . . . Socialism is also unselfishness embraced as an axiom: the gratifying *emotion* of unselfishness, experienced alternately as resentment against others and titillating satisfaction with oneself. The philosophy of Rousseau, which elevated what he called the "indescribably sweet" feeling of virtue into a political imperative, is socialism *in ovo*. "Man is born free," Rousseau famously exclaimed, "but is everywhere in chains." That heart-stopping conundrum—too thrilling to be corrected by mere experience—is the fundamental motor of socialism. It is a motor fueled by this corollary: that the multitude unaccountably colludes in perpetuating its own bondage and must therefore be, in Rousseau's ominous phrase, "forced to be free."
>
> . . . The socialist pretends to have glimpsed paradise on earth. Those who decline the invitation to embrace the vision are not just ungrateful: they are traitors to the cause of human perfection. Dissent is therefore not mere disagreement but treachery. Treachery is properly met not with arguments but (as circumstances permit) the guillotine, the concentration camp, the purge.[7]

Kimball is surgically correct about the socialist pathos, but it has little to do with the socialist program as it actually operates. Government-enforced charity is of course coercive by its nature; the use of the state to execute the redistribution of wealth, income, or other goods is both morally and economically complicated. But it is not sufficient, on its own, to constitute socialism. Central planning, not simple redistribution, is the defining feature of socialism. Under socialism, THE PLAN is everything.

The presence of THE PLAN, and the empowerment of THE PLANNERS, is to socialism what the Eucharistic sacraments are to Christians, what the Mosaic Law is to the Jews, what enlightenment is to the Buddhists: it is the fundamental expression of what is good and true.

When THE PLAN conflicts with the desire to redistribute income or to subsidize the poor and the working class, THE PLAN always prevails. Indeed, even Mikhail Gorbachev, a committed socialist who believed he could save the Soviet Union by reforming it, gave up on the idea of equalizing incomes when doing so interfered with the ability of central authorities to implement THE PLAN. "Wage-leveling," he told the Soviets' Central Committee in a 1988 speech, "has a destructive impact not only on the economy but also on people's morality, and their entire way of thinking and acting. It diminishes the prestige of conscientious, creative labor, weakens discipline, destroys interest in improving skills, and is detrimental to the competitive spirit in work. We must say bluntly that wage-leveling is a reflection of petty bourgeois views which have nothing in common with Marxism-Leninism or scientific socialism."[8] Such sentiments would be at home at the annual luncheon of any American Chamber of Commerce—except for the scientific socialism part.

What Gorbachev is making clear here—and what too many critics of socialism fail to understand—is that the necessary thing from the socialists' point of view is not egalitarian economic outcomes, but state control. And that control need not be enacted nationwide or imposed by a single-party dictatorship of the Chinese or Soviet sort. State direction comes in many degrees and can take many forms, from Venezuela's nationalizations to FDR's cartels to Richard Nixon's regime of wage-and-price controls. American socialists for years have been eager to use the Medicare/Medicaid system to impose a system of price controls on pharmaceutical companies and other medical-service providers—and the 2010 legislation we know as ObamaCare today lays the groundwork for empowering them to further do so. Stalin argued for "socialism in one country," while American progressive argue for socialism in one industry—or, one industry at a time.

The modern experience suggests that the economist Ludwig von Mises was only partly correct when he wrote, "The socialistic State owns all material factors of production and thus directs it."[9] That was true for the authoritarian, single-party powers of his day. In our own time, the converse is a more accurate description of the real economic arrangement: under socialism, the state directs the material factors of production *as if it owned them*. The state does not have to actually own factories, mines, or data centers if it has the power to dictate, in minute detail, how business is conducted within them. Regulation acts as a proxy for direct state ownership of the means of production.

Even in its more dispersed modern forms, socialist central planning is fairly easy to spot because it has an easily identifiable signature: failure. Socialism reliably produces economic dysfunction when applied nationally (the USSR, China, India, Chile, Vietnam), when applied in modified forms across mixed economies (postwar Britain's nationalized industries), and when applied to particular sectors within largely capitalist economies (national healthcare programs). Pockets of socialism found within largely liberal countries can be evaluated—*as socialism*—regardless of the fact that they are operating within a largely non-socialist context, just as the limited free-market activities that were permitted within Soviet Russia or Deng Xiaoping's China can be evaluated as free-enterprise initiatives. Socialist economic failures spring from well-understood defects within the form of organization itself; those failures are not dependent upon the intelligence, goodwill, or moral character of those who are attempting to implement a socialist system, though often enough venal human failings have magnified the inherent problems of socialism.

Socialism's main defects are the inability of political decision-makers to make rational decisions without the information provided by prices generated by marketplace transactions; the misalignment of incentives and resources; and the subjugation of economic necessities to political mandates with no basis in material economic reality. It is the last of these, above all, that makes socialism dangerous. As Mises's colleague F. A. Hayek argued in *The Road to Serfdom*, central planners frustrated by their inability to mold the economic world to their will inevitably are tempted to run roughshod over the rights and interests of the individuals they purport to serve. Sometimes this takes the relatively innocuous form of high-handed officials in the Canadian public-health service denying a procedure or timely access to care; sometimes it takes one of the diverse forms explored with such horrific vigor by Kim Jong Il.

Hayek's diagnosis, which is widely misunderstood and exaggerated, is not perfect, but he was correct that there is a path that connects the various permutations of state planning; in other words, those rotting oranges in California, that soured milk in Venezuela, the petty depredations of India's license raj, and the purges of Castro and Kim are all stops on the road to serfdom.

Chapter Two

YES, "REAL SOCIALISM" HAS BEEN TRIED—AND IT HAS FAILED

"Real socialism has never been tried." That is a standard line of argument from socialism's apologists, and it is a high-school debaters' trick. The shortcomings of socialism, as practiced in the real world—shortcomings that range from those mountains of oranges in California to the mountains of skulls that Pol Pot piled up in Cambodia—are dismissed as deviations from "real socialism." This line of argument might be restated in this way: "The ideal version of my system is preferable to the non-ideal version of your system."

Of course it is true that a pure, undiluted, uncorrupted, ideal expression of the socialist state has never existed, just as an entirely unfettered, perfectly competitive expression of capitalism has never existed. There never has been an ideal constitutional republic, liberal democracy, or technocratic management state. Ideals do not exist; the literal meaning of the word *utopia* is "no place." Utopias exist only in the imaginations of political idealists and stoned poli-sci undergraduates.

A variation on this is the argument that goes, "Socialism is great in theory, but it doesn't work in practice." Is socialism great in theory? And if the theory is so great, why do the results always disappoint? In truth, the theory behind socialism is deeply flawed: it is intellectually narrow, inhumane, and deeply irrational in that it fails to account for the ways in

Guess What?

★ Socialism in theory is just as defective as socialism in practice

★ The dysfunctions of socialism stem partly from Marx's moralizing

★ Capitalism invests more faith in everyday people than does socialism

which knowledge works in a society. Socialism in theory is every bit as bad as socialism in practice, once you understand the theory and stop mistaking it for the common and humane charitable impulse.

Comparing the socialist ideal to the capitalist one is an exercise in intellectual frippery. What we can do, however, is look at how socialism has operated in the real world. To do this is to operate under the radical theory that *socialism is what socialism does*, not what socialists would like socialism to be. But the idea that the USSR, Cuba, Venezuela, Vietnam, China, and others have failed socialism—not that socialism has failed them—persists. And it persists at relatively high levels of intellectual discourse, as in left-wing patron saint Noam Chomsky's shameful defense of the genocidal Khmer Rouge.

But it also exists in low-level discourse, where this notion perhaps does the most damage. Consider this admittedly unsophisticated but entirely typical exchange from an online debate: "Just for the record—communism has never existed, not a single day. Today you can only judge the idea of it. [The] USSR tried to build communism, but they've failed. China is still on its way. Communism is utopia—everyone is equal, there's no money, everyone just gets what they need."[1] This was followed by, "Communism in theory, great; in practice it just doesn't work."[2] Other observations included these: "Sure, most communism has failed; however, this is not due to a fundamental flaw in the theory, rather it is due to a flaw in implementation,"[3] and "Obviously, absolute communism doesn't work. Nor does absolute capitalism. However, in direction and ideals, it leaves the overwhelming majority much better off. Look at Venezuela, Cuba, and even much of Europe. They don't have nearly the disparity and class warfare problems that hardcore capitalists do. It leaves the masses in a much better and happier environment rather than allowing a select few to inherent wealth generation after generation."[4]

Such is the sophomoric appeal of socialism, but we need not limit ourselves to actual sophomores. An extraordinary number of national leaders, many of them among the world's best-educated people, have fallen for the fool's gold of central planning. In the West, this has contributed to economic stagnation and political calcification. In the Third World, it has led to absolutely tragedy. As former secretary of state Zbigniew Brzezenski notes in *The Grand Failure*:

> In different ways, the new governments of such major countries as India or Indonesia and of the new African states adopted some form of state socialism as the norm, though in every case insisting that they were blending it with their own specific national cultures. The leader of West Africa's new state of Guinea, Sékou Touré, responding to [Soviet leader Nikita] Krushchev, expressed that mood when he stated, "The Marxism which served to mobilize the African populations, and in particular the working class, has been amputated of those of its characteristics which did not correspond to the African realities." Nonetheless, the new leaders did find the Soviet support helpful and were inclined to flirt with Soviet-propagated doctrines, especially for political reasons. They were particularly attracted by Leninist techniques for the seizure and maintenance of power, and the concept of a disciplined and hierarchical ruling party was especially appealing to the new generation of rulers.
>
> . . . In the 1970s, several African countries thus embraced Marxism as their doctrine and proclaimed themselves to be engaged in the task of building socialism. Six—Angola, Mozambique, Madagascar, the Congo, Benin, and Ethiopia— even went so far as to adopt Marxism-Leninism as their guiding framework and stressed their fidelity to the broad outlines of the Soviet experience in building socialism. Nine others— Algeria, Libya, Cape Verde, Guinea-Bissau, Guinea, Sao Tome

and Principe, Zambia, Tanzania, and the Seychelles—became self-avowed socialist regimes, though stressing the centrality of their own national conditions in the actual implementation of socialist goals and avoiding any explicit identification with Leninism. All of them, however, did elevate the state into the central organ of socioeconomic change.[5]

Crime and Punishment in a Workers' Paradise

"The [Cuban] government claims it takes no political prisoners. The numbers provided by human rights agencies—an estimated 500,000 since 1959, with thousands executed—tell a different story. In Castro's Cuba, it is a crime to meet to discuss the economy, to write letters to the government, to report on political developments, to speak to international reporters, to advocate human rights, to visit friends or relatives outside your local area of residence without government permission. Cubans are arrested without warrants and prosecuted for 'failing to denounce' fellow citizens, for general 'dangerousness,' and, should some crime not be covered by these criminal code provisions, for 'other acts against state security.'

"...Cubans found guilty under this criminal justice system—and their fate is rarely in doubt—often serve 10 to 20 years in jail for political crimes. But most Cuban criminals are not political. A large proportion of the estimated 180,000 to 200,000 common criminals in Cuba's 500 prisons are people who broke the law by killing their own pigs, cattle and horses and selling the excess meat on the black market."

Larry Solomon, *National Post*, May 2003

Of course our anonymous online commenter, praising the wonders of Cuba and Venezuela, would not want to deal with such basketcases as Ethiopia or the Congo. But the Congo is easy pickings for the critic of socialism. Let us do that commentator the courtesy of examining the cases he holds up as exemplars of socialism: the Venezuela-Cuba model and the more socialist corners of Europe. There is something to his observations. (Not much, and not what he thinks, but something.) Let us look at the world's various models of socialism and the representative countries. Let us look at their prosperity, disparity, and class-warfare problems, as compared to more capitalist countries. And, above all, let us look, as our commentator suggested, at the directions and ideals at work. In fact, let us begin with those.

Karl Marx, Lady Gaga, and the Labor Theory of Value

At the heart of the difference between capitalism and socialism is a question about the calculation of economic value. In a free-market economy, economic values are established economically; that is, a product is worth what you can sell it for on the marketplace. Ayn Rand's followers, who are some of the most energetic defenders of capitalism in the world, call themselves "Objectivists," but in truth capitalism assumes a radical *subjectivism* in the marketplace. The real, objective economic value of things is identical to how people subjectively value them.

We can debate whether Lady Gaga or J. S. Bach is the superior musical composer (okay, *no we can't*, but never mind that for now), but what is certain is that in the first decade of the twenty-first century, Her Ladyship commanded a larger market share than did Mr. Bach. Likewise, pornographic actresses may command higher salaries than do professors of philosophy. Consumers may have bad taste, they may have immoral tastes, but their tastes are what their tastes are, and the market allows us to understand them.

Look at it this way: a top-flight surgeon does not command high wages because of his intelligence, his skill, or his expensive education, important as those things may be. He earns a big salary because his services are highly valued by the people who want them. He may be a brain surgeon doing life-saving work, or he may be a cosmetic surgeon tweaking a nose in Beverly Hills. A surgeon's work may be, in some sense, more socially important than a professional basketball player's or a pop star's. It may be socially less important than a priest's or a teacher's. But the reason your average surgeon earns more than a priest or a teacher, but less than an NBA point guard or a pop princess, has nothing to do with any objective features or qualities of his work. It has nothing to do with the moral value of his work: boob-jobs pay just as well as treating kids for cancer. Capitalism's approach, in other words, is to answer economic questions *economically*. This theory is not normative; it has nothing to say about whether people *should* value goods and services in the way they do.

Socialism breaks with capitalism on precisely this issue. It seeks to infuse the fundamental, deep processes of the economy—the setting of prices—with moral meaning. Indeed, normative, moralistic methods for calculating economic values have obsessed socialists and other utopian thinkers for more than a century. It is one of history's great ironies that capitalists built decent and humane societies on the basis of an amoral approach to the economics of pricing, whereas socialists built exploitative and inhumane societies on the basis of a morally inflamed approach to economics. Of those normative approaches to prices and wages, the best known comes from the father of socialism, Karl Marx, and it is called the "Labor Theory of Value."

In broad strokes, Marx holds that the real value of a product is measured by the labor necessary to produce it, regardless of the market price or value of other material inputs. If it takes twice as much labor to produce widgets as it does to produce gadgets, then widgets are twice as valuable, to Marx, in real economic terms, as gadgets are. "That which determines the magnitude of the value of any article," he writes in *Capital*, "is the amount of labour socially necessary, or the labor-time socially necessary, for its production."[6] Marx's analysis is morally normative in that he insists that, since labor is the measure of value, wages must equal the price of the product. The mere existence of profits—squeezing economic value out of a product beyond what workers are paid—for Marx was proof of capitalists' exploitation of workers. It was indistinguishable from outright theft.

Marx was not entirely simplistic, and he made room for the fact that some kinds of labor are going to be worth more than others. (He is, it must be said, sometimes vague, sometimes abstruse; one can derive many meanings from conflicting and inconsistent passages in his work. One may quote Marx to all ends, just as one may quote Scripture to all ends.) In *The Poverty of Philosophy* he writes:

> Does labor time, as the measure of value, suppose at least that the days are *equivalent*, and that one man's day is worth as much as another's? No.

Jokes: The One Thing Communism Produces in Abundance

A poor, starving citizen of North Korea takes it upon himself to protest in front of Kim Jong Il's official residence. He yells over the fence, "We have no food! We have no electricity! We have no water! We have nothing!"

Naturally, he is seized by the local gestapo, who take him into one of Pyongyang's many police dungeons and interrogate him. After they're done, they decide to give him a good scare, so they tie him to a chair and point a gun at his head. He doesn't know it's full of blanks. The policeman pulls the trigger—BANG!—and says, "Let that be a lesson to you." To which the dissident replies, "We have no food! No electricity! No bullets! Nothing!"

Let us suppose for a moment that a jeweler's day is equivalent to three days of a weaver; the fact remains that any change in the value of jewels relative to that of woven materials, unless it be the transitory result of the fluctuation of demand and supply, must have as its cause a reduction or an increase in the labor time expended in the production of one or the other. If three working days of different workers be related to one another in the ratio 1:2:3, then a change in the relative value of their products will be a change in the same proportion of 1:2:3. Thus values can be measured by labour time, in spite of the inequality of value of different working days.[7]

Got that? Good. Adam Smith, the supreme anti-Marx in the popular imagination, entertained a version of a labor theory of value himself, and he explains the issue slightly differently in *The Wealth of Nations*:

But though labor be the real measure of the exchangeable value of all commodities, it is not that by which their value is commonly estimated. It is often difficult to ascertain the proportion between two different quantities of labour. The time spent in two different sorts of work will not alone determine this proportion. The different degrees of hardship endured, and of ingenuity exercised, must likewise be taken into account. There may be more labor in an hour's hard work, than in two hours easy business; or, an hour's application to a trade which it costs ten years' labor to learn, than in a month's industry at an ordinary and obvious employment. But it is not easy to find any accurate measure, either of hardship or ingenuity. In exchanging, indeed, the different productions of different sorts of labor for one another, some allowance is commonly made for both. It is adjusted, however, not by any accurate measure, but by the higgling and bargaining of the market, according to that sort of rough equality, which though not exact, is suffi-cient for carrying on the business of common life.[8]

Here we begin to understand the real moral flavor of socialism. Adam Smith, a classical liberal, created a school of economics that took into account human error, human foibles, and human shortcomings. Eschew-ing any rigid ideology, he had faith in the "higgling and bargaining of the market"—which is to say, faith in people—and was satisfied with a sys-tem that, for all its imperfections, is "sufficient for carrying on the busi-ness of common life."

Socialism, on the other hand, became a creed of revolutionaries, and it retains its revolutionary characteristics even today, when the dream of worldwide socialist revolution is as limp and dingy as a sweaty Che Gue-vara T-shirt. That kernel of, "Hey, let's pick up an AK-47 and solve this problem" think-ing always is there. It does not begin with Marx, but Marx made it orthodoxy, and his writing is florid with angry, puritanical moralism. His critique of liberalism is not just economic, but moral, and scaldingly so: "Capital is dead labor, which, vampire-like, lives only by sucking living labor, and lives the more, the more labor it sucks."[9] When it comes to philosophy, Marx wrote, "The point is not merely to understand the world, but to change it."[10]

The question of how we set prices and wages may seem, at some level, like a trivial one, but it is the cornerstone of socialism. Once a socialist central-planner is empow-ered to go into the marketplace and start

...And Goodnight, Liberty

Together,
We can take everything:
Factories, arsenals, houses, ships,
Railroads, forests, fields, orchards
And turn 'em over to the people who work.
Rule 'em and run 'em for us people who work.

Langston Hughes, "Good Morning, Revolution"

issuing *diktats*—that the value of X is something other than what the producer and consumer of X have agreed it is, and that the world must bend to that judgment—then a cascading array of political problems and questions must follow. The first one is this: if prices aren't set in the marketplace, then who sets them? And how do our new lawgivers know what they should be? That is the topic of our next chapter.

Chapter Three

THE PRICE OF BEING WRONG: SOCIALISM AND THE GREAT CALCULATION DEBATE

Marx's attitude toward economics was energetically moral, and responses to socialism have been energetically moral as well. But the most important objection to socialism is a technical one, not a moral one. Although the moral case against socialism is indeed powerful, and will be discussed later in this book, its real intellectual deathblow was dealt in 1920 by Ludwig von Mises based on the relatively dry and technical question of the use and nature of prices in an economy.

As we know from our discussion of the Labor Theory of Value, socialists of the Marxian bent hold prices to be at some level *objective*. In part, this is an outgrowth of socialism's pretense that it is a scientific system for understanding and organizing a society. If economic values are in constant flux—as is known by anybody who has followed the stock market or observed pricing trends at your local grocery store—then central planning is impossible. To counteract that criticism, socialism posits that economic values are fixed and knowable. For the socialist, a product has a certain value, and it is a moral imperative that the worker be compensated at a level equal to the value of the thing produced.

Under the socialist understanding, prices are endogenous, an aspect of the thing itself, reflecting the material, resources, time, expertise, and—above all—the labor involved in its creation. But for Mises, and for practically all modern economists, prices are exogenous, reflecting only how

Guess What?

★ Socialism is an intellectual parasite of capitalism

★ Rational planning, to the extent socialism requires, is impossible

★ "Socialist prices" is an oxymoron

people value a particular product. This may seem like an oversimplification—a product is only worth what you can sell it for—but, in practice, the radical subjectivism of Mises provides an infinitely richer and more nuanced model of pricing—and thus of human action—than does the static Marxist model. That's because the Mises model asks not only, "What is it worth?" but, "What is it worth? To whom? At what time? In what context? In relation to what other goods?"

Mises not only rejected Marx's theory of pricing, he went a step further, arguing that the lack of real market prices in a socialist economy would make economic calculation *impossible*. If we define socialism as economic central planning conducted in accord with rational economic calculation, Mises argued, socialism is not just impractical, but beyond realization. That is to say, *socialism is impossible*, because without prices there can be no economic calculation, and therefore, no economic planning in the real sense of the phrase. To the extent that the socialist powers of Mises' day—the Soviet Union prominent among them—engaged in economic calculation, they were able to do so only because prices were being calculated in the capitalist economies.

Socialism, Mises argued, was not only a material and economic parasite succored by capitalist prosperity, but also an intellectual parasite. In other words, socialism needed capitalism to do its thinking for it. As Mises put it in his magisterial *Socialism*:

> The problem of economic calculation is the fundamental problem of Socialism. That for decades people could write and talk about Socialism without touching this problem only shows how devastating were the effects of the Marxian prohibition on scientific scrutiny of the nature and working of a socialist economy.
>
> To prove that economic calculation would be impossible in the socialist community is to prove also that Socialism is

impracticable. Everything brought forward in favour of Socialism during the last hundred years, in thousands of writings and speeches, all the blood which has been spilt by the supporters of Socialism, cannot make socialism workable. The masses may long for it ever so ardently, innumerable revolutions and wars may be fought for it, still it will never be realised. Every attempt to carry it out will lead to syndicalism or, by some other route, to chaos, which will quickly dissolve the society, based upon the division of labour, into tiny autarkous groups.

.... The attempt of the Russian Bolsheviks to transfer Socialism from a party programme into real life has not encountered the problem of economic calculation under Socialism, for the Soviet Republics exist within a world which forms money prices for all means of production. The rulers of the Soviet Republics base the calculations on which they make their decisions on those prices. Without the help of these prices their actions would be aimless and planless. Only so far as they refer to this price system, are they able to calculate and keep books and prepare their plans.

.... We know indeed that socialist enterprises in single branches of production are practicable only because of the help they get from their non-socialist environment. State and municipality can carry on their own enterprises because the taxes which capitalist enterprises pay, cover their losses. In a similar manner Russia, which left to herself would long ago have collapsed, has been supported by finance from capitalist countries. But incomparably more important than this material assistance, which the capitalist economy gives to socialist enterprises, is the mental assistance. Without the basis for calculation which Capitalism places at the disposal of Socialism, in the shape of market prices, socialist enterprises would never be carried on, even within single branches of production or individual countries.[1]

Socialist thinkers misunderstand the role of prices. Prices are not a static measure of the effort that went into making a product. Rather, prices are a kind of epistemological interface, facilitating the exchange of information about what producers are producing and what consumers are consuming, what producers want to produce and what consumers want to consume.

Milk: It Does an Economy Good

Take a simple example: milk. Imagine what it would take, in terms of sheer information, to run a socialist distribution network for milk in the United States. Some people, such as vegans or the lactose intolerant, consume no milk. But some households consume large quantities of the drink: those with many kids, those who use lots of milk products in their cooking, etc. Others may consume varying amounts; in July, when it's hot and humid, a family might prefer lemonade, but it might consume a lot of milk in August if it's whipping up a bunch of home-made ice cream for a big family reunion.

In addition to quantity calculations, there are various questions to answer, too: whole milk or skim, 1 percent or 2 percent? Do you prefer more expensive organic milk or cheaper factory-farmed milk? And if you prefer the pricier organic stuff, how much more are you willing to pay for it? What about soy milk? Chocolate milk? The delicious Pennsylvania Dutch treat known as vanilla milk?

There are 115 million households in the United States. If we imagine a weekly milk-consumption budget for each of them, that's 5.98 billion household-weeks to plan for. Adding in a fairly restrictive list of variables—

call it zero to twenty quarts a week, four levels of fat content, organic/nonorganic, soy/dairy, and three flavor options—you end up with around 6 *trillion* options to choose from.

These are the choices facing our committee of central planners—and let's just assume our planners are the best and brightest the world has to offer, with the temperaments of angels, totally unswayed by the quotidian concerns of politics or the influence of the various competing dairy lobbies (i.e., let's assume they are not human beings as we know them to exist), and that they have at their disposal a vast array of top-flight supercomputers. If they took just one second to consider each of these options, it would take them 190,128 years just to run through the possibilities of one year's milk consumption in the United States. That's a lot of calculation. When cen-

And Don't Even Get Me Started on the Milk!

"How can you govern a country in which there are 246 kinds of cheese?"

———

Charles de Gaulle, saying more than he knew

tral planners say they're considering all the options and taking all the information into account, they are never telling the truth. They do not even know what the options are—because they *cannot* know.

But even if the planners had some miraculous way to consider all the options and to take all of the information into account, where would they get the information? They could send out surveys to every household, asking them about their milk-consumption preferences for the following year. But would they get accurate answers? Probably not. People often lie on opinion surveys, providing answers that simply communicate what they imagine to be some desirable quality about themselves. For instance, newspaper companies, terrified about their declining readerships, frequently survey Americans about what they want in a newspaper, and the answers usually are:

1. More foreign news
2. More in-depth/investigative reporting
3. More cultural news

In truth, the most-read sections of most newspapers are:

1. Obituaries
2. Sports scores
3. Letters to the editor

In other words, consumers' *stated* preferences are at odds with their *revealed* preferences. We say we want to watch culturally enriching PBS programs, but we actually watch *American Idol*.

Another complicating factor is that consumers do not know what their future needs and desires will be. If you're planning your household's milk consumption in January, you may not plan adequately for August's family reunion—because you do not know there will be a family reunion in August. You do not know how many kids are coming to your daughter's birthday party in May. You may not know that you're going to have a new baby in nine months. (Granted, the more assertive socialist regimes are pretty aggressive about helping you to "plan" that last contingency—ask a Chinese family.)

But what Hayek and Mises understood was that this end-consumer question was only a tiny part of the problem facing central planners. As difficult as it is to plan for consumers' actual preferences—Mises would say *impossible*—the much larger and more intractable problem is the capital structure necessary to meet those needs. Imagine that the planners calculate that 10 percent of consumers will prefer organic milk to non-organic milk. (Of course, in a non-price economy more people will prefer the more expensive options, but let's set aside that problem for the moment.) Calculating that one-tenth of the dairy output should be organic, they order the construction of one organic dairy for every nine non-organic dairies.

Dairies are large and complex operations. Roads must be built to service them, along with fleets of trucks, vast arrays of machinery and tools for maintaining the machinery, housing for the workers, etc. And, of course, in a centrally planned economy, you can't just go out and buy those trucks on the free market; you have to plan and build factories, mines and steelworks, rubber plantations, oil wells, and gasoline refineries. All of this adds to the information overload that makes it impossible to rationally plan an economy when you lack the information communicated through prices.

Inevitably, the central planners are going to get some of their calculations wrong, because they won't be making calculations, but educated guesses—at best. Say the demand for organic milk turns out to be much stronger than 10 percent—say it's 30 percent. How can the planners meet their citizens' milk-consumption preferences then? They've already built their dairies, and 90 percent of their output is non-organic. They've already built roads, transportation systems, apartment buildings, and a vast infrastructure to support their assumption of a 10 percent organic milk preference. Their choices are not good: they can try to retrofit the old non-organic dairies to make them organic, or they can build new organic dairies and let the surplus capacity at their non-organic dairies fall into disuse, an enormous waste of resources and effort.

Most likely, the central planners will simply refuse to accommodate their citizens' preferences. They will condemn their taste for organic milk as a bourgeois extravagance. In the more robustly socialist economies, the planners will inform the citizens what their preferences are rather than the other way around. In any case, you can be sure of three things:

1. Consumers' actual preferences will not be satisfied.

2. Resources will be inefficiently allocated.

3. Something other than rational, disinterested economic planning will be the real guiding force behind the central planners' decisions.

We Will Bury You...Unless We're Wrong about That Planning Thing

This is not a fanciful example, incidentally. In the hardcore socialist economies of the twentieth century, the production and distribution of foodstuffs was horribly dysfunctional. As murderous as tyrants such as Stalin and Mao were, far more people died from unnecessary starvation under socialist management of food production. In fact, of the 100 million or so deaths attributable to socialism worldwide in the twentieth century, most came through starvation. And the inescapable problem of socialism's ineffective production and distribution of food is still evident today in the vast stores of food rotting in Venezuelan government warehouses while Hugo Chávez's subjects go hungry.

But it can also be seen in the United States, where a federally chartered cartel sets a minimum price for milk. That is, under American law, it is illegal for a merchant to sell a gallon of milk to a poor mother to give to her hungry baby for less than the milk cartel says is a fair market price. Given what we've learned about the complexities of calculating a rational plan for a milk distribution system, you'll not be surprised to learn that that poor American mother is paying more than the market price would be for her milk. In other words, in the United States of America, the heartland of capitalism, a little bit of dairy socialism is literally keeping milk out of the mouths of hungry babies. (The Left has long argued that a capitalist is a guy who steals candy from a baby; in fact, a socialist is a guy who steals *milk* from a baby.)

America's Great Bastion of Would-Be Central Planners

"Like every other group, academics like to exert influence and feel important. Few scholars in the social sciences and humanities are content just to observe, describe, and explain society; most want to improve society and are naive enough to believe that they could do so if only they had sufficient influence. The existence of a huge government offers academics the real possibility of living out their reformist fantasies."

Dwight Lee, *Go to Harvard and Turn Left*, 1994

"After the collapse of central planning in Eastern Europe and the former U.S.S.R., the only place in the world where Marxists were still thriving was the Harvard political science department."

Peter G. Klein, *Why Intellectuals Still Support Socialism*, 2006

Naturally, in this situation the interests that are being served are not those of the poor and the hungry, but the interests of the dairy producers. The pattern repeats itself wherever there is government planning of economic activity, whether it is in a socialized sector of a non-socialist country, as in the case of the U.S. milk producers, or in the broader economy of a socialist country.

It is no accident that in every socialist country, the central planners and government officials enjoy a substantially higher standard of living than do the poor proletarians on whose behalf, allegedly, they manage the economy. This has proven true across long periods of time, in different countries with very different cultures and social habits. It is not a feature of some alleged misapplication of socialism, but of socialism itself. The disastrous economy of Cuba and the disastrous economy of North Korea are regional expressions of a single phenomenon.

Though most socialists today attempt to distance their beliefs and ideology from Marxism—mostly because of the horrors inflicted upon the world by Marxist governments—the belief that a complex economy can be rationally planned is quintessentially Marxist. In his famous 1938 essay, "Dialectical and Historical Materialism," Joseph Stalin clearly laid out the philosophical case:

> Contrary to idealism, which denies the possibility of knowing the world and its laws, which does not believe in the authenticity of our knowledge, does not recognize objective truth, and holds that the world is full of "things-in-themselves" that can never be known to science, Marxist philosophical materialism holds that the world and its laws are fully knowable, that our knowledge of the laws of nature, tested by experiment and practice, is authentic knowledge having the validity of objective truth, and that there are no things in the world which are unknowable, but only things which are as yet not known, but which will be disclosed and made known by the efforts of science and practice.[2]

Stalin here is engaged in one of the characteristic intellectual errors of the twentieth century: conflating the hard-and-fast, objective knowledge of the natural sciences with the tenuous, contingent, temporary knowledge of the social sciences—and, more important, the scattershot knowledge of daily life. Knowing how many protons are in a uranium atom is not very much like knowing whether you should plant corn or wheat in a particular field in western Ukraine. Stalin would turn out to be pretty good about getting the former kind of knowledge but not the latter, which is why the USSR could build a terrifying, cutting-edge nuclear arsenal but starved millions of its people to death.

Russians are a mathematically and scientifically gifted people, and perhaps that is part of the reason why the allegedly scientific nature of central planning appealed to them. Nikita Khrushchev, in one of the all-time great moments of hubris in the history of politics, promised a 1961 Communist Party congress that by 1980 at the latest, scientific socialism would surpass, in both quantity and quality, the best that Western capitalism could produce.

Years before the rise of information technology transformed capitalism, the Soviets were counting on "cybernetics"—applied computer science—to provide the information-management solutions that marketplace calculations provide in capitalist economies. In his fascinating look at Soviet economics, *Red Plenty*, Francis Spufford places that project in context:

> For much of the 80 years during which the USSR was a unique experiment in running a non-market economy, the experiment was a stupid experiment, a brute-force experiment. But during the Soviet moment there was a serious attempt to apply the intellectual resources of the educated country the Bolsheviks had kicked and bludgeoned into being. All of the perversities in the Soviet economy... are the classic consequences of running a system without the flow of information provided by market exchange; and it was clear at the beginning of the 60s that for the system to move on up to the plenty promised so insanely for 1980, there would have to be informational fixes for each deficiency. Hence the emphasis on cybernetics, which had gone in a handful of years from being condemned as a "bourgeois pseudo-science" to being an official panacea.

The USSR's pioneering computer scientists were heavily involved, and so was the authentic genius Leonid Kantorovich, nearest Soviet counterpart to John Von Neumann and later to be the only ever Soviet winner of the Nobel prize for economics. Their thinking drew on the uncorrupted traditions of Soviet mathematics. While parts of it merely smuggled elements of rational pricing into the Soviet context, other parts were truly directed at outdoing market processes. The effort failed, of course, for reasons which are an irony-laminated comedy in themselves. The sumps of the command economy were dark and deep and not accessible to academics; Stalinist industrialisation had welded a set of incentives into place which clever software could not touch; the system was administered by rent-seeking gangsters; the mathematicians were relying (at two removes) on conventional neoclassical economics to characterise the market processes they were trying to simulate, and the neoclassicists may just be wrong about how capitalism works.[3]

Today, Khrushchev's "cybernetic" approach has passed into disrepute—to the dust-bin of history—but faith in "scientific" and "rational" management of incomprehensibly complex economic systems remains a fixed fact of political life. Other models of scientific understanding have replaced Soviet cybernetics—evolutionary biology, network systems, complexity theory—but the central conceit remains as fatal as ever. The main question is the scale of the attempted planning; the socialism applied to the U.S. healthcare, agriculture, and education sectors is fairly limited, so its effects are relatively mild. More comprehensive central-planning regimes produce more comprehensive failures—and a more comprehensively perverse feedback loop for the central planners.

If the Shoe Fits, It Wasn't Produced by Socialism

"By keeping the prices of consumer goods artificially low, the Soviet planners created the ubiquitous 'waiting line.' Around that institution grew 'an elaborate subculture…with its own habits and rules.' The odd thing is that shortages appeared in product lines of which the Soviet Union was the largest producer in the world. In the late 1980s, the USSR produced more than three pairs of shoes for each citizen, but people had to wait to buy shoes. The problem was that the available shoes did not reflect consumers' tastes: the shoes were made to fulfill a government plan, not to satisfy market demand."

—James Dorn, Cato scholar, 1994

The scientific hubris of socialism turned out to be one of its deadliest features, and the misapplication of scientific knowledge—the literalization of scientific metaphor—is a recurring theme. For instance, the Juche Idea, the socialist philosophy of North Korea, is deeply influenced by a shallow and misunderstood reading of the science of biological evolution. Referring to the state as the "socio-political organism," with the great leader as its brain, the Juche Idea assumes that central planning is as necessary to a society as a nervous system is to a biological organism. (Woodrow Wilson, years before the advent of the Juche Idea, made a similar argument, describing the ideal leader as an autocrat who acts as the brain of the body politic. His administration would also pursue a bush-league version of Juche, American-style. More on that later.)

As consecutive iterations of the central-planning ideology have become less metaphorical and more literal—the Pyongyang regime really does want to do all of North Korean society's thinking for it, as though it were a literal biological organism and not a metaphorical one—the belief in the necessity of central planning has become ever more deeply ingrained, even as the disastrous results of central planning have become impossible to ignore.

The central planners, of course, have no incentive to admit that their powers to act rationally are limited. When THE PLAN fails—as THE PLAN ultimately must fail, being based on faulty and inadequate information— the planners invariably attempt to force society to conform to their plan, rather than reform their plan to conform to society. In truth, they cannot reform their plans to conform to society's actual needs, because they do not know what those needs are and have no way of finding out.

The case of milk is a relatively simple and straightforward one; imagine how much more complicated healthcare is. Knowing that planners have little access to useful information but easy access to brute political force, Hayek predicted that attempts at central planning would lead to authoritarian misrule of the sort that characterized the socialist regimes of the mid-twentieth century, an argument he spelled out at great length in *The Road to Serfdom*.

Hayek's Revenge

Mises and Hayek are today synonymous with what is known as the Austrian school of economics, and they had first-hand experience to show them where the road to serfdom ends. The Austrians, in an ironic historical twist, did not do most of their intellectual work in Austria, which became inhospitable to them after the rise of one of the twentieth century's most notable socialist movements, one which marched into Vienna in the form of the Austrian National Socialist Workers' Party, a.k.a. the Austrian Nazi Party. Mises spent most of the rest of his life in the United States, Hayek in Britain. Each was troubled by the rise of the central-planning ethos in the West and by the romantic spirit that became attached to socialism. Each would have recognized the governments of contemporary North Korea or Venezuela as familiar to those who experienced the twin totalitarianisms of the 1930s.

Mises was one of the first to fully appreciate that the Stalin-Hitler, socialist-fascist, Left-Right split was an illusion, and that the totalitarian movement based in Berlin was substantially similar to the one based in Moscow. "The usual terminology of political language is stupid," he wrote.

> What is "left" and what is "right"? Why should Hitler be "right" and Stalin, his temporary friend, be "left"? Who is "reactionary" and who is "progressive"? Reaction against an unwise policy is not to be condemned. And progress towards chaos is not to be commended. Nothing should find acceptance just because it is new, radical, and fashionable. "Orthodoxy" is not an evil if the doctrine on which the "orthodox" stand is sound. Who is anti-labor, those who want to lower labor to the Russian level, or those who want for labor the capitalistic standard of the United States? Who is "nationalist," those who want to bring their nation under the heel of the Nazis, or those who want to preserve its independence?[4]

Modern American socialists and their apologists have done relatively little to wrestle with the substance of the Austrians' critique. A few exceptions to that rule are writers associated with *Dissent* magazine, an American socialist journal. Those socialists who have addressed the Austrians' criticisms have mostly ignored Mises and concentrated on Hayek, whose analysis is more holistic and less technically economic.

Liberal Fascism

"Socialists should be delighted to find at last a socialist who speaks and thinks as responsible rulers do."

George Bernard Shaw, on fascist kingpin Benito Mussolini

Their lines of criticism are familiar and, if not quite obvious, certainly inadequate.

One is that Hayek's prophesied "Road to Serfdom" has not come to pass; Sweden, rather famously, is not an authoritarian hellhole, in spite of its large and expensive welfare state. The second objection is that all governments engage in some level of central planning. Hayek's "spontaneous orders," they argue, are not in truth spontaneous; they rely upon the rule of law and other institutions that can only be created and guaranteed by the state. If the state can create a regime of the rule of law, they implicitly ask, why can't it create a regime in which economic affairs are arranged in ways that maximize social benefits (however those social benefits might be defined)? In a 1994 *Dissent* article, David Miller made both cases:

> Hayek's view of the world was Manichaean. On one side stood liberty, limited government, and the market economy; on the other stood coercion, authoritarian government, and planning. It was essential to his argument that there should be no halfway houses. Full-scale planning would be economically disastrous, but trying to *compromise* between the market and planning, using government agencies to direct investment while relying on market pricing of consumer goods, for instance, would be worse still. Behind this lay his view that the two political systems were the embodiments of two opposed philosophies, both with deep roots in European culture. The first of these embraced those who emphasized the limits and fallibilities of the human intellect, drawing from this the conclusion that in social affairs we must proceed cautiously and pragmatically, using trial and error and relying to a large extent on inherited traditions.... Ultimately, then, the question of economic freedom versus planning was

a question of knowledge. Those who advocated the latter were not simply making an empirical error, they were supposing that the human mind was capable of acquiring a kind of knowledge that, according to Hayek, was categorically unobtainable. And for that reason, no compromise with the enemy was possible.

. . . . Plainly he belonged to that generation of European liberals who had to confront the combined impact of Soviet communism and Fascism, and it is tempting to suppose that Hayek's attacks on planning and socialism are motivated by a wish to protect liberal democracies from totalitarian infection. Evidence to support this suggestion might be found in *The Road to Serfdom,* where Hayek lays a good deal of stress on the socialist origins of Nazism, and argues that the adoption of socialist policies elsewhere might be expected to culminate in a form of Fascism. Reduced to its essentials, the argument is that economic planning cannot even be attempted in a parliamentary democracy, so power must gravitate into the hands of a small group of officials, and eventually into those of a single dictator.[5]

Mr. Miller responds to Hayek with an ethical argument positing equality as a good to be considered with weight equal to (perhaps greater than) the moral weight that Hayek gives to liberty. Consequently, he considers all sorts of limitations on property rights, from differential rights to different kinds of property, to highly redistributive tax systems, to disallowing the inheritance of property. The relative weight of equality and freedom is an old and difficult question of political morality, and it goes well beyond our brief here. But what Mr. Miller and his fellow socialists have not adequately dealt with is this: even if they are right about the moral question—even if we conclude that material equality (as opposed to political equality) is to be considered as important or more important than liberty—the freedom that makes marketplace capitalism possible is not merely a moral concern but also a practical one.

Without the liberty that makes real markets possible, we still are left with either a central-planning regime or an incoherent system that attempts to install a partial-planning program parasitically upon the market economy. Hayek was demonstrably correct that the most robust central-planning regimes end in inhumane dictatorships. The jury is still out on the partial-planning regimes; bear in mind that it has only been a short time, historically speaking, since World War II. Within the memory of men still playing dominoes in VFW halls today, most of Europe was under authoritarian dictatorships. Within my own lifetime (and, as of this writing, I am well under forty) such paragons of Western European enlightenment as Spain, Portugal, and Greece have been subject to wretched dictatorships.

Today, the European Union grows ever more intrusive and ever more hostile to the democratically exercised sovereignty of its constituent states. Meanwhile, far-right nationalist movements and far-left socialist movements still have a lot of life left in them in Europe—and both far left and far right call not for capitalism and personal freedom, but for central planning, economic nationalism, autarky, and various expressions of neo-mercantilism. Do not be too sure that Europe has found an off ramp from the Road to Serfdom.

Chapter Four

INDIA: A CASE STUDY IN SOCIALIST FAILURE

The most extreme forms of socialism have usually been implemented by political movements describing themselves as "communist." And though socialism was a fundamental part of the ideology of Adolf Hitler's government—*Nazi*, it is essential to remember, is an abbreviation of national *socialist*—the particularities of the Third Reich's ideology, with its eliminationist anti-Semitism, its racial romanticism, and its delusional imperial ambitions, make it an imperfect example. My colleague Jonah Goldberg is absolutely correct to argue, as he does in *Liberal Fascism*, that the twin totalitarianisms of the twentieth century are variations on the same phenomenon rather than philosophically opposed phenomena, but for our purposes here we will disaggregate the two, though our doing so should offer no comfort to the modern-day apologists for socialism; Stalin was no less a monster than Hitler, Lenin no less a monster than Stalin, and Trotsky not much less a monster than Lenin or Che Guevara.

"But that's communism!" the modern-day socialist will object. "We're talking about socialism! Decent, humane, democratic socialism! We're talking about Swedish socialism, not Soviet communism."

What, precisely, is the difference between socialism and communism? Socialists invariably maintain, in essence, that all the bad stuff done in the name of socialism is communism, and all the good stuff is socialism. Free healthcare? That's socialism. Political repression? That's communism.

Guess What?

★ Gandhi set the stage for decades of Indian poverty

★ Socialism, not the legacy of colonialism, largely caused India's post–World War II economic misery

★ Indians viewed their central planners as similar to their former colonial masters

Public pensions? Socialism. Gulag? Communism. But this is obviously facile and dishonest. It is also a gross oversimplification. Whether one describes a particular arrangement as socialist or communist, one is talking about different expressions of a single phenomenon: Marxism. The great communist leaders regularly describe themselves, their work, and their philosophy as *socialist*.

Still, today's socialists and central planners, from Europe to the Obama administration, argue that it is unfair to locate them in the same camp as Lenin or Ho Chi Minh. That objection will not wash, for many reasons. One is that we must deal with the world as it is, not as the philosophers wish it were. Another is that the relationship between democratic socialism and the authoritarian nightmares enacted under such dictators as Stalin and Mao is not so distant as the socialists in the West would have us believe.

We have their own word for that. The contrarian Marxist Christopher Hitchens, who spent much of his lifetime as a foot soldier and influential thinker in various socialist factions, is forthright in admitting that even the anti-Stalinists of the democratic-socialist Left were eager to extend the influence of their forthrightly communist colleagues in the Eastern Bloc. "Where it was easy to do so," he writes, "we supported causes—the National Liberation Front in Vietnam in particular—whose objects were to extend Soviet power."[1] His brother Peter, a fellow veteran of the International Socialists who eventually broke entirely with their utopian aims, tells a similar story: "The [other socialists] were more honest than we were. Ours was the extreme version of pretending that the U.S.S.R. was not the fault of socialists, or even of Bolsheviks (which we wished to be). Of course it was their fault, the fault of people exactly like us, but we closed our minds to this with a web of excuses. We pretended not to be who we were, and that the U.S.S.R. was not what it was."[2]

We also have the benefit of being able to turn to the words of our own leading socialist thinkers to get a better appreciation for the relationship between democratic socialism and authoritarian communism. The leading socialist journal in the United States is called *Monthly Review*. It was founded by the late Harvard economist Paul Sweezy, whom the *New York Times* described as "the nation's leading Marxist intellectual."[3] The journal is quite prestigious—its first issue contained an article written by Albert Einstein titled "Why Socialism?" Professor Sweezy and his colleague Leo Huberman published an instructive collection of epigrams relating socialism to communism. In their own words:

> What is the difference between socialism and communism?
>
> Socialism and communism are alike in that both are systems of production for use based on public ownership of the means of production and centralized planning. Socialism grows directly out of capitalism; it is the first form of the new society. Communism is a further development or "higher stage" of socialism.
>
> . . . Socialism is . . . the necessary transition stage from capitalism to communism.
>
> It must not be assumed, from the distinction between socialism and communism, that the political parties all over the world which call themselves Socialist advocate socialism, while those which call themselves Communist advocate communism. That is not the case. Since the immediate successor to capitalism can only be socialism, the Communist parties, like the Socialist parties, have as their goal the establishment of socialism.[4]

Socialism, then, in the words of its leading exponents, is a stage in the development of communism—the chrysalis from which the full-blown Marxist insect will emerge. The differences between the two, as Sweezy and Huberman argue, are largely tactical and technical:

The Communists believe that as soon as the working class and its allies are in a position to do so they must make a basic change in the character of the state; they must replace capitalist dictatorship over the working class with workers' dictatorship over the capitalist class as the first step in the process by which the existence of capitalists as a class (but not as individuals) is ended and a classless society is eventually ushered in. Socialism cannot be built merely by taking over and using the old capitalist machinery of government; the workers must destroy the old and set up their own new state apparatus. The workers' state must give the old ruling class no opportunity to organize a counter-revolution; it must use its armed strength to crush capitalist resistance when it arises.

The Socialists, on the other hand, believe that it is possible to make the transition from capitalism to socialism without a basic change in the character of the state. They hold this view because they do not think of the capitalist state as essentially an institution for the dictatorship of the capitalist class, but rather as a perfectly good piece of machinery which can be used in the interest of whichever class gets command of it. No need, then, for the working class in power to smash the old capitalist state apparatus and set up its own—the march to socialism can be made step by step within the framework of the democratic forms of the capitalist state.

The attitude of both parties toward the Soviet Union grows directly out of their approach to this problem. Generally speaking, Communist parties praise the Soviet Union; Socialist parties denounce it in varying degrees. For the Communists, the Soviet Union merits the applause of all true believers in socialism because it has transformed the socialist dream into a reality; for the Socialists, the Soviet Union deserves only condemnation because it has not built socialism at all—at least not the socialism they dreamed of.[5]

Not the socialism they dreamed of! That is the essence of modern socialist apologetics: never mind the socialism we have, the socialism that the world has experienced—judge us by the socialism we dream of. (Do they judge capitalists by the capitalism they dream of? The capitalism in which competitive, market-driven innovation means that inner-city schools improve as quickly, in terms of both quality and price, as the iPhones in the pockets of the schools' students? *That* capitalism?)

Interestingly, Sweezy and Huberman echo Hayek and Mises in emphasizing the difference between consumer goods (your personal groceries, your household possessions) and capital goods (the means of production: factories, mines, industrial facilities, and the like). The Austrians understood the misallocation of capital goods (they call it "malinvestment") to be the principal challenge to the socialist economy. For Sweezy and Huberman, the different attitudes toward capital goods and consumer goods define the difference between socialism and communism.

Under socialism, they argue, consumer goods can remain private property. In fact, they predict that the intelligent application of central planning will produce a superabundance of consumer goods, a state of

Free to Choose

"A major source of objection to a free economy is precisely that it gives people what they want instead of what a particular group thinks they ought to want. Underlying most arguments against the free market is a lack of belief in freedom itself."

Milton Friedman, *Capitalism and Freedom*, 1962

plenitude enabling the radically egalitarian reconstruction of society they seek. Under communism, they argue, consumer goods must be abolished with other forms of private property:

> There are two kinds of private property. There is property which is personal in nature, consumers' goods, used for private enjoyment. Then there is the kind of private property which is not personal in nature, property in the means of production. This kind of property is not used for private enjoyment, but to produce the consumer's goods which are. Socialism does not mean taking away the first kind of private property, e.g., your suit of clothes; it does mean taking away the second kind of private property, e.g. your factory for making suits of clothes.[6]

In other words, when it comes to the deep structural issues in the economy—investment, infrastructure, large-scale property rights, capital markets, trade, etc.—socialism and communism are, in the analysis of America's leading socialist thinkers, *identical*. Other than the theoretical legal status of personal consumer goods, communist economics and socialist economics must then be substantially the same. The authors minimize questions of political organization, although there is a telling bit of self-awareness in their contention that "capitalists as a class (but not as individuals)" are to be eradicated; obviously, the murderous history of socialism-in-arms is not entirely lost on its American apologists.

But as Hayek ably demonstrates, the political arrangements of socialism are in no small part a response to the economic contradictions inherent in the system. That is to say, if socialist and communist *economics* are substantially the same, then we should expect socialist and communist *political arrangements* to be substantially the same. This does not necessarily mean we should expect Sweden to be as repressive and backward as the Soviet Union was; it means we should expect Sweden under socialism to very much resemble Sweden under communism.

It is difficult to disaggregate such factors as Russian nationalism, Russian peasant culture, the political legacy of tsarism, and Russian war experiences from the political character of the Soviet Union. But it is possible to extract from the various experience of very different countries and cultures, with very different kinds of socialism, commonalities that tell us something about the characteristics of socialism itself.

Socialisms in Theory, Socialisms in Practice

For better and for worse, history has provided us with a pretty good case study for how socialism works within a single culture, and how kinds of socialism work in similar cultures. In fact, we have an experiment conducted at the crossroads of two of the world's great civilizations at one of the most dynamic and fraught moments in human history: China and India at the close of World War II.

At the time of its winning its independence in 1947, India was many years ahead of China, better off in almost every conceivable way. India had escaped the ravages of World War II, whereas China had been torn apart by civil war and a brutal Japanese invasion. In India, British colonial rule came to a largely peaceful end thanks to the efforts of Mohandas K. Gandhi, and the departing English left behind a well-developed economic infrastructure and such critical social and economic institutions as a highly disciplined professional civil service and independent courts. Perhaps most important, they left behind a legal code based on English Common Law, arguably the greatest political institution developed by mankind, and one that left India well positioned to integrate easily into the global network of trade that would thrive in the emerging postwar order, catapulting the United States, Japan, and a reformed Germany to undreamt-of heights of prosperity.

In the Sinosphere, things were different. British colonial rule had left a much less productive legacy to the Chinese, whose proud and ancient culture was less flexible than India's and less syncretic. Whereas India had a long history of incorporating influences from cultures as different as Portugal and the Mughal Empire into its social and economic practices, China, styling itself the Middle Kingdom and the center of the world, had always stood apart.

As World War II came to a close, the Japanese withdrew from China and the British began to withdraw from India. China's civil war ended in a *modus vivendi* that saw the mainland under the rule of the communist forces of Mao Zedong, the nationalists establishing a single-party dictatorship in Taiwan, and Hong Kong reverting to British rule after the exit of the Japanese. The final distribution of power and sovereignties produced one of the great experiments in socialism in world history, a fascinating case study—and a tragic one, resulting in the deaths of millions of Chinese and the impoverishment of generations of Indians.

In mainland China, there was utter socialism under Mao, but the same Chinese people would soon find their way to nearly unbridled capitalism in Hong Kong. And while much lip-service would be given to the

A Commissar Walks into a Bar...

A Soviet agricultural commissar visits a collective farm and demands to know how the potato harvest is proceeding. "Marvelously!" replies the head of the farm. "We have so many potatoes that if we put them all in one pile, it would reach the foot of God!" The commissar turns grim and thunders, "This is the Soviet Union! There is no God!" To which the farmer replies, "That's alright, there are no potatoes, either."

Hindocentric doctrines of *swaraj* (self-rule) and Gandhi's *satyagraha* philosophy, India would in fact look to the West and its former colonial master, embracing a democratic form of Cambridge-Fabian socialism under the leadership of Jawaharlal Nehru. Meanwhile, on the outlying edges of the Sinosphere, a formerly obscure possession of the Sultanate of Johor, Singapore, would find itself on the road to independence, which it achieved in 1965—and, more important, on the road to becoming one of the most capitalistic, globalized nations in the world.

In many senses, each of these societies was rebuilding itself anew, and only India had been spared the storm of fire and steel that was the Second World War. Chinese people starting from the ashes of a double war attempted to build a socialist utopia in mainland China, while their estranged compatriots—sharing a culture, a language, and a history—eschewed socialism, first in Hong Kong, and later in Taiwan. Meanwhile, the enormously diverse but heavily Chinese enclave of Singapore would find its own way ahead. Within a few decades, the world would have a vivid example illustrating the practical differences among totalitarian socialism in China, democratic socialism in India, and capitalism in Hong Kong. The results of that experiment should have been the dispositive case against socialism, but socialism's apologists remain curiously immune to evidence.

What Gandhi Has Wrought

India defies generalities. Its people are wildly diverse. It has a topsy-turvy history and helter-skelter politics. The bewildering welter of its cities and villages contains practically every aspect of the human experience, the sublime and the horrible never far apart. Alexander the Great, Islam, Buddhism, the British Empire, the Mughal Empire, the Portuguese Empire—all have come pouring into and out of the Indus valley, and all of them have been transformed by the encounter with its culture.

It is no surprise, then, that two of the twentieth century's towering figures found their way onto history's stage in India. Ironically, both of these historical giants were physically diminutive: Mother Teresa, the Albanian nun who provided an example of modern sainthood, and Mohandas Karamchand Gandhi, known as the "Mahatma" or "great soul," a similarly saintly figure who made his career in a very spiritualized form of politics.

In the West, Gandhi is uniformly admired. If anything, he is even more revered than is Mother Teresa; it is hard to imagine a book about Gandhi like Christopher Hitchens' *The Missionary Position*, a brutal and malicious assault on Mother Teresa, being published in the United States. It might find more of a market in India, where Gandhi's legacy is much more hotly contested, despite his being rightly regarded as the father of his country.

Indians are of two minds about Gandhi for many reasons, the main one being his consent to India's partition, which resulted in the Muslim-leaning west being broken off into a separate country, Pakistan. But there is also a quiet reassessment under way of Gandhi's political and economic ideas, and they are an odd, mixed bag.

Gandhi, like most socialists, was at heart a moral thinker, not an economic thinker. Unlike most Western socialists, he was reasonably forthright in admitting he would rather see Indians poor under his system than rich under another. He advocated a kind of radical self-reliance that calls to mind Thomas Jefferson more than it does Marx or his epigones. He described his thinking in a letter to Leo Tolstoy:

> Independence begins at the bottom.... A society must be built in which every village has to be self sustained and capable of managing its own affairs.... It will be trained and prepared to perish in the attempt to defend itself against any onslaught from without.... This does not exclude dependence on and willing help from neighbours or from the world. It will be a free and voluntary play of mutual forces.... In this structure composed of

innumerable villages, there will be ever widening, never ascend-
ing circles. Life will not be a pyramid with the apex sustained
by the bottom, but it will be an oceanic circle whose center will
be the individual. Therefore the outermost circumference will
not wield power to crush the inner circle but will give strength
to all within and derive its own strength from it.[7]

This system of self-sufficient but interlinked villages was known as *gram
swaraj*, and it bears the unique stamp of Gandhi's moral and aesthetic imagination. It also bears the stamp of his naivety, which was willful, and led
him to reject trade, investment, and technology, creating a moral and political culture that left his people ripe for impoverishment and extraordinarily vulnerable to the normal economic vicissitudes that more sophisticated
economic cultures weather with relative ease. He was especially hostile to
industrial and technological investment, falling victim to the make-work
fallacy that conflates the value of employment with the value of the products that employed people produce. "Don't rush into technologically ori-
ented development," he advised, "First make sure what impact it will have
on employment, and through this on the well-being of the poor people."[8]

Here we have Gandhi articulating something akin to Marx's Labor Theory of Value, inasmuch as he misunderstands the problem of valuing
labor. He did not understand that performing labor is not inherently valuable, that the value of labor comes from the value of the things labor produces. You can have full national employment by paying people to dig
holes in the morning and fill them up in the afternoon, but your society
will be none the richer for it. Gandhi's concern for the poorest among us
was every bit as admirable as Mother Teresa's. Unlike Mother Teresa,
however, he had a hand in creating a disastrous system of politics and
economics that was especially devastating to the poor.

In much the same way that Gandhi was hostile to technological development, which could have multiplied the value of the labor of India's

poor many times over, greatly enriching them and their country, he was hostile to trade, both domestic and foreign. Much of this was no doubt a reaction to India's historical colonization by big trading powers—particularly the Portuguese and the British—and the fact that India's vast peasantry, subsisting on low-level agriculture and crafts, had long been exploited by the local potentates who were themselves enriched by India's trade or in league with the trading powers.

Swadeshi, Gandhi's philosophy of self-sufficiency, eschews trade in goods and capital, by implication rejecting such fundamental economic ideas as the division of labor and comparative advantage. As was his wont, Gandhi gave little thought to the practical economic consequences of his philosophy, concentrating instead on the moral aspects of the argument: "*Swadeshi* is that spirit in us which requires us to serve our immediate neighbours before others," he wrote, "and to use things produced in our neighbourhood in preference to those more remote. So doing, we serve humanity to the best of our capacity. We cannot serve humanity by neglecting our neighbours."[9]

Classical economic thinking holds that if we are really good at growing rice and our neighbors are really good at catching fish, then we specialize in rice, they specialize in fish, and both sides trade, resulting in more rice and fish for everybody. By having multiple parties each specialize in the area where they perform best, the overall productivity of the economy rises, and all enjoy a higher standard of living. Classical economists call this *gains from trade*—but Gandhi was having none of it. He simply rejected the concept out of hand on moral grounds. Rather than helping his people to grow prosperous the same way the great trading powers had enriched themselves in India, he encouraged everybody to adopt precisely the same model of subsistence economics—a little bit of farming, a little bit of weaving homespun fabric—that had left Indians vulnerable to colonial exploitation in the first place.

Gandhi argued that he was placing humanity and human interest at the center of his economics. Once challenged by a militant Marxist critic, who told him that his spiritualism was worthless because it did not make economic sense, Gandhi retorted that no economics was worth anything unless it made moral sense in accord with the human spirit. Someone might have asked Gandhi, "What good is your concern for the poor if your philosophy leaves them poor—if, indeed, it leaves them even worse off than they were before?"

At a 1973 lecture on Gandhian economics, E. F. Schumacher expanded on Gandhi's view, arguing that the economic development model of the time left the poor in a hopeless situation, abandoned in a Malthusian resource deficit:

> It is now widely accepted that there are limits to growth on the established pattern, so that, in all probability, the trends established over the last twenty-five years could not be continued even if everybody wished to do so. The requisite physical resources were simply not there, and living nature all around us, the ecosystem, could not stand the strain. Gandhi had always known, and rich countries are now reluctantly beginning to realise, that their affluence was based on stripping the world. The U.S.A. with 5.6 percent of the world population was consuming up to 40 percent of the world's resources, most of them non-renewable. Such a lifestyle could not spread to the whole of mankind. In fact, the truth is now dawning that the world could not really afford the U.S.A., let alone the U.S.A. plus Europe plus Japan plus other highly industrialised countries.[10]

Ironically, these observations were published in *Gandhi and the Contemporary World*—in 1997, just as India was starting to embrace the

Western-style capitalism that was anathema to Gandhi and his contemporaries. Lost on Schumacher, as it would have been on Gandhi, was that the very same U.S.A. that was consuming 40 percent of the world's resources was also producing 40 percent of the world's wealth. In other words, the shocking fact was not that so few people were *consuming* so much, but that so few people were *producing* so much. Gandhian economics, obsessed with the problem of unemployment, might have benefited mightily from such a realization.

Instead of looking to the capitalist model of the United States, Gandhi's immediate political heir, Jawaharlal Nehru, looked to the managerial socialism that had been in vogue during his time as a student at Cambridge. Whereas Gandhi's ideas were airy and philosophical, a nebulous tangle of ideals and ideology, prejudice and superstition, Nehru's ideas were straight democratic socialism of the Fabian variety, and he set about appending a neutered version of Marxism onto the moral foundations laid by Gandhi. Whereas Gandhi talked about "soul force" and deploying moral power, Nehru would begin to build an industrialized, concrete-and-steel socialist state, enacting Soviet-style "five-year plans" that failed exactly as Hayek and Mises would have predicted—and which set India on the road to serfdom, as the bureaucratization of central planning was accompanied by the inevitable centralization of power. One generation after embracing democratic socialism, India would slide into autocracy as Nehru's more masterfully socialist daughter, Indira Gandhi, installed herself as dictator. Economically and politically, socialism would prove a disaster for the emerging republic—one from which it would take nearly fifty years to begin to recover.

Socialist India: Spreading the Poverty Around

By way of contrast, consider that by the time India got around to opening its economy in the late 1990s, plucky little Hong Kong—a former pirates' haven that had been ravaged by World War II, occupied by the Japanese, seen two-thirds of its population disappear as refugees and war casualties, menaced by Mao's China, and governed by a foreign colonial power—had become one of the richest nations in the world in just a few decades. Whereas Gandhi's heirs were worrying about how to create make-work jobs for India's legions of unemployed, Hong Kong was advertising its "human capital"—the enormously productive labor force that had helped to transform its economy. And it's no accident that "human capital" is what Hong Kong chose to rely upon; other than being geographically well-positioned to benefit from ocean trade, Hong Kong had practically no natural resources to speak of, whereas India had vast swaths of arable land, forests, minerals, warm-water ports, and the like.

Hong Kong's per capita GDP grew 8,700 percent from 1961 to 1997, its ports rivaling the world's giants in New York and Rotterdam, its shipping companies rising to challenge the longstanding dominance of the Greeks. And Hong Kong's ascent was not just a rich man's boom; as measured by

Answer: No Socialism

"According to the latest figures I have, per capita income in Hong Kong is almost identical with that in the United States. That is close to incredible. Here we are—a country of 260 million people that stretches from sea to shining sea, with enormous resources, and a two-hundred-year background of more or less steady growth, supposedly the strongest and richest country in the world, and yet six million people living on a tiny spit of land with negligible resources manage to produce as high a per capita income. How come?"

Milton Friedman, *The Hong Kong Experiment*, 1998

the Gini Coefficient, the territory's population became more economically equal as Hong Kong became richer.

India meanwhile remained a highly stratified society. Instead of turning outward to trade, India turned inward, guided by the romantic ideas of socialism and self-sufficiency. The result was poverty. "India discovered that tiny Hong Kong could earn more from its exports than the whole of India," writes Indian economist Gurcharan Das. "India's share of world trade declined from 2.2 percent in 1947 to 0.5 percent in 1990."[11] That is to say, after forty-three years of independence and self-rule, India lost 77 percent of its share of world trade.

India's road to serfdom began with Gandhi's spiritualized politics, but it was Nehru, inspired by the British socialist Harold Laski, who built the socialist state under which India would sweat and founder for decades. Nehru's brand of socialism was democratic, but it should come as no surprise to the student of socialism that he identified closely with the two great undemocratic socialist states of his time—the Soviet Union and Mao's China—and looked to them for guidance. Though he would have drawn a different conclusion from the fact than do modern critics of socialism, Nehru seemed to understand that the political organization of socialist states, while an issue of real consequence, is secondary to and subordinate to the economic organization of those states. Socialism in democratic India very much resembled socialism in the undemocratic USSR.

Nehru, like most of his fellow Fabians, was deeply romantic in his view of socialism, a fact that blinded him to the military threat posed by his socialist neighbor to the east. Operating under the socialist slogan *Hindi-Chini bhai bhai*—"Indians and Chinese are brothers"—Nehru took no precautions against the festering predations of Mao Zedong. Socialists were all self-declared partisans of peace, and that fact seems to have been enough for Nehru, who was caught entirely off guard when China's Red Army invaded his country in 1962 and annexed the disputed territory of Aksai Chin near the Tibetan border while the rest of the world was distracted by the Cuban Missile Crisis, another curious case of socialist pacifism.

Even though Nehru had been one of the first world leaders to recognize Communist China and had defended its aggression in Korea, an armed invasion was enough to sour even a socialist romantic like him on China. But Nehru remained enamored with the Soviet Union, and in particular with its narrow model of central economic management, the *piatiletka*, or five-year plan.

The Indian version of the five-year plan was a cornerstone of Nehru's approach to economic development, and its development and implementation suggests that Nehru's version of socialism was somewhat looser and less ideological than the versions being executed in Moscow and Beijing, though that is a fairly low bar to clear. Rather than direct state management of all aspects of economic life, Nehru preferred a mixed system, with the government nationalizing industries in the commanding heights of the economy, such as steel and major manufacturing, while using a system of licenses, subsidies, regulation, and cartelization to achieve socialistic economic and political goals throughout both the public and private sector. Nehru was open to a level of entrepreneurship, but he wanted the state to be the main entrepreneur in society.

To aid him in achieving this vision, Nehru (like FDR before him, and like socialists of all parties ever since) turned to the best and brightest central-planning talent available to him, and found his instrument in the person of P. C. Mahalanobis, a gifted mathematician and statistician. Milton Friedman, one of the twentieth century's greatest economists and no friend of central planning, was acquainted with Mahalanobis, and offered some insightful observations in private, which were published years later: "Mahalanobis began as a mathematician and is a very able one. Able mathematicians are usually recognized for their ability at a relatively early age. Realizing their own ability as they do and working in a field of absolutes, tends, in my opinion, to make them dangerous when they apply themselves to economic planning. They produce specific and detailed plans in which they have confidence, without perhaps realizing that economic planning is not the absolute science that mathematics is."[12]

Indeed it is not, and central planning of the Indian economy turned out to be every bit as disastrous as central planning of the Russian and Chinese economies, even though it was not accompanied by the near-genocidal political violence that was unleashed in those two bastions of socialist purity. There are libraries' worth of statistics documenting the miserable performance of the Indian economy during this period, but those numbers do not capture the consequent stagnation of Indian society and the enormous squandering of human lives that this needless impoverishment produced.

While statistics are one useful measure, it is perhaps more telling that the two most popular terms used to characterize the Indian economy during this period were expressions of national disgust and self-abasement. The regulating-and-licensing apparatus that Nehru bequeathed to the country in order to look after the interests of the poor, of course, did no such thing and instead became, as it has in every other socialist country, a source of petty corruption. Indians therefore nicknamed that system the "License Raj"—*raj* being the term used to describe the hated British colonial occupiers. Indians, to whom history has bequeathed a sense of irony that surely functions as a psychological survival mechanism, understood that their socialist planners had, in the name of national liberation and national development, become precise analogues of their former colonial masters. They were in the same position as the animals at the end of *Animal Farm*, unable to tell the newly masterful pigs from the farmers against whom they had risen.

The second term described the paltry gains the Indian economy made from the time of its independence until major economic reforms were implemented in the 1990s, while formerly backward and impoverished peoples in South Korea and Hong Kong grew rich during the ascent of the "Asian Tigers." No doubt recognizing that India's economic stagnation was in no small part a legacy of Gandhi's spiritualized politics and moralized economics, this legacy was wryly described as the "Hindu rate of growth."

The prominence of those two terms is a small but telling thing. Nations, like individuals, can suffer crises of confidence and can be self-loathing. And India's decline under socialism, the most progressive economic doctrine of its time, an idea endorsed by the most celebrated intellectuals of the day, must surely have been inexplicable. Still more perplexing must have been the fact that those who had eschewed socialism and the rational planning of the economy, operating in resourceless enclaves in Hong Kong, Singapore, and Taiwan, had grown stupendously

Private Services for Me, Not for Thee

"K. N. Raj, widely respected development economist and teacher and one of the architects of the Indian Plan edifice, passed away here on Wednesday. He was 85.

"Dr. Raj—who was the economic adviser to Prime Ministers from Jawaharlal Nehru to P.V. Narasimha Rao, and set the pace of India's economic growth story from the First Five-Year Plan—had been keeping indifferent health for some time. He was admitted to a *private hospital* here on Saturday with fever and breathing trouble and died following a cardiac arrest at 2:40 p.m." [emphasis added]

Obituary of K. N. Raj, who helped to draft India's first five-year plan, *The Hindu*, 2010

rich. India's performance wasn't only dwarfed by the meteoric rise of Hong Kong, it was a full 1.5 percentage points below the Third World's average rate of growth from 1950 to 1980.

"History has its unforeseen ironies," Jagdish Bhagwati wrote in *India in Transition*, an intelligent analysis of the country's early economic reforms. He continued,

> The post-war period, now spanning four decades through the 1980s, began with both a strong economic performance and Western empathy and approbation of India's developmental efforts and ideas. It ended with an economy in serious difficulty and, worse, the perception that India had not merely chosen the wrong economic path but had also marginalized herself in world economic affairs in consequence. The economic realities cannot be ignored, even as India's failures must be carefully analyzed, since they and their causes are more complex than commonly believed, while there are countervailing successes as well.[13]

Perceptively, he titled that chapter "The Model That Couldn't," and he added:

> Let me first stress that countries such as South Korea and Taiwan, which have grown much faster than India in the post-war period to date, have had a substantial impact on their living standards. To see the force of the argument, that India's poor growth performance has affected its prospects for raising living standards, it is useful to understand the force of compound interest. Had India's GDP grown as rapidly from 1960 to 1980 as South Korea's, it would stand at $531 billion today rather than $150 billion—surpassing that of the UK, equal to that of France, and more than twice that of China. India's per capita

income would have been $740 instead of $260; even with the benefits of growth inequitably distributed, it is not unreasonable to believe that most of the poor would have been substantially better off.[14]

The other great irony is that India once was the world's byword for extravagant wealth. In assessing their sorry situation before their free-market reforms, Indians knew that the Mughals, the Portuguese, and the British hadn't come to India because India was poor, but because India was rich—fabulously rich, in fact, accounting for more than one-fifth of the entire world's economic output in the early eighteenth century. India had been a major manufacturing power at the same time, with its textiles industry the envy of the world. It had a sophisticated system of banking and finance. Additionally, while the political repression and exploitation of the colonial era should not be underestimated, it had emerged as an independent nation with the benefit of British systems and standards of law and public administration on its side—and it was the lack of such fruitful institutions, as Hernando de Soto documented in *The Mystery of Capital*, that had doomed so many other nations to poverty and dysfunction. "Given the enormous financial surplus, a skilled artisan class, large exports, plenty of arable land and reasonable productivity," Das asks, "the question is: Why didn't a modern industrial economy emerge in India? Instead, why did India become impoverished?"[15]

Where It All Went Wrong

While Marxists and postcolonialist critics have attributed India's impoverishment to the predations of the British colonial powers, there is little evidence to support such a claim. As Das notes, the economic evidence suggests that Britain's colonial operations constituted a net economic gain for India. The problem, as Hayek and Mises would have predicted, was central economic planning. While India's socialism was politically different from the hardcore socialism of the Soviet Union and Mao's China, and while its economic regimentation was certainly less radical and more liberal, it was implemented through the same apparatus: the government plan, the government planner, and the government-planning authority.

Because of the impossibility of securing and organizing the knowledge necessary to conduct rational economic planning, India's five-year plans were just as defective as the Soviet plans that became the object of scorn

Still a Ways to Go

While India in recent years has developed a high-growth economy by dismantling much of the license raj architecture, it is still plagued by vestiges of socialism, as shown in the following report: "Farmers in Vidarbha [India] are forced to sell their land to the socialist regime at a value much less than its market worth. Indian socialist/communist laws, which show negligible reverence for property rights of an individual, authorizes the administration to appropriate and take away an individual's land and property, and allows the government itself to set the value for the land. The sellers, who are victimized, can't bargain, nor can they reject [demands] to sell the land. The government will snatch it, anyway—it has authority to do so: It is the biggest mafia, and all that stealing and looting and impounding will be done legally; the victim even cannot complain against it....The very continuation of such a dictatorial law is justified by its communists/socialist supporters, saying that, in view of the fact that the government will use the property for public welfare (roads, etc), it should be empowered to capture land from unruly land owners."

Sudha Amit, Indian commentator, *Don't Steal: The Government Hates Competition*, 2007

and ridicule in the Cold War years, both in the free world and behind the Iron Curtain.

Nehru's planner, Mahalanobis, was by all accounts a brilliant man, utterly committed to the betterment of his nation. But his plan, as Das documents, was deeply and irredeemably flawed. Not only were the five-year plans unrealistic, the act of attempting central planning was itself destructive to India's development and left its public policy deeply deformed. In accord with Gandhi's *swadeshi* philosophy, it sought substitutes for import and shunned trade, in the process becoming internally focused. In accord with Nehru's Fabian socialist prescriptions, it established a massive array of public-sector enterprises in which the state attempted to play the role of entrepreneur, a system that was not only grossly inefficient but also monopolistic, since government-run enterprises displaced private competition from the marketplace.

Likewise, the "License Raj" choked private entrepreneurship and ensured that what little capital made it into India from the outside world found few projects to nourish. The consequent distortion of private enterprise and the massive public sector together ensured that huge amounts of capital were misallocated into bad investments and unproductive, politically driven enterprises. Cut off from the outside world by hostility to trade and foreign investment, Indians lost touch with the dynamic currents of thought, especially as regards the development and use of technology.

Underlying all of this was a hostility to competition, a sentiment that still is heard today in the voices of those who oppose global trade and the opening of markets. Mahalanobis, Das writes, "assumed that competition was wasteful."[16] But competition—unlike central planning—improves productivity, making more and better goods available at lower prices. Competition necessitates innovation and investment. Competition is the reason that Hong Kong and Singapore got rich while India foundered until 1997, when it opened up its economy and began its remarkable transformation into a major world economic power. Competition is the antithesis to central planning. It's also the reason the iPhone in your pocket is a marvel of engineering and economics but the public school on the corner stinks.

Chapter Five

THE PRUSSIAN ROOTS OF AMERICAN SOCIALISM

The literature documenting the ideas that created Indian socialism provides some wonderful reading—philosophical, deeply moral, deeply serious. Reading the words of Mohandas K. Gandhi, one sincerely wishes that the humane essence of his vision could have been implemented without the immiseration of the very people Gandhi's *swadeshi* was intended to elevate. Gandhi was a moral giant, just as Marx, in his way, was a moral giant—each had a plan to radically transform the world with the effect of bettering the lives of the poor. The problem, as the Austrian economists argued, is not so much with the content of THE PLAN, and not necessarily with the moral intent of the men who draw up THE PLAN, but with the fact of THE PLAN itself.

Unlike India, Hong Kong was very lucky in having its affairs shaped by two men who were not moral giants but who did have full command of a crucial piece of wisdom: "In the long run," wrote Sir John James Cowperthwaite, Hong Kong's financial secretary from 1961 to 1971, "the aggregate of decisions of individual businessmen, exercising individual judgment in a free economy, even if often mistaken, is less likely to do harm than the centralized decisions of a government, and certainly the harm is likely to be counteracted faster."[1]

In Hong Kong, this idea is known as "positive non-interventionism," and it was the bedrock of the city-state's nearly unprecedented economic

Guess What?

★ American progressivism was heavily influenced by authoritarian and socialist Prussian policies

★ The U.S. public school system is based on the nineteenth-century Prussian model

★ Public education strives to turn students into useful servants of the state

69

success. Cowperthwaite's sentiments were echoed by his successor, Sir Charles Phillip Haddon-Cave, who hewed closely to Hayek's view: "Positive non-interventionism involves taking the view that it is normally futile and damaging to the growth rate of an economy, particularly an open economy, for the government to attempt to plan the allocation of resources available to the private sector and to frustrate the operation of market forces."[2] That's a kind of wisdom that lacks the satisfying moral charge of Gandhi's view, or the romantic declarations of the socialists who throughout history have claimed to labor on behalf of the poor and the exploited.

The United States, for many cultural reasons, has long been resistant to highly romanticized political ideologies, preferring instead to follow its own Anglo-Protestant model of classical liberalism, one not far removed from the "positive non-interventionism" of Cowperthwaite and Haddon-Cave. But the United States has not been entirely immune, to be sure—such phenomena as the Ku Klux Klan, the survivalist/militia movement, the sixties counterculture, the Black Panthers, and the utopian communities that dotted the American landscape in the nineteenth century are expressions of a deep political romanticism, as were more mainstream developments such as Kennedy's "Camelot," FDR's New Deal, LBJ's Great Society, and the contemporary, right-wing, anti-trade and anti-globalization faction associated with Pat Buchanan and the *American Conservative*. That romanticism, which always necessitates a rejection of positive non-interventionism, is not a left-right, liberal-conservative development in the United States. Libertarian and paleoconservative critics are right to point to an axis of romanticism that runs from Theodore Roosevelt's progressivism to George W. Bush's determination to rid the world, or at least the world's governments, of evil.

Perhaps the most romantic movement in American political history—and, not accidentally, the most European movement—was the progressivism of Woodrow Wilson, which combined the pragmatism of the

American spirit with the German romanticism that undergirded the Prussian model of government under Otto von Bismarck, the patron saint of progressivism. Conservative and libertarian critics of American progressivism, notably *Liberal Fascism* author Jonah Goldberg, have explored the intellectual and political linkages between the policies pursued by the contemporary Left and those pursued by Bismarck and, more to the point, to his more radical political epigones, who range from Lenin to Mussolini, but include, most notably, the democratic socialists.

This line of criticism often is met with flat rejection and no small amount of derision: "How could any thinking person link Bismarck and the socialists?" they demand. "Bismarck was the sworn enemy of the socialists." And that is true, so far as it goes—which is not very far.

From the Guy Who Later Vowed to Make the World Safe for Democracy

"[In Prussia] administration has been most studied and most nearly perfected. Frederic the Great, stern and masterful as was his rule, still sincerely professed to regard himself as only the chief servant of the state, to consider his great office a public trust; and it was he who, building upon the foundations laid by his father, began to organize the public service of Prussia as in very earnest a service of the public. His no less absolute successor, Frederic William III... in his turn, advanced the work still further, planning many of the broader structural features which give firmness and form to Prussian administration today. Almost the whole of the admirable system has been developed by kingly initiative."

Woodrow Wilson, *The Study of Administration*, 1886

Bismarck was deeply troubled by the emerging influence of the Social Democratic Party and in particular its radical wing, whose members had been linked to the attempted assassination of Kaiser Wilhelm. The Iron Chancellor, much more closely allied in the historic mind with German nationalism than with German socialism, adopted the *Sozialistengesetze,* a set of legal reforms specifically designed to suffocate the Social Democratic Party by forbidding its members to meet, shuttering its newspapers and journals, dissolving unions affiliated with the movement, and similarly repressive measures.

The most illuminating political analogy here is the rift between the Stalin and Trotsky factions in the Soviet Union. The Stalinists were socialists and the Trotskyists were socialists; they were merely competing factions fighting for power. Bismarck's longrunning battle with the Social Democratic Party in fact tells us very little about Bismarck's ideological kinship with, or aversity toward, socialism as we now understand it.

Let us go ahead and grant that Bismarck was no socialist in the sense that we are using that word here—he did not advocate the public ownership of capital, the suppression of private property, the establishment of a classless society, or any of the other fundamental goals that socialism purports to pursue. Bismarck called his philosophy, such as it was, *Realpolitik*, which we might render in English as *pragmatism*. In Bismarck's time, that meant "The Great Game," the fine art of balancing the major European powers, playing each off against the others. But there was a domestic side to *Realpolitik*, too; even as his government was laboring to suppress the Social Democratic Party, Bismarck was busily enacting those parts of its agenda that he thought would serve his own purposes by pacifying the poor and the working classes.

It was *Realpolitik*, and not romantic socialism, that thereby led to the establishment of Europe's first major welfare state as Bismarck oversaw the creation of a social-insurance program, a health-insurance entitlement, old-age pensions, disability benefits, and restrictive labor laws. These were the first programs of their kind, and they were adopted in no small part to reduce the appeal of the socialist movement that was promising even more generous subsidies and benefits. Bismarck's calculating *Realpolitik* caught the attention of another group of political visionaries inclined to describe themselves as pragmatists, though today we know them more commonly as the progressives.

The most prominent of them were John Dewey, America's leading public intellectual, and Woodrow Wilson, the Bryn Mawr and Princeton don who went on to become president of the United States. But well before these men found themselves intoxicated by the allure of masterful Prussian pragmatism, they were beaten to the discovery by Horace Mann, known today as the father of the American public school system, the most notable island of socialism in the once-uproarious, presently diminishing sea of American capitalism.

Not by Rational Planning?

"The great questions of the day will not be settled by means of speeches and majority decisions but by iron and blood."

Otto von Bismarck, Prussian autocrat and intellectual godfather of American progressivism

Public Schools: American Socialism in Action

While the Prussian model of education would eventually come to be adopted in the United States, the public provision of schooling in America far precedes the establishment of the country itself. The later Prussian-style schooling would be explicitly presented as a component of national economic planning; students would be taught skills that would make them productive workers, national examinations would be used to channel them into suitable jobs, and the whole enterprise would be integrated into a rational plan of economic development. This was the essence of the progressive vision for education. But the earliest public schooling project in the United States had a very different goal: to curb the influence of Satan.

The first public-education law in the United States was the "Old Deluder Satan Law," named for its citation of Old Hickory in its opening passage. Unlike most of our modern laws, this 1647 statute is quite readable, and it is worth considering in full:

> It being one chief project of that old deluder, Satan, to keep men from the knowledge of the Scriptures, as in former times by keeping them in an unknown tongue, so in these latter times by persuading from the use of tongues, that so that at least the true sense and meaning of the original might be clouded and corrupted with false glosses of saint-seeming deceivers; and to the end that learning may not be buried in the grave of our forefathers, in church and commonwealth, the Lord assisting our endeavors. It is therefore ordered that every township in this jurisdiction, after the Lord hath increased them to fifty households shall forthwith appoint one within their town to teach all such children as shall resort to him to write and read, whose wages shall be paid either by the parents or masters of such children, or by the inhabitants in general, by way of supply, as the major part of those that order the prudentials of the town shall appoint; provided those that send their children be not oppressed by paying much more than they can have them taught for in other towns. And it is further ordered, that when any town shall increase to the number of one hundred families or householders, they shall set up a grammar school, the master thereof being able to instruct youth so far as they may be fitted for the university, provided that if any town neglect the performance hereof above one year that every such town

> shall pay 5 pounds to the next school till they shall perform
> this order.[3]

Hayek had a lot to say about central planning as an approach to economic problems, but very little to say about it as a strategy for fighting Satan. It only takes a little reading between the lines, however, to decode the language and discover the true intent of this law. The program being described by the Old Deluder Satan Law is not about instruction in the liberal arts, but about indoctrination—*indoctrination* literally, as Christians use the word—using the schools, under political discipline, to enforce uniformity of opinion, which is to say: conformity of all opinion with the official dogma of the governing powers. Public schools have served the same function ever since.

This was hardly unprecedented. The first mandatory-education laws appeared in Germany in the sixteenth century, and the schools were used to impose Lutheran orthodoxy on heterogeneous populations. Martin Luther himself was an energetic advocate of mandatory education as a means of enforcing religious orthodoxy, and the teacup totalitarian John Calvin had similar ideas in Geneva. The Empress Maria Theresa in Austria, another monarch struggling with religious dissent, was quick to adopt the Prussian model and use it to impose orthodoxy. The Soviet Union would later adopt compulsory education for much the same reason, though it was imposing a rather different kind of orthodoxy.

The Austrian economist Murray Rothbard quotes Luther's argument for the establishment of compulsory schools:

> I maintain that the civil authorities are under obligation to
> compel the people to send their children to school. . . . If the
> government can compel such citizens as are fit for military
> service to bear spear and rifle, to mount ramparts, and perform
> other martial duties in time of war, how much more has it a

right to the people to send their children to school, because in this case we are warring with the devil, whose object it is secretly to exhaust our cities and principalities.[4]

And that argument was easily mutated into a less religious and more explicitly statist formulation by the progressive thinker Calvin Stowes, who was influential in seeing the Prussian model adopted in the United States:

> If a regard to the public safety makes it right for a government to compel the citizens to do military duty when the country is invaded, the same reason authorizes the government to compel them to provide for the education of their children .... A man has no more right to endanger the state by throwing upon it a family of ignorant and vicious children, than he has to give admission to the spies of an invading army.[5]

The leap from doing war with Satan (who was euphemistically referred to as "The Enemy") to doing war with the Enemy of the State was a very short and brief one, and it illustrates an important point about public education, which is that its point is not educating the public. The point of public education is, and has always been, to make members of the public better and more productive servants of the state—and it is therefore unsurprising that socialists have taken up the cause. President Obama, speaking to an audience of schoolchildren, described in some detail how he expects the schools to produce students that will serve the needs of the state; unsurprisingly, he cast the situation in terms of his own agenda, emphasizing healthcare, racial discrimination, and job-creation:

> What you make of your education will decide nothing less than the future of this country. What you're learning in school today will determine whether we as a nation can meet our greatest challenges in the future.

You'll need the knowledge and problem-solving skills you learn in science and math to cure diseases like cancer and AIDS, and to develop new energy technologies and protect our environment. You'll need the insights and critical thinking skills you gain in history and social studies to fight poverty and homelessness, crime and discrimination, and make our nation more fair and more free. You'll need the creativity and ingenuity you develop in all your classes to build new companies that will create new jobs and boost our economy.

We need every single one of you to develop your talents, skills, and intellect so you can help solve our most difficult problems. If you don't do that—if you quit on school—you're not just quitting on yourself, you're quitting on your country.[6]

Education: Good for Putting People in Their Place

"We want one class of persons to have a liberal education, and we want another class of persons, a very much larger class, of necessity, in every society, to forgo the privileges of a liberal education and fit themselves to perform specific difficult manual tasks....We are either trying to make liberally educated persons out of them, or we are trying to make skillful servants of society along mechanical lines, or else we do not know what we are trying to do."

Woodrow Wilson, speech to high-school teachers' convention, 1909

Obama here is describing a right of eminent domain over the lives of American children, without putting it quite in those words. Other social-education activists have been more explicit, and it is undeniable that the public provision of educational services is understood today, and has always been understood, as a component of national economic planning.

It would be difficult to find in the United States any profession so dedicated to socialism as that of educators, and difficult to find any argument for socialism as popular as the cause of public education. When some parents objected to the Obama speech quoted above being broadcast into all the nation's government-run schools, on the grounds that it constituted political indoctrination, they were roundly mocked by the Left. One diarist at the left-wing website *Daily Kos*, noting that some of Obama's critics had described his platform as a "socialist agenda," wrote, "If your kids are in public school, they're already living that agenda."[7] To make his point especially clear, he headlined the post, "Public Schools Are Socialist."

Likewise, writing in a forum for *The Nation* titled "Reimagining Socialism," Emory University history professor Patrick Allitt cited public schools as evidence that "millions of Americans...are ardent supporters of socialism." "It's odd," he wrote, "that so many critics of [the Obama] administration should use 'socialism' as a devil word."[8] *Devil word*: perhaps he's never heard of the Old Deluder Satan Law.

At any rate, this is a common trope on the Left: *"socialism" sounds scary, but we're really talking about things like public schools and public highways*. Education blogger Jerry Webster, writing at About.com, headlined his post on nationalizing teacher-pay decisions "Give Socialism a Chance."[9] Writing in the arts and humanities journal *Helium*, Daniel Reneau asks, "Like public schools? Then say, 'Thank you, socialism!'"[10] Other writers on the Left have similarly argued that the popularity of the public schools suggests that Americans are more comfortable with socialism than they let on.

As indeed they are. The public schools constitute one of the most popular instantiations of socialism in American life, though Social Security and government-funded transportation systems no doubt rank nearly as high. But popular with whom? Certainly the educators and administrators who run the system are largely pleased with it, as they should be; the noncompetitive nature of government-run education provides them with salaries and benefits far exceeding what they plausibly could earn in the private sector. Some parents and property owners are very happy with the public schools as well. The well-off and well-connected tend to enjoy reasonably good public schools, which help sustain high residential real-estate values in the largely suburban communities that host them.

Equal Opportunity Failure

But other Americans are much less pleased with their government schools, particularly the poor, non-whites, and those living in inner cities. Black families in particular consistently rate their government schools as performing poorly, and their subjective impressions are borne out by empirical data. Writing in 1973, Murray Rothbard understood that this was a socialist central-planning problem of the classical variety:

> Bureaucratic convenience has invariably led the states to pre-scribe geographical public school districts, to place one school in each district, and then to force each public school child to attend school in the district closest to his residence.... The present system compels a monopoly of one school per district, ✓ and thereby coerces uniformity throughout each area. Children who, for whatever reason, would prefer to attend a school in another district are prohibited from doing so. The result is enforced geographic homogeneity, and it also means that the character of each school is completely dependent on its

residential neighborhood. It is then inevitable that public schools, instead of being totally uniform, will be uniform *within* each district, and the composition of pupils, the financing of each school, and the quality of education will come to depend upon the values, the wealth, and the tax base, of each geographical area. The fact that wealthy school districts will have costlier and higher-quality teaching, higher teaching salaries, and better working conditions than the poorer districts, then becomes inevitable. Teachers will regard the better schools as the superior teaching posts, and the better teachers will gravitate to the better school districts, while the poorer ones must remain in the lower-income areas. Hence, the operation of district public schools inevitably results in the negation of the very egalitarian goal which is supposed to be a major aim of the public school system in the first place.[11]

Rothbard goes on to cite nineteenth-century public-schooling advocate Newton Bateman, who called for a socialist model of mandatory schooling; education, he wrote, was too important to be left to the marketplace, a good that "cannot be left to the caprices and contingencies of individuals."[12] Prefiguring President Obama, he cited the state's "right of eminent domain" over the "hearts and minds and bodies" of the nation's children in support of his case.[13]

Bateman's reasoning was extended to its natural conclusion in the state of Oregon, which attempted not only to create mandatory government schools but in 1922 tried to ban all private schools as well, citing the need to provide a uniform education that would make good citizens and productive workers of all its wards. The driving force behind the proposal was the Ku Klux Klan, which wanted to make sure that new immigrants, particularly Catholics, were sufficiently Americanized—by which they presumably meant much the same thing that Martin Luther had meant, i.e. that they should be conformed to the religious-political orthodoxy of the time. The particular content of that orthodoxy has changed from time to time—Robert Dale Owen, another progressive-era proponent of state-run education, wrote of a "national, rational, republican education, for the honor, the happiness, the virtue, and the *salvation* of the state."[14] But what has remained constant is that the political mission of the socialist education system in the United States dominates its nominal educational mission.

Sheldon Friedman of the *Freeman* cites a particularly brazen expression of that fact in an article touching on public-school advocate William Seawell, a professor at the University of Virginia, who argued that state schools, unlike private schools, "promote civic rather than individual pursuits... creating citizens for the good of society.... *Each child belongs to the state.*"[15] A Venezuelan oil rig, a Russian wheat field, an American child—all the property of the state, all grist for the socialist central-planning mill. Friedman noted that this sentiment was echoed in an even more illiberal promise from Winnie Mandela, the South African politician who gave campaign speeches promising that "parents not sending their children to school will be the first prisoners" of her government.[16]

Despite the wildly exaggerated claims made by partisans of socialist education, its results in the United States are similar to the results of the socialist cartels in India or the socialist collective farms of the USSR: resources are misallocated or squandered, the programs' intended beneficiaries are shortchanged, and the interests of the central planners themselves are those that are most astutely upheld. The inner-city schools are a nightmare from coast to coast. Education spending has skyrocketed while educational outcomes have stagnated in many schools and declined in many others. The first state to adopt a mandatory public education program, Massachusetts, had a higher literacy rate in 1850, the year it adopted its compulsory-attendance law, than it does today.

Is That Really the Purpose of Comparative Government Classes?

"Without comparative studies in government we cannot rid ourselves of the misconception that administration stands upon an essentially different basis in a democratic state from that on which it stands in a non-democratic state."

Woodrow Wilson, *The Study of Administration*, 1886

The public schools of Medfield, Massachusetts, recently invited parents to participate in the development of a five-year plan—what *is* it with statists and five-year plans?—and it's an instructive case study. Medfield is about as good as you could ask for when it comes to public schools. It's an extraordinarily affluent community, with an average household income above $100,000 and average home valuations (the basis of public-school revenue) above a half-million dollars. It's very wealthy and very white—so white that it does not even disaggregate test scores for black or Hispanic students. It spends a tremendous amount of money per student, an amount comparable to the tuition at many good private schools.

So, how is socialism working out in the Medfield schools? To take one typical example, the district's "report card" under the No Child Left Behind law reports that fourth-grade math scores are much lower than one would expect in such a high-flying community. Fourteen percent of students were graded "advanced," 36 percent "proficient," 45 percent "needs improvement," and 4 percent "warning," the lowest rating offered. Even taking out the extremes, there are nearly one-third more students in the non-proficient category than in the proficient category.

Overall, the state of Massachusetts has highly rated public schools, a fact attended by much rhetoric about serving the poor and the disadvantaged. Statewide, Massachusetts's fourth-grade math-score breakdown for black students is: 5 percent advanced, 20 percent proficient, 51 percent needs improvement, 25 percent warning. Notably, the scores for black students are even worse, marginally, than the scores for low-income students, whose breakdown is: 6 percent advanced, 22 percent proficient, 51 percent needs improvement, and 22 percent warning.

And these are among the best state-run schools *in the country*. The situation is much worse in other states, particularly for black and low-income students. The *Wall Street Journal* reports, "In the year 2000's standardized NAEP test for math achievement, this is the percentage of black eighth graders who passed respectively in some famous states: New York, 8%; California, 6%; Michigan, 6%; Tennessee, 6%; Texas, 7%; Arkansas, 2%. Indeed the national average for black eighth graders is 6% compared to 40% for white students, a 34% achievement gap."[17]

Why would black parents and poor parents be "ardent supporters of socialism," to use Professor Allitt's words, when school socialism produces those kinds of results? The truth is they aren't. School-choice programs are wildly popular with black families and poor families; the Washington, D.C. scholarship program, recently destroyed by congressional Democrats at the behest of the teachers' unions, had thousands of applications for each of its handful of slots. The results strongly indicated that the students were achieving far superior educational outcomes under the private-school program than they were in the socialist schools. The *Washington Post* reports, "Students awarded vouchers to attend private schools in the District had significantly better chances of graduating from high school, and parents who sent their children to schools using scholarships were happy with having a choice of good, safe schools. These latest findings on D.C. school vouchers underscore the value of this program and show how wrong-headed it is to deny future students this opportunity."[18] But future students are indeed being denied the opportunity, and they will be sentenced to 13-year terms in Washington's failed and failing socialist schools. Why?

If the well-off and white in leafy Medfield, Massachusetts, cannot make a socialist five-year plan work for their state-run schools, it is unlikely that the largely poor urban blacks in Washington's schools will be able to, either. If the knowledge problem identified by Mises and Hayek make rational central planning impossible for something as simple as a quart of milk, what chance do central planners have to make rational, effective plans for something as complex and difficult as educating the children of a diverse nation of more than 300 million?

The educational establishment claims a "right of eminent domain" over the "hearts, minds, and bodies" of the children, but to what end? Clearly, the end is not education, and it never was—not from the time of Martin Luther and the Old Deceiver Satan Law forward. The interests of the children in the socialist education system are no more being served than were the interests of the millions of Indians consigned to poverty by their socialist rulers or the interests of Venezuelans who were left hungry as tons of food mouldered away in the warehouses of Hugo Chávez's socialist government.

So, whose interests are served under socialism? That vital question is the topic of the next chapter.

Chapter Six

OTHER PEOPLE'S MONEY: SOCIALIST EDUCATION AND THE PROBLEM OF INCENTIVES

s we've seen, socialism cannot serve citizens' interests because central planners have no way of knowing what those interests are. In the absence of the information conveyed through marketplace activity—particularly through prices—economic planners are left with highly defective sources of information: opinion polling, surveys, stated preferences (which normally differ dramatically from real or revealed preferences), and the like.

Under democratic socialism, the main communicator of citizens' preferences will be election results, but these, too, are highly unreliable. Voters will support a particular candidate or party for any number of reasons, and the mere fact that a majority of voters supports Candidate A over Candidate B does not mean that the voters endorse Candidate A's agenda *in toto*, or even the most important parts of it. Barack Obama, for instance, won election as president of the United States very convincingly, yet voters opposed—strongly, in many cases—much of his core agenda, including his economic program (most notably the stimulus bill) and his healthcare overhaul. The available data suggest voters did not select Obama because of their support for particular items on his platform, but because they had negative feelings about George W. Bush that were transferred onto other members of Bush's party, including John McCain and Sarah Palin, along with many congressional candidates.

Guess What?

★ The planners are the biggest beneficiaries of socialism

★ Public school policy is formulated to benefit specific interest groups

★ Unlike socialism, capitalism serves the interest of consumers

Most developed democracies have relatively few political parties, so voters' decisions tell us little about their real preferences. Imagine a United States in which consumers could choose from only two models of automobile: black, four-door, four-cylinder economy sedans, or red, two-door, eight-cylinder sports coupes that cost twice as much. Sedan buyers might be expressing a preference for economy cars, or they may not have enough money to buy the more expensive sports car. But it could be that they simply hate red cars. It could be that, in general, they prefer sports coupes but do not like the design or drivetrain on the one sports car available in the marketplace. The fact that a majority of consumers chose one car or the other would tell us little about their overall preferences, and the same is true for voters given a choice between two major-party presidential candidates, or three competing parties in a parliamentary system.

Election results tell us even less at the local level, which is where school boards are elected and thus where most day-to-day public-school decisions are made. Relatively few voters cast their ballots in presidential races, but an even smaller number—much smaller, proportionally—cast their ballots in school-board elections. The general population in any given community knows very little about its school board, about its members and their policy agendas, or about how and why it makes decisions. Because so few people vote in school-board races, and because the general population pays so little attention to school-board politics and policymaking, a small group of highly motivated voters tends to have a disproportionate influence in public-school decision-making.

Usually, that highly influential group is dominated by people with children in the public schools, though education is far from their only motive. Prestigious public-school systems tend to increase real-estate values, so property owners are more likely to take an interest in public-school politics than are renters. Because people who own homes also tend to be people whose children attend public schools—renters more often are younger and childless or older people with adult children—they have a double incentive to shape school-board decisions, and their incentives are to maximize the amount of resources put into public schools. Their neighbors might in fact prefer to spend a bit less on schools, or to be more vigilant about linking funding increases to performance gains. But since the people who are least enthusiastic about public-school spending also tend to be renters—who pay school taxes only indirectly, through higher rents—they are less likely to be as energetic in seeing to it that their interests are served by the school board.

The branch of economics known as "public choice theory" is particularly interested in those kinds of problems, usually described as "concentrated benefits vs. dispersed costs." If you own a great deal of residential real estate in a particular school district, you have a strong incentive to support higher public-school spending. But if you rent, and the only impact of higher spending is a $10-per-month increase in rent, you have a relatively weak incentive to counteract higher spending. On a larger scale, the petroleum companies that collect billions of dollars a year in subsidies through the U.S. ethanol program (BP collected $600 million in

A Lesson in Incentives

"In New York City, landlord arson became so common [after the imposition of rent control] that the city responded with special welfare allowances. For a while, burned-out tenants were moved to the top of the list for coveted public housing. That then gave tenants an incentive to burn down the buildings in which they lived—which they did, often moving television sets and furniture out onto the sidewalk before starting the fire."

William Tucker, *Zoning, Rent Control, and Affordable Housing*, 1991

ethanol subsidies in 2010, even as members of Congress declared the oil company Public Enemy No. 1) have a strong incentive to defend those subsidies and to lobby for their expansion. But consumers paying an extra 10 cents a gallon at the pump may not even know they are contributing to a $5 billion annual payoff to the energy industry. An industry with $5 billion on the line is going invest a lot of money in lobbying and garnering political influence; a commuter with 10 cents on the line is not.

The problem of concentrated benefits vs. dispersed costs means that the one source of information that central planners have access to—voters' decisions—is distorted, usually beyond recognition. It is that distortion of knowledge and incentives—and not (usually) corruption or malfeasance on the part of elected officials—that explains the paradoxical outcomes so familiar in democracies: a majority-rules system that produces policies that the majority would not choose, policies that are in many cases exactly the opposite of what the majority would prefer.

The more socialist a system is, the more it must suffer from this problem. In a highly competitive marketplace, consumers make decisions for themselves and—most important—are forced to spend their own resources in accordance with those decisions. Under a socialist system, consumers of government-provided goods and services use the power of politics to consume at a higher level than they would if they had to pay the entire cost themselves. Most people probably would prefer owning a Ferrari to owning a Hyundai, but Hyundai sells a lot more cars, because Ferraris are expensive. If people could vote to acquire Ferraris for themselves at Hyundai prices—with their neighbors being forced to make up the price difference through higher taxes—then Ferrari would sell a lot more cars.

Who Reaps the Profits of Socialism?

But consumers are not the only interest group that is able to game the system under the socialist model of providing goods and services. As strong as highly motivated consumers' incentives may be, there is another group of people with an even stronger set of incentives: the central planners themselves, i.e. the government employees who staff the socialist bureaucracies. Again, the American public-school system provides a telling example of how these incentives play out.

Though the United States is a broadly capitalist country, primary-secondary education is conducted under an almost exclusively socialist model. Indeed, the U.S. school system is more deeply socialized than Soviet agriculture was under Stalin. About 90 percent of U.S. students attend government schools for primary and secondary education, and practically 100 percent of taxpayers pay into the system. The Soviets, for all their effort, never managed to achieve 90 percent socialization of agriculture.

This comparison is not a facetious one; just as Soviet apparatchiks used their positions of influence to command better wages, better food, better housing, and other privileges not accorded to the vast proletariat on whose behalf they alleged to labor, American government workers—and government-school workers in particular—enjoy far higher wages, better healthcare benefits, more job security, guaranteed pensions, generous paid vacations, and other benefits not dreamt of by the working people on whose behalf they allegedly engage in "public service." And the economics of the U.S. public-school system would be readily familiar to any student of the Soviet economy.

The economist Paul Craig Roberts tells a relevant anecdote about the shortcomings of Soviet economic planning: when the output of a nail factory was measured in total units of production, the managers of the factory decided to produce great quantities of small, thin nails. When the measure of output was changed to gross tonnage, the managers switched to making big, heavy nails. In both cases, the producers produced what the measurers measured, regardless of whether the economy actually needed lots of small nails or a fewer number of heavy nails.

The socialist economics of the U.S. public-school system operates in precisely the same way: when schools were measured by their gradua-tion rates, they lowered standards and graduated more students. When they were measured by standardized-test scores, they neglected general education to focus on the subjects covered by the tests and lobbied to have the tests designed in such a way as to maximize their students' scores. (In some instances, educators organized their students to system-atically cheat on standardized tests.) When extra money became available for "special needs" students, educators began to classify more and more of their students as "special needs." While reporting on school budgets in a school district outside Philadelphia, I found one school district went so far as to classify its gifted-and-talented program as a "special needs" program, thereby maximizing both its funding and its measured success in educating special-needs students.

Of course, the best way for managers to meet the goals set for them by the central planners is to take over the process of writing the central plan themselves. Studying Soviet industrial production, Professor Roberts observed,

> When I first examined this system, it was clear to me that sig-nals interpreted by managers constituted the main difference between the Soviet economy and a normal market economy. In a normal market, managers organize production by interpret-ing price and profit signals. In the Soviet economy, managers interpreted gross output indicators. The critical difference is that gross output indicators are irrational from the standpoint of economic efficiency. Soviet managers were as autonomous as their market counterparts. They set their own plan targets by disguising their productive capacity and overstating their resource needs. Soviet planners served primarily as supply agents for enterprises, endeavoring to supply the enterprises

with sufficient inputs to fulfill their gross output targets. The system of material supply could seldom perform this task, and Soviet factory managers made barter arrangements with one another and produced their own inputs. This activity led me to the conclusion that the Soviet economy, like a market, was organized polycentrically and not hierarchically as a planning system. The "central plan" was little more than the summation of the factory managers' individual plans.[1]

The New York City public schools formulated a five-year plan in 2008, and they conducted their business in much the same way as the Soviet factory managers did: their collective five-year plan was simply a summation of the pre-existing preferences of the "factory managers," in this case the teachers, as represented through their unions, along with the principals and other administrators. In fact, the teachers so dominated the process that the five-year plan was focused on a single central desire of the education-factory managers: reducing class sizes.

The educational-achievement literature shows little connection between class size and student achievement. But smaller classes mean much less work for educators—but not less pay—so reducing classroom headcounts has long been a key goal for educators and the education bureaucracies. Likewise, the teachers' unions have long fought for the requirement of advanced degrees for many teachers, or for significantly higher pay for teachers who hold masters' degrees or better. The research shows no relationship between teachers' holding advanced degrees and student performance. But more advanced degrees mean higher aggregate salaries for educators—as well as for administrators—and, perhaps more important, significantly higher pension benefits, because pensions are directly related to salaries during the last years of a teacher's career.

Professor Roberts had a difficult time assembling meaningful economic data for his studies of Soviet industrial production. Happily for students of mixed-economy socialism, we have much better data about the economics of American public education, and they mirror the trends in socialist production across industries and nations. Inputs are misaligned and resources are misallocated; consumers' interests are not served but the apparatchik's interests' are. In short, real spending (which is to say, inflation-adjusted spending) on education in the United States has skyrocketed—and not just over recent decades. Real spending on schooling in the United States has grown an average of 3.5 percent above and beyond the rate of inflation for a century, as reported by Eric A. Hanushek and Dale W. Jorgensen in their National Research Council study, "Improving America's Schools."[2] While real expenditures have been climbing, real educational achievement has flatlined in most cases, but in many cases has declined, and in some cases has declined radically. More spending for less output—that's a good working definition of socialist economic outcomes.

The spending on U.S. education, Hanushek and Jorgensen find, has been driven by three factors: educators' salaries, reductions in classroom size, and spending on non-instructional expenses. That lattermost category includes things like administrative costs and the salaries of non-educator personnel such as counselors, assistants, nurses, and the like. But it also hides a good deal of money directed into the pockets of teachers. Retirees' expenses, for instance—the generous pensions and lavishly funded healthcare benefits that teachers' unions demand from taxpayers—are classified as non-instructional costs, since they go to retired educators instead of active classroom teachers. Taken together, these three factors add up to a program of paying teachers much more to do much less work, without any concomitant demand that they get better results from their reduced workloads. As Hanushek and Jorgensen put it:

> Matched against the growth in spending, student performance has, at best, stayed constant and may have fallen. While

aggregate performance measures are somewhat imprecise, all point to no gains in student performance over the past two decades. . . . While there has been slight movement, the overall picture is one of stagnating performance.

Perhaps the most dramatic finding of analyses of schools is that smaller class sizes usually have had no general impact on student performance, even though they have obvious implications for school costs. Moreover, the basic econometric evidence is supported by experimental evidence, making it one of the clearest results from an extensively researched topic. Although some specific instruction may be enhanced by smaller classes, student performance in most classes is unaffected by variations in class size in standard operations of, say, 15 to 40 students. Nevertheless, even in the face of high costs that yield no apparent performance benefits, the overall policy of states and local districts has been to reduce class sizes in order to try to increase quality.

A second, almost equally dramatic, example is that obtaining an advanced degree does little to ensure that teachers do a better job in the classroom. It is just as likely that a teacher with a bachelor's degree would elicit high performance from students as would a teacher with a master's degree. Again, since a teacher's salary invariably increases with the completion of a master's degree, this is another example of increased expenditures yielding no gains in student performance.

These resource effects are important for two reasons. First, variations in instructional expenditures across classrooms are largely determined by the pupil-teacher ratio and the salary of the teacher, which, in turn, is largely determined by the teacher's degree and experience. If these factors have no systematic influence on student performance—which the evidence shows they do not—expansion of resources in the ways of the past are unlikely to improve performance. Second, either explicitly or implicitly schools have pursued a program of adding these specific resources. . . . Schools currently have record-low pupil-teacher ratios, record-high numbers for completion of master's degrees, and more experienced teachers than at any time at least since 1960. These factors are the result of many specific programs that have contributed to the rapid growth in per-pupil spending but have not led to improvements in student performance. Schools do not try to ensure that increased student performance flows from increased expenditures.[3]

The Lure of Other People's Money

"There are four ways in which you can spend money. You can spend your own money on yourself. When you do that, why then you really watch out what you're doing, and you try to get the most for your money. Then you can spend your own money on somebody else. For example, I buy a birthday present for someone. Well, then I'm not so careful about the content of the present, but I'm very careful about the cost. Then, I can spend somebody else's money on myself. And if I spend somebody else's money on myself, then I'm sure going to have a good lunch! Finally, I can spend somebody else's money on somebody else. And if I spend somebody else's money on somebody else, I'm not concerned about how much it is, and I'm not concerned about what I get. And that's government. And that's close to 40 percent of our national income."

Milton Friedman, Fox News interview, 2004

That last sentence is particularly telling: educators do not try to ensure that increased student performance flows from increased expenditures. But why? For the people who run the schools, increased expenditures are a net benefit in and of themselves, regardless of whether they produce superior results; the bigger the budget, the bigger the salary of the administrator charged with managing it. The more money in the system, the more will be paid out in salaries and benefits.

It is worth noting that much of the spending classified as "non-instructional costs" ends up enriching school-system employees through pension and medical-benefit programs. When there is no link between payment and performance, prices inevitably rise and quality decreases, which is precisely what has happened in American public schools. But because the price is hidden through a byzantine system of taxes and subsidies, rather than being explicit, as in the form of an annual tuition check, the consumers of those services do not directly experience the economic dysfunction of the system.

Calling Gordon Gekko

Compare this model of providing goods and services with practically any product provided through the competitive marketplace. Government-education advocates such as Barack Obama give passionate speeches about the need for education, about the critical role it plays in our society, but they continue to advocate what is—let us remember—a nineteenth-century Prussian approach to education.

The United States in the twenty-first century is not very much like nineteenth-century Prussia (Prussia today isn't much like Prussia then, either), but we still use its educational methods. We would never think of using its transportation methods (horsepower was literally *horse*-power), its communication methods (telegraphs), or its military technology (muzzle-loaders and bayonets). But government-run systems have a way of preserving themselves well past any rational point, which is why the United States still maintains the helium reserve it established for dirigible warfare—presumably to fight those nineteenth-century Prussians.

Compare our failing public schools with our cellular phones. Cell phones and cell-phone service are enormously competitive industries in which innovation and capital from around the world are channeled—with no five-year plan, amazingly enough—to serve the needs of consumers. They have improved immeasurably over a short period of time. In 2010, movie-goers watching the trailer for the Oliver Stone film *Wall Street: Money Never Sleeps* got a big laugh out of the 1985-vintage cell phone that white-collar criminal Gordon Gekko reclaims from the property room as he is released from prison. It's a great gag—the thing is as big as a cinderblock. But there's more to the joke than the clunky aesthetic of Reagan-era technology. Gordon Gekko's cell phone, the Motorola DynaTac, cost the equivalent of just under $10,000 in 2010 dollars. Monthly service fees ran into hundreds of dollars. Basic features of 2010 cell phones, like text-messaging and e-mail, were unheard of—even a Wall Street titan like Gordon Gekko couldn't download a song from the iTunes store. In 2010, you couldn't give Gordon Gekko's cell phone—his prized status symbol, his most conspicuous indicator of wealth and sophistication—to a kid in a housing project in the South Bronx.

But that same South Bronx kid who has access to some of the best communication technology in the history of mankind is stuck with a failing public school—a third-rate version of a nineteenth-century Prussian model that at its best probably would not serve his interests. The difference is that the socialist model of education *is not designed to serve his interests*, while the private enterprise model, which must compete for customers and their money, has no choice but to serve its customers' interests. The free-market model has its shortcomings, too, but in most cases a bad product or defective service is driven out of the marketplace by competition. Under a socialist model, there is no competition to drive out bad products and rotten services, which is why a visitor from 1929 would recognize your public schools but would be amazed by the cell phones they give away for free at your local mall.

What is worth noting—and what must be most amazing to the true-believers among the central-planning authorities—is that something as miraculous as the cellular-phone network, which has brought technology that was once the stuff of Buck Rogers comics into the hands of ordinary people, including poor people, lacked any coordinated national or global plan to do so. In fact, is it precisely the absence of a central plan that has allowed the industry to thrive and to innovate.

If we had structured the provision of cellular-phone service the way we have education, the incentives would have been radically different: the guy selling the 1985 DynaTac would make the same profit as the guy selling the iPhone; consumers would have no choice between Verizon's good network and AT&T's spotty one, and would simply be assigned a network based on which street they live on. Because everybody would be taxed to provide cell phones for everybody else, only the wealthy would have enough money left over to enter the private cell-phone market, so innovation would be stifled. With no competition, there would be no incentive to drive down prices—in fact, there would be every incentive to drive up prices.

Given the inherent defects of the socialist model of providing goods and services, one has to wonder: why would anybody choose socialism in the first place? There are lots of possible answers to that question: class resentment, socio-economic envy, risk-aversion, irrational distrust of profit-seeking entrepreneurs, etc. The best answer, however, may surprise many people: Sweden.

Chapter Seven

WHY SWEDEN STINKS

Venezuela, North Korea, the Soviet Union, Mao's China, pre-reform India, American inner-city schools, Amtrak, Sri Lanka's graphite industry, Mexico's nationalized banks in the 1980s, Cuba, Laos, Vietnam, Bangladesh, Libya, the Sandinista regime—there's an expansive catalogue of socialism, from the national to the local, from the general to the particular, that socialists do not want us to talk about when we talk about socialism. The list of nations they do want to talk about is very short, and it reads: Sweden.

Writing in Britain's *Independent*, Hamish McRae called Sweden "The Most Successful Society on the Planet."[1] Not to be outdone, Polly Toynbee of the *Guardian* christened it "The Most Successful Society the World Has Ever Known."[2] In 1976, *Time* described Sweden as a veritable utopia operating under *samhället*, Sweden's more liberal answer to Marx's dictatorship of the proletariat and North Korea's "Juche Idea":

> It is a country whose very name has become a synonym for a materialist paradise. Its citizens enjoy one of the world's highest living standards, and a great many possess symbols of individual affluence: a private home or a modern apartment, a family car, a *stuga* (summer cottage) and often a sailboat. No slums disfigure their cities, their air and water are largely pollution-free, and they have ever more leisure to indulge a collective passion

Guess What?

★ Swedes in capitalist America fare better than those who live in socialist Sweden

★ Sweden's socialist "successes" can't be repeated in most countries

★ Socialism has turned Sweden into a nation of petty swindlers

for being *ut i naturen* (out in nature) in their half-forested country. Neither ill-health, unemployment nor old age pose the terror of financial hardship. In short, Sweden's 8.2 million citizens have ample reasons for being satisfied. In fact, most are.

...The *samhället*'s cradle-to-grave benefits are unmatched in any other free society outside Scandinavia. Swedes enjoy free public education through college, four weeks' annual vacation and comprehensive retraining programs if they want to switch careers....In pursuit of new ways to ease the *Angst* of life, a local politician actually proposed that the government provide free sex partners for the lonely.[3]

Sweden in particular, and the Scandinavian model of socialism more generally, has given American socialists the best piece of evidence for their case. One of the more perceptive among them, Jesse Larner of *Dissent* magazine, attributes the supposed success of Swedish-style socialism to its disinclination to centrally plan the entire economy. "Hayek understood at least one very big thing," Larner writes, "that the vision of a perfectible society leads inevitably to the gulag."[4] But the Scandinavian model, he argues, makes room for a less authoritarian, more genuinely democratic expression of socialism, one that is not held hostage by the petty corruption and endemic misallocation of resources associated with other kinds of socialism. "The possibility of nontotalitarian models of social democracy, like those that emerged in Europe after the war, should alert the reader to Hayek's limitations," he claims.[5]

Can one have socialism without central planning? Larner argues for exactly such a thing, and other likeminded "market socialists" have pressed for similar arrangements. Hayek was writing about Lenin, Stalin, and Hitler. The limitations articulated by Hayek, they argue, do not apply to other, less centralized kinds of socialism. Larner writes:

Comprehensive models of how society should work reject the wisdom of solutions that work and deny the legitimacy (indeed, from Lenin to Mussolini to Mao to Ho to Castro to Qutb, deny the very right to *exist*) of individuals who demonstrate anti-orthodox wisdom. Defenders of these models are required by their own rigidity to invent the category of the *counterrevolutionary*. To Hayek, this is what socialism, communism, and collectivism—he makes little distinction between them—mean: the dangerous illusion of perfectibility. The only kind of socialism he considers in *Road* is state-managed, perfect-society utopianism, in which the direction of the economy and all of its inputs and outputs are planned, with the accompanying political and moral degradation that Hayek demonstrates quite convincingly.[6]

In many ways, the Scandinavian model is superficially attractive, and no critic of socialism can afford to ignore its successes. While Venezuela's state-run grocery stores exhibit failures that have obvious parallels in American public schools, the Scandinavian countries seem to offer an exception. Why?

To understand the apparent success of Scandinavian socialism, it is first necessary to understand the cultural and economic conditions that gave rise to this system, which on the surface appears to be radically more successful than alternative models of socialism. The free-market economist Milton Friedman was among those who understood that there is something deep in Scandinavian culture that greases the machinery of socialism. When a Scandinavian socialist boasted to Friedman, "In Scandinavia, we have no poverty," his reply was astute: "That's interesting—because in America, among Scandinavians, we have no poverty, either."[7] That isn't quite true: the poverty rate for Swedish Americans is about 6.7 percent, according to economists Geranda Notten and Chris de Neubourg. The poverty rate in Sweden? Also 6.7 percent.

What seems undeniable is that the Scandinavian countries, especially Sweden, have much more effective government institutions than does the United States. "Sure, the taxes are sky-high," say admirers of Swedish socialism, "but at least they get something in return." One of the things they get in return is a relatively efficient government, and one with low levels of corruption. Effective public institutions are characteristic of societies with high levels of social trust, and Sweden is just such a society. The bad news for the rest of the world—but especially for highly complex societies such as the United States, India, and China—is that the social conditions that produce these high levels of trust are not generally transmutable. (And it's bad news for Sweden, too, which is rapidly transforming itself into the sort of society that will not be able to support the relatively successful welfare-state arrangements that characterized it throughout most of the twentieth century.)

Highly trusting societies tend to be ethnically, religiously, and linguistically homogenous, relatively small, and often culturally insulated by the use of a rare language such as Swedish or Icelandic. So culturally homogenous are the Scandinavian-style socialist success stories that most of them (Iceland, Norway, Denmark, Finland) still have taxpayer-supported state churches, something that would be anathema in a religiously complex society such as the United States. Sweden itself had a state church until 2000, and the Church of Sweden, a

He Fought Socialism... And Socialism Won

"Carl Bildt, Sweden's new 42-year-old conservative prime minister, aims to steer Sweden back into the family of free-market nations. 'Collectivism and socialism have been thrown on the scrap heap of history,' he told us during a recent visit. 'There is no compromise worth having between state control and capitalism.'"

Wall Street Journal, April 1992

Lutheran congregation, still enjoys something close to an official status, listing 73 percent of Swedes as members—in a country that is 85 percent atheist.

Even if diversity-celebrating Americans wanted to reproduce the social conditions underpinning Swedish socialism, it would be impossible for them to do so, just as it would be impossible for them to become a nation of less than 10 million rather than the world's third-most-populous country, with more than 300 million residents. At times, this obvious fact becomes apparent even to American policymakers predisposed toward Swedish-style socialism. President Obama, challenged by a critic to explain why Sweden managed its banking crisis with relative aplomb compared to the United States, said,

> They took over the banks, nationalized them, got rid of the bad assets, resold the banks, and, a couple years later, they were going again. So you'd think, looking at it, Sweden looks like a good model. Here's the problem; Sweden had like five banks. We've got thousands of banks. You know, the scale of the U.S. economy and the capital markets are so vast and the problems in terms of managing and overseeing anything of that scale, I think, would—our assessment was that it wouldn't make sense. And we also have different traditions in this country.[8]

Somehow, a precisely parallel set of facts and equally obvious conclusions eluded him and his party when it came to reforming American healthcare policy. (More on that later.)

The Dark Side of a Socialist Paradise

Sweden's high level of cultural cohesion, like that of its Scandinavian neighbors, has its drawbacks, however. Sweden in recent years opened itself up to high levels of immigration; about 13 percent of its population today is foreign-born, though it is worth noting that the largest group of immigrants to Sweden are *Finlandsvensk*—Swedish-speaking people from neighboring Finland—who share similar cultural traditions and are easily assimilated into Swedish society. For non-Scandinavian immigrants, who include refugees from the Balkans, Africa, and the Middle East, prospects are very different. The British journalist Christina Patterson, who spent her childhood summers in Sweden, laments the country's "near-universal conformism" and describes the situation thus: "In a country where pretty much everyone is blonde and beautiful (Goering, I discovered, spent a happy summer at my childhood seaside resort), the non-white immigrant is greeted with generous welfare benefits and a hefty dose of suspicion."[9]

What they are not greeted with are jobs. While immigrants constitute nearly 15 percent of the working-age population, they make up a far higher proportion of the unemployed. In fact, Sweden has one of the highest disparities between immigrants' unemployment and native-born unemployment in the developed world. Its labor market is severely segregated along racial lines, as the Swedish economist Johan Norberg reports:

> Unemployment problems in turn result in de facto segregation. Despite little history of racial conflict, the labor market is more segregated than in America, Britain, Germany, France or Denmark—countries with far more troublesome racial histories than Sweden. A report from the free-market Liberal Party ahead of the election 2002 showed that more than 5 percent of all precincts in Sweden had employment levels lower than 60 percent, with much higher crime rates and inferior school results than in other places. Most of these precincts are suburban, so outsiders rarely see them. The number of segregated precincts has continued to grow. In some neighborhoods, chil-

dren grow up without ever seeing someone who goes to work in the morning. Pockets of unemployment and social exclusion form, especially in areas with many non-European immigrants. When Swedes see that so many immigrants live off the government, their interest in contributing to the system fades.

Like in other parts of western Europe, the segregation of immigrant areas leads to insularity, crime and, in some cases, radicalism. Last year, Nalin Pekgul, the Kurdish chairman of the National Federation of Social Democratic Women, explained that she was forced to move out of a suburb of Stockholm because of crime and the rise of Islamic radicalism. The announcement sent shock waves through the entire political system. "A bomb waiting to explode" is one of the most common metaphors used when social exclusion in Sweden is discussed.

Those immigrants who do keep their entrepreneurial spirit intact often take it elsewhere. Hundreds of unemployed Somalis and Iranians leave Sweden every year and move to Britain, where they are often successful in finding work. The contrast in experience can be staggering. The Swedish economic historian Benny Carlson recently compared the experiences of Somali immigrants in Sweden with those of Somali immigrants in Minneapolis, Minnesota. Only 30 percent had a job in Sweden, about half as many as in Minneapolis. And there are about 800 businesses run by Somalis in Minneapolis, compared to only 38 in Sweden. Carlson quoted two immigrants who together summed up the disparity. "There are opportunities here," said Jamal Hashi, who runs an African restaurant in Minneapolis. His friend, who migrated to Sweden instead, told a different story: "You feel like a fly trapped under a glass. Your dreams are shattered."[10]

Just as Somalis in the United States have far different economic outcomes than do Somalis in Sweden, Swedes in the United States fare far better than do their kinsmen in the mother country. The average income for a Swede in Sweden is $36,600, while the average income in the United States is $45,500—and the average income for a Swede in the United States is $56,900—55 percent more than the Swedish average.

In fact, if Sweden were a state in the United States, it would be the poorest. The poorest demographic cohort in the United States, African Americans, enjoy an average household income slightly higher than the Swedish average. The more extreme the socialism, the more extreme the poverty; while black Americans enjoy a higher standard of living than do Swedes, black South Africans under apartheid by many measures enjoyed a higher standard of living than did their contemporaries living under Russian socialism. For instance, black South Africans owned more cars per capita in 1983 than did Soviet subjects,[11] suggesting that even a system of intentional, wicked oppression did not enact as much material privation on its victims as did the socialist system intended to help its victims.

Sweden does not seem poor, but it is relatively poor, and it is getting relatively poorer; in 1970, Sweden had the fourth-highest average income in the world, but by 2000 it had fallen to fourteenth place, and it appears likely to head further downward.

One reason for that is that fewer Swedes are working. And that in itself is a strange development, inasmuch as Swedes once were among the hardest-working peoples in the developed world, working more hours than Americans and nearly as many as the workaholic South Koreans. Today, 10 percent of all Swedes of working age are in early retirement, collecting disability payments. About 16 percent of the national government's expenditures goes to subsidizing workers' sick days, and employee absenteeism is at epidemic levels. How is it that one of the healthiest group of citizens on the planet are so frequently disabled and so often too sick to work? Was there some sort of terrible accident? A 13,000-Saab pileup? A Scandinavian epidemic?

The most likely answer is this: they aren't disabled, and they aren't sick. In Sweden, a society once defined as much by its Protestant work ethic as by its egalitarian social ideals, gaming the system—defrauding one's taxpaying neighbors—has become socially acceptable, something that would have been unthinkable to Swedes a generation ago. Norberg argues that this shift in national psychology is a direct reaction to the incentives created by the Swedish model of socialism:

Good Thing They Have Free Healthcare!

Sweden has the "sickest work force in the world," reports Swedish journalist Ulf Nilson. And Monday is the "sickest day of the week." "Another way of describing *Svenska sjukan* (the Swedish disease) is to say that around one million Swedes of working age (of whom there are some five million) are not going to work today," he writes. "Or tomorrow. Or the day after. In other words, some 20 percent. Every fifth [working-age Swede]. In spite of everything being said the disease does *not* strike old women...worse than any other group. To the contrary: according to the reports, the sickliest Swedes are young men, generally believed to be among the healthiest specimens on earth.

"At which point you might say: Oops, there must be something fishy here."
And indeed there is.

"...Most of the young men, thousands of them every day, lie when they call in sick. The same goes for thousands of young women. And older people, too. They call in sick, without being sick—and why? Because it has become a habit. And because—very important this!—given the idiotic tax system, you lose very little by not working."

Mentalities have a tendency of changing when incentives change. The growth of taxes and benefits punished hard work and encouraged absenteeism. Immigrants and younger generations of Swedes have faced distorted incentives and have not developed the work ethic that was nurtured before the effects of the welfare state began to erode them. When others cheat the system and get away with it, suddenly you are considered a fool if you get up early every morning and work late. According to polls, about half of all Swedes now think it is acceptable to call in sick for reasons other than sickness. Almost half think that they can do it when someone in the family is not feeling well, and almost as many think that they can do it if there is too much to do at work. Our ancestors worked even when they were sick. Today, we are "off sick" even when we feel fine.[12]

If we are to take Swedes at their word, then they are the sickest society in the developed world. Some 20 percent of all working-age Swedes receive some form of unemployment benefit, many of them related to sickness and disability—and many of them almost certainly fraudulent.

What is perhaps most interesting about this change in national psychology is that Swedish socialism, despite its high rates of taxation and its generous array of welfare benefits, is not an especially redistributive system. Whereas welfare benefits in the United States tend to result in a great deal of interpersonal transfers—taxing Peter to subsidize Paul—Swedish welfare historically has been geared more toward intertemporal transfers—taxing young Peter to fund old Peter's pension benefits. By some estimates, Swedish social benefits are 80–85 percent "self-financing," meaning that beneficiaries mostly get out of the system what they have paid into it, minus the (substantial) overhead costs imposed by government management of the programs.

Swedes are well aware of this fact; indeed, the "you get out of it what you put into it" mentality is one of the reasons that Swedes have accepted such high levels of taxation and such a large and expensive welfare state. But defrauding the system through phony sick days and overstated disability claims undermines that mentality. It not only makes the system of transfers more interpersonal and less intertemporal, it also diminishes the high levels of social trust that have made such a system possible in the first place.

It will come as no surprise, then, to learn that the Swedish model is on the socialist skids. In fact, it looks increasingly likely that Sweden's socialist system will end up undermining the country's historically egalitarian, trusting, and hard-working ethos—leaving Swedes with the high taxes, expense, and dysfunctional public sector familiar to students of the European welfare state, but depriving them of whatever benefits such a system may have offered.

Furthermore, it is not entirely clear what those benefits may be. Swedes are a very healthy and long-lived people, for instance, and aficionados of European socialism have argued that this speaks well of the country's centralized, single-payer healthcare system. Sweden has very low rates of poverty and an apparently egalitarian economic climate, which also are taken as evidence that Swedish-style socialism works wonderfully. But the fact is that all of that was true of Sweden long before the establishment of the Swedish socialist state. In 1950, Swedes already were living, on average, 2.6 years longer than Americans, according to the Swedish think tank Captus.[13] Sixty years of "The Most Successful Society the World Has Ever Known" brought that differential all the way up to ... 2.7 years. As late as 1980, Sweden's per capita GDP was 20 percent higher than that of the United States, but by 2001 the U.S. per capita GDP was 56 percent higher. A big part of the reason for that is high levels of taxation; whereas the Sweden of 1960 was taxed at levels approximately equal to those of the United States today, the country's tax rate is more than 52 percent of GDP—half of all economic output is seized by the state.

The irony is that all of this socialism has left Sweden with a society that is, in many important ways, less egalitarian and less generous than that created by the allegedly pitiless capitalism of the United States. While Sweden's income is much more evenly distributed throughout its society than it is in the United States, its wealth is less evenly distributed. Unsurprisingly, income and wealth are highly correlated in the United States, where most rich people get rich through high-paying work and by starting businesses. In Sweden, wealth is in fact less correlated with income than it is in the United States, suggesting that wealthy Swedes are less likely to have worked for their money than wealthy Americans, and more likely to have inherited it or otherwise obtained it through family connections.

Jobs Swedes Won't Do

"Some in Washington jokingly refer to IKEA as the Swedish Embassy. And there is no doubt it is the most successful Swedish retail outlet throughout the world. IKEA is well-known for its lack of staff both on the floor and in the back office. Shoppers experience IKEA as a do-it-yourself store. The shopping style stems from the high cost of Swedish employees. Ingvar Kemprad, founder of IKEA, constructed an employment model that minimized state-imposed labor costs."

Washington Times, 2007

Not only is Swedish socialism in many ways less egalitarian than American capitalism, the Scandinavians cannot even pride themselves on being more generous toward the poor and the disadvantaged than are the cowboy capitalists in the United States. While studies based on Organization for Economic Cooperation and Development statistics generally find a wide disparity between social spending in socialist Scandinavia than in the capitalist United States, those numbers fail to account for an important fact: Sweden and other northern European welfare states tax many of the benefits they pay out, whereas in the United States most benefits are untaxed and the tax code itself is used to provide social subsidies, through programs such as the Earned-Income Tax Credit.

Further, that social spending usually is calculated as a percentage of GDP, but the GDP of the United States is far larger than that of the Scandinavian socialist countries. Accounting for differences in GDP, the tax system, and the tax treatment of welfare benefits, the United States actually ranks right in the middle of the European socialist utopias when it comes to welfare spending, at a far lower rate of taxation, with a much more robust and dynamic economy.

Spending more, getting less: Swedish socialism looks a lot like the American public schools.

Chapter Eight

NORTH KOREA: FIGHTING FOR A FAILED SYSTEM

It is difficult to believe that history just happens to throw up monsters every time an unusually powerful central government is created. What are the chances, really, that Kim Il Sung, the very definition of a monster in politics, would have an equally monstrous, if not more monstrous, son to whom to bequeath his empire? What are the chances that the great demon of the twentieth century, Vladimir Lenin, would have an equally wicked lieutenant, Joseph Stalin, to take over for him when he died? And what are the chances that Stalin would find his mirror image in Adolf Hitler, another monster who clawed his way up from the penumbras of politics at precisely the same moment in history?

There is much to be said about the private immorality of such men, but there is at least as much to be said—probably more—about the ideas they embraced. Ideas move the world. A political idea is what makes the difference between a common criminal and a genocidal tyrant. A political idea is what turns a bitter art student into Hitler, a petty bank-robber into Stalin.

One has to wonder: what kind of idea turned the father-son, tag-team tyrants of North Korea into the masters of an anachronistic, starving slave-state, an island of antique Stalinism in the sea of resurgent Asian capitalism? The idea has a name, and it is "Juche."

Guess What?

★ Socialism has directly led to millions of famine-related deaths in North Korea

★ North Korean policy is more attributable to socialism than to the whims of its dictators

★ Like other socialist tyrants, Kim Jong Il mixes politics with biology

On the occasion of the seventieth birthday of North Korean dictator Kim Il Sung, his son Kim Jong Il, a future dictator, published an essay on the "Juche Idea," the guiding philosophy of his family's socialist regime. It is a largely banal and bombastic document, but it is remarkable for its robust—indeed, *fanatical*—commitment to the idea of socialist central planning. The Juche Idea holds that man is the center of the universe and that his powers to transform the universe are, in effect, unlimited, so long as he has the right kind of political leadership and acts under the right principles. As another leader of an effort to fundamentally transform his society might have put it, the Juche Idea holds that "we are the change we've been waiting for." Kim writes,

> The Juche Idea is a new philosophical thought which centers on man. As the leader [Kim Il Sung] said, the Juche Idea is based on the philosophical principle that man is the master of everything and decides everything. The Juche Idea raised the fundamental question of philosophy by regarding man as the main factor, and elucidated the philosophical principle that man is the master of everything and decides everything.[1]

That kind of heroic, anthropocentric thinking will be familiar to students of Jean-Jacques Rousseau, who saw the sovereign (in his case, an abstract sovereign: the "rule of law") as a kind of vessel by means of which the "general will" is collected and channeled into the state, the cauldron in which it is boiled down into policy through means obscure. Echoes of Rousseau can be heard throughout the history of socialism, and it is no coincidence that defenders of the anti-democratic Hugo Chávez describe him, in apologetic tones, as a "Rousseauean democrat," which is to say, no kind of democrat at all.

It is surely not any kind of familiar democracy that the North Koreans have in mind when they describe their state as the *Democratic* People's

Republic. If not through democracy, how is it that man "decides everything"? And what does Kim mean by the term? Helpfully, he explained his thinking:

> That man is the master of everything means that he is the master of the world and of his own destiny; that man decides ✓ everything means that he plays the decisive role in transforming the world and in shaping his destiny.
>
> The philosophical principle of the Juche Idea is the principle of man-centered philosophy which explains man's position and role in the world. The leader made it clear that man is a social being with Chajusong [a peculiar Korean expression meaning, roughly "social consciousness"], creativity and consciousness.
>
> Man, though material existence, is not a simple material being. He is the most developed material being, a special product of the evolution of the material world.
>
> Man was already outstanding as he emerged from the world of nature. He exists and develops by cognizing and changing the world to make it serve him, whereas all other material lives maintain.
>
> ... Man cannot, of course, live outside the world; he lives and conducts his activity in the world. Nature is the object of man's labor and also is the material source of his life. Society is a community where people live and conduct activities. Natural environments and social conditions have a great effect on human activity. Whether natural environments are good or bad and, in particular, whether the political and economic systems of a society are progressive or reactionary—these factors may favorably affect human endeavor to remake nature and develop society or limit and restrict that activity.

But man does not merely adapt himself to environments and conditions. By his independent, creative and conscious activity, man continuously transforms nature and society, changing as he desires what does not meet his needs, and replacing what is outdated and reactionary with what is new and progressive.[2]

What it means, then, is that reality is not reality, only the raw material from which the all-powerful MAN—by which Kim clearly means the all-powerful STATE—shapes a new reality according to the mandates of politics.

Aside from the Cannibalism, How's That Socialism Working Out?

"Tens of thousands starved in the latest [North Korean] famine, from 1995 to 1997. Lee, who asked that her given name not be used, was a clerk in a government office who notarized the deaths in her town. She is a pretty young woman, 29, with tumbling hair curling to her shoulders and smooth, flawless skin that belies the hardships she has faced and struggles to explain. 'We started seeing cannibalism,' she recalled, pausing. 'You probably won't understand.' She went on: 'When one is very hungry, one can go crazy.'

"... 'I can't condemn cannibalism. Not that I wanted to eat human meat, but we were so hungry.... I witnessed a woman being questioned for cannibalism. She said it tasted good.'

"Massive international food aid gradually stemmed the famine after a death toll estimated at anywhere from 300,000 to 2 million."

Washington Post, 2003

There is probably no more dangerous idea than the belief that a society can be perfected, and that the men who reside in it can be perfected as well, that we can, at will, start "replacing what is outdated and reactionary with what is new and progressive." Not that we haven't tried: Lenin, Stalin, and Mao all found great swathes of their societies outdated and reactionary, and worked to eliminate them. Hitler was known to protest that "the Jew is not a socialist!" in explaining his anti-Semitism. But if you believe that it is possible to command all of the relevant knowledge in a society, that you can make rational decisions governing every aspect of life, and that you have a historical mandate to do so, then you must believe that you can create a kind of utopia, a political heaven on Earth.

However, when THE PLAN fails—and THE PLAN always fails—then it is time to find somebody to blame. Over the course of the twentieth century, political movements understanding themselves to be socialist were responsible for the deaths of some 100 million people.[3] In China, in Cambodia, in the USSR, the belief in the perfectibility of society led not to heaven on Earth but to hell on Earth, especially for those poor unfortunates who found themselves labeled "outdated and reactionary" by socialist regimes applying the best "scientific" thinking they could muster to the management of human affairs.

Under the Juche Idea, that allegedly scientific thinking has three components. They are *chaju*, or independence in politics; *charip*, or economic independence (a concept not very different from Gandhi's *swadeshi* ideology); and *chawi*, or assertive national defense. As for independence in politics, the thought that any typical North Korean should have any say in the affairs of the state is clearly anathema to Kim's regime, and *chaju*, if it means anything, is shorthand for North Korean nationalism. Likewise, there is relatively little to say here about *chawi*: North Korea has been nothing if not assertive in its military operations, terrorizing its neighbors, torpedoing the occasional ship, and using its nuclear arsenal as a tool of blackmail. Nationalism and militarism are fairly common features of socialist states—particularly of the more comprehensively socialist states—but there is nothing uniquely socialistic about them. Kim's *charip*, though—the Juche Idea's philosophy of economic independence—is of interest, and is worth exploring as a strain of socialist economics.

Charip, like *swadeshi*, is a creed of self-reliance. As such, it rejects international trade and investment. At some level, it is inconceivable that a socialist state would fail to reject international trade with non-socialist economies. Believing that profit-oriented private enterprise is, by definition, an act of exploitation of the working classes, a socialist regime that partook of the fruit of that purportedly poisonous tree would be enriching itself at the cost of the very same workers whose liberation from capitalism is its reason for being. Under a comprehensively socialist regime, profits would not exist, inasmuch as profits are, under the Labor Theory of Value, evidence of a capitalist crime being committed. Without profits, of course, there is nothing with which to finance trade; socialists have always hoped to finesse that problem by achieving large surpluses of industrial and agricultural production, but of course socialist economies rarely if ever produce those kinds of surpluses.

As a result, socialist societies often resort to a crude form of economic nationalism, insisting that all that is necessary in life can be produced locally under socialist conditions. That kind of nationalistic rhetoric is fairly common in state-planned sectors in non-socialist countries, too; one can hear *charip*-style rhetoric in the speeches of American progressives who bemoan the country's "addiction to foreign oil." North Korea not only rejects dependence upon foreign oil, but upon foreign anything—in theory, at least. In practice, North Korea is supported by food aid from the West, by medical assistance and energy aid from South Korea, and by other forms of international humanitarian assistance.

Juche and *charip* are written right into North Korea's constitution, and the country's decision to stand alone economically produced the inevitable consequences familiar to any student of socialism. As the journalist Mitchell Lerner reports, Kim Il Sung's five-year plan of the late 1950s met with some measure of success. From dietary staples such as bean paste and soy sauce to Western-style consumer items such as beer

Shorting the Future

"At 16, Myung Bok is old enough to join the North Korean army. But you wouldn't believe it from his appearance. The teenager stands 4-feet-7, the height of an American fifth- or sixth-grader.

"Myung Bok escaped the communist North last summer to join his mother and younger sisters, who had fled to China earlier. When he arrived, 14-year-old sister Eun Hang did not recognize the scrawny little kid walking up the dirt path to their cottage in a village near the North Korean border, whom she hadn't seen for four years.

"'I can't believe he used to be my big brother,' Eun Hang said sadly as she recalled their early childhood, when Myung Bok was always a full head taller. Now she can peek over the crown of his head without standing on her tiptoes.

"The teenagers go through an almost daily ritual: They stand against a wooden wardrobe in which they've carved notches with a penknife, hoping that after eating a regular diet, Myung Bok will grow tall enough to reclaim his status as a big brother.

"…The World Food Program and UNICEF reported last year that chronic malnutrition had left 42 percent of North Korean children stunted—meaning their growth was seriously impaired, most likely permanently. An earlier report by the U.N. agencies warned that there was strong evidence that physical stunting could be accompanied by intellectual impairment."

Los Angeles Times, 2004

and soft drinks, the socialist regime was successful in nationalizing almost all production, from 90 percent to 100 percent by most estimates.

But socialist regimes will not normally limit themselves to planning the soft-drink industry. Kim Il Sung embarked on a wide-ranging campaign to achieve massive and rapid industrialization, redistribution of land and agricultural resources, and similar large-scale projects of economic reorganization. Within a few years, Kim's subjects were starving. Housing was in short supply, electricity nonexistent in much of the country and unreliable in the rest, water and sewer services were falling apart, and the country's infrastructure was quickly decaying into ruin, where it remains today—except for the 500-foot-tall, gleaming white granite Juche Tower, a monument to Kim Il Sung composed of a granite block for each day he had lived until the tower's construction.

Soon enough, famine struck, and millions died. Lerner relates a cheery state-run radio broadcast from the 1990s: "Today I will introduce you to tasty and healthy ways to eat wild grass."[4] At the famine's worst, North Koreans were reduced to worse than that—reports of cannibalism made the rounds in intelligence circles and in the international press.

"Madman" Kim Jong Il: An Insult to Madmen

To many, all of this sounds like utter madness. Outsiders, particularly in the West, frequently describe Kim Jong Il as being "insane" or "irrational," and characterize his government's behavior as "bizarre." "We don't know much about North Korea and who this Kim Jong Il is," California congressman Jay Kim once said. "I understand he is not a rational individual."[5]

What they almost always fail to appreciate is that Kim is proceeding in accordance with the Juche ideology, a form of socialism that is eccentric, to be sure, but which ought to be familiar enough to us, from our experience with other expressions of socialism, that we can understand

Pyongyang's seemingly erratic behavior. North Korea is not the personality of Kim Jong Il spread thin across the land, but socialism spread thick upon it.

It often has been noted that Kim's regime becomes most bellicose at precisely those moments that it is most vulnerable, when it is seeking assistance from South Korea and from the West. But Kim's behavior is much less unpredictable in light of the mandates of the Juche Idea, which holds that North Korea has a mandate from history to achieve full socialism on its own terms, following its own interests (which are defined as being identical to the narrow self-interest of the governing regime), independent of outside influence.

Under Juche, North Korea rejects foreign values for precisely the same reasons that it rejects (in theory) foreign goods: because they are incompatible with socialism. If this is madness, it is madness of a catchy kind: Stalin suffered from the same disease. So did Lenin. So did Mao. So does Hugo Chávez today. The "madman theory" of world history sheds very little light on the behavior of such regimes; an understanding of socialist ideology, and its application to the messy realities of economic life as it actually is lived, is much more illuminating.

"I could not use a word like madman" to describe Kim, says North Korea specialist Kongdan Oh in an interview with journalist Laura McClure. "He is a very bright, very daring, very bold dictator who knows how to control his society and act strategically to shock his people and the globe. In that sense he's no different from a person like Stalin or Saddam Hussein, and in many ways he's actually been more successful. . . . The economy has been devastated since the early 1990s and yet the country is still standing together. Something is holding them together."[6]

Oh believes that what is holding North Korea together is Kim's iron fist, a government based on state terrorism, and the regime's violent retribution against its critics. But it is as likely that what is holding North Korea together is the Juche ideology, which is interwoven into every aspect of North Korean life in a way that is difficult to appreciate for those who have never lived in an entirely closed, hermetically sealed society. As one North Korean defector put it, "I never thought that Juche was a closed or oppressive ideology. I simply believed it as truth. I could not imagine being disloyal to Kim Il Sung. When he died, I was sad—much as when my father died."[7]

These lessons, unfortunately, remain lost on the modern Left, and on those who continue to romanticize socialism. Writing in the quarterly journal *International Socialism*, Owen Miller rehearses the familiar litany of socialist apologetics when it comes to regimes such as the Democratic People's Republic of Korea: what's going on in Pyongyang isn't "real socialism"—it's "state capitalism." It isn't the fault of socialism, but the result of the malign influence of Joseph Stalin, whose agents dominated North Korea in its early days. It's because North Korea is insufficiently democratic, superabundantly nationalist, inauthentically a "workers' state." In a bizarre exercise in moral equivalence, he writes that in its early days "the North Korean regime was a 'puppet government' of a variety not significantly different from the current regime in occupied Iraq."[8] But of course there is a significant difference: socialism.

North Korea is not the only state that has used hunger as a weapon of mass terrorism: Stalin's "Holodomor" starved to death as many as 10 million Ukrainians, and untold millions died under Mao's politically induced famines.

It is worth considering that the cause of all this suffering was not the presence of evil men, but the presence of mistaken ideas. When Americans look back at their Founders, they often marvel at how lucky

That's One Way to Put It

"Twilight in the Evil Kingdom of the Hermit Midgets."

Mario Loyola, describing the crisis in the North Korean regime, *National Review*, 2010 they were to have present at the creation of the republic a group of men including the austere aristocrat George Washington, the democratic Thomas Jefferson, the practical Alexander Hamilton, the skeptical Benjamin Franklin, the idealistic Tom Paine, and the rest of the luminaries of 1776. And they were all great men, to be sure—but if the revolution had worked out differently, if it had gone the way of the French revolution and descended into terror, oppression, and repression, then our opinions of these men would be considerably different.

The American Founders were great men, but they were also working in the service of great ideas—namely, the skeptical Yankee belief that, given a modest republican government to defend the borders and hang thieves, people would be better off more or less left to their own devices. Similarly, the dictators of the twentieth century each looked uniquely evil—until his evil was matched or surpassed by the dictator next door. How likely was it that remarkably evil men would come to power, at roughly the same time, in Germany, Italy, Russia, and China? A more likely explanation is that, wicked as those dictators were, it was the ideology they followed, and not the peculiar moral character of the men involved, that was the decisive factor. Indeed, the ideology of central planning is itself an invitation to the exercise of dictatorial power and repression, as Hayek argued so ably in *The Road to Serfdom*.

But we do not need to reach back into twentieth century history to explore that question. In our own time, there remains in the world one truly, comprehensively, committed socialist enterprise: The Democratic People's Republic of North Korea. Though it is largely cut off from the world, a fact that led to its being nicknamed "The Hermit Kingdom," North Korea has done us the service of making its governing socialist ideology a matter of public knowledge. Kim Jong Il has published considerably on the subject, and Pyongyang even has clubs of admirers in Western capitals: The Juche Idea Study Group of England, to take one example, advertises itself as "open to those who (1) support the Juche Idea whole-heartedly, (2) want to apply the Juche Idea in England, (3) love the DPRK, the WPK, Kim Il Sung, and Kim Jong Il."[9] For the sake of England, let us hope that their numbers are small.

And the Ape Stood and Became...A Socialist

The Juche Idea takes the scientific pretense of socialism—the belief that all of a society's knowledge can be known, organized, and deployed by a central authority—and extends it to its most extreme conclusion. Not only does the Juche Idea hold that running a society is a science, it suggests that it is a particular science: biology.

The misapplication of scientific theories to social life was a remarkably common and influential feature of twentieth-century intellectual life, and no scientific insight was more widely or more consistently misapplied than Charles Darwin's theory of evolution. While Social Darwinism, the most nefarious misappropriation of evolutionary thinking, is largely (if unfairly) associated in the public mind with various right-wing organizations and movements, there was a fair amount of Social Darwinism afoot on what we would now call the Left or progressive side of the political spectrum. Planned Parenthood founder Margaret Sanger—who envisioned planning family life very much the way Lenin imagined planning the world economy—was a notable exponent of the racial-eugenic variation of Social Darwinism. Aldous Huxley was another.

The Social Darwinists tended to see in the theory of evolution a guideline for the state's interaction with the individual and with groups of individuals. Sanger wanted rigorous state intervention to prevent the birth of "unfit" citizens, an opinion shared by the iconic liberal Supreme Court justice, Oliver Wendell Holmes. (Years later, socialist Sweden would fall into scandal for its programs of involuntary sterilization and other eugenics-related activities.)

But for socialists, Darwin's ideas also were thought to shed light on the evolution of entire societies. Marx himself believed in an iron law of socio-economic evolution, one in which feudalism was displaced by capitalism, which was itself destined to be displaced by a provisional form of socialism, which was to be replaced by fully realized socialism. Even today, socialists and other sympathetic anti-capitalists speak of socio-economic evolution as though it were a punctuated equilibrium like speciation; they speak of "Late Capitalism," "Financial Capitalism," and, with hope in their eyes, of "Post-Capitalism." Stalin was taking a very Darwinian view of political evolution when he wrote,

> Contrary to metaphysics, dialectics does not regard the process of development as a simple process of growth, where quantitative changes do not lead to qualitative changes, but as a development which passes from insignificant and imperceptible quantitative changes to open 'fundamental changes' to qualitative changes; a development in which the qualitative changes occur not gradually, but rapidly and abruptly, taking the form of a leap from one state to another; they occur not accidentally but as the natural result of an accumulation of imperceptible and gradual quantitative changes.[10]

Elsewhere, Stalin expands on this evolutionary view of politics, arguing that the study of political history should yield "laws" comparable to those of the natural sciences—as though human beings, and their aspirations, were so many electronics in so many orbits around the nucleus of the almighty state:

> Hence, social life, the history of society, ceases to be an agglomeration of "accidents," for the history of society becomes a development of society according to regular laws, and the study of the history of society becomes a science.

Hence, the practical activity of the party of the proletariat must not be based on the good wishes of "outstanding individuals," not on the dictates of "reason," "universal morals," etc., but on the laws of development of society and on the study of these laws.

Further, if the world is knowable and our knowledge of the laws of development of nature is authentic knowledge, having the validity of objective truth, it follows that social life, the development of society, is also knowable, and that the data of science regarding the laws of development of society are authentic data having the validity of objective truths.

Hence, the science of the history of society, despite all the complexity of the phenomena of social life, can become as precise a science as, let us say, biology, and capable of making use of the laws of development of society for practical purposes.[11]

As Hayek might have pointed out—or as Darwin himself would no doubt have observed—the difference between biological evolution and the socialist view of socio-economic evolution is this: nobody is in charge of biological evolution. Nobody plans biological evolution—it represents a kind of spontaneous order, resulting from the complex interaction of billions and billions of individual factors. That is to say, biological evolution much more closely resembles the market economy than it does socialist central planning. Ironically, given the secular leanings of most socialists, what their ideas really most closely resemble is the anti-Darwinian theory of "Intelligent Design."

Stalin, for all of his shortcomings, benefited from the cleverness and the cynicism native to his youthful occupation of bank-robbing. He might have had philosophical essays published under his name (and may even have written them—who knows?) but he was, at heart, a simple tyrant. Even simple tyrants, however, have a set of operating ideas that guide them. The "politics as biology" theme that is implicit in Stalin and Marx becomes more explicit under the Juche Idea, which finds Kim Jong Il writing,

> Since the leader is the center of the life of a socio-political community, revolutionary duty and comradeship must also be centered on the leader... loyalty to the leader and comradeship towards him are absolute and unconditional because the leader, as the top brain of the socio-political organism, represents the integrity of the community. It is only when the leader, the party and the masses are integrated that they can become an immortal socio-political organism .... Being at the center of unity and leadership, he plays the decisive role in shaping the destiny of the popular masses. This is similar to the brain of a man playing the decisive role in his activities.[12]

Kim's language here ranges from the bombastic to the lifeless, though some of that may be an artifact of translation from Kim's own eccentric Korean. But it is worth considering that North Korean socialism is only radical in its breadth and depth, not in its fundamental assumptions about the nature of society and the possibilities of governance. The North Korean communists are simply attempting to do to an entire country what political authorities have done to K-12 education in the United States: run it politically, through central planning under state authority.

The results, unsurprisingly, are the same: American government schools fail to produce educated students, while North Korean government farms fail to produce crops. The costs are much more dramatic and readily apparent in the case of North Korea—starvation is a shocking thing—though it is of course the case that there are many countervailing institutions in the United States that make the costs of the crumbling educational system less obvious.

Communism: The *Real* Opiate of the Masses

"The North Korean state-sanctioned philosophy of Juche is the 10th-largest religion in the world with 19 million adherents, according to Adherents.com, a Web site that tracks world religions.

"It's bigger than Judaism, bigger than Jainism, bigger than Baha'i. Sorry Tom Cruise, but it's nearly 40 times bigger than the Church of Scientology.

"Not bad for a religion that isn't even considered a religion by its followers.

"If you told a loyal North Korean that Juche (pronounced 'JOOCH-ay') is a religion, he might punch you in your shamelessly heretical mouth.

"'Juche,' he might say, 'is definitely NOT a religion: We're atheists, for heaven's sake.'

"And then he might tell you how Comrade Kim Il Sung, Juche's founder and Kim Jong Il's dad, is laid to rest within the Sacred Temple of Juche, near signs that read 'The great leader Comrade Kim Il Sung will always be with us!'

"If religion is a duck, says Tom Belke, author of *Juche: A Christian Study of North Korea's State Religion*, Juche quacks big time. In an attempt to run away from religion, North Korea has run smack dab into it. 'They have their holy sites, they have their ceremonies, they have their own exclusive belief system,' Belke said. 'It's something that demands one's all.'"

Chicago Tribune, 2007

What is more surprising is this: the North Koreans in some ways are more open to reforming their system than are American educators. In 2010, while the Obama administration was shutting down the school-choice scholarship program that had allowed thousands of poor students in Washington, D.C., to escape from the capital's horrific government schools, Kim's regime was loosening restrictions on the private sale of food and essential supplies in reaction to the deterioration of the North Korean economy. Unfortunately, it is not clear how extensive this liberalization will prove to be or whether it will last: similar reforms were enacted in the 1990s after Kim's catastrophic attempts at collective management of the North Korean agricultural economy produced famines that killed up to 2 million people.

But at least Kim eventually changed his policies in response to myriad disasters. In the U.S. public school system, the more disastrous schools become, the more teachers and education bureaucrats insist on *expanding* the policies—union power, lack of competition, ever-expanding budgets regardless of performance, prioritizing teachers' and administrators' length of service over merit—that made them that way. One thing's for sure: when your industry makes Kim Jong Il look flexible by comparison, you're not achieving good results.

Chapter Nine

SOCIALISM IS DIRTY

There's a term of art on the right for the former socialists who diverted their political efforts away from economic central planning and channeled them into the environmental movement. They are known as "watermelons"—green on the outside, red on the inside. There is something to that perspective on things.

From the end of the Cold War until the advent of the financial crisis of 2008, socialism was, politically speaking, a dirty word. Britain's socialist party, which goes by the name of Labour, excised the word from its rhetoric. While socialist parties and the occasional outright communist party still rotate in and out of power in places such as France and India, in most of the world socialists were compelled to pretend, to some degree, to be something other than what they were. In the environmental movement, they found a convenient ally—and a first-rate source of political camouflage.

The idea that capitalism is inherently bad for the environment, and the corollary notion that socialism provides a preferable alternative, is deeply engrained in the environmental movement, particularly in the "Anglosphere"—the capitalist countries of the United States, the United Kingdom, Australia, Canada, and New Zealand. And from the most deep-dyed sectors of the socialist world, the green gospel has come pouring forth: capitalism kills planets, the Left argues, and socialism can save us.

Guess What?

★ Socialism destroyed one of Earth's biggest lakes

★ Capitalism is a far better system for environmental protection than socialism

★ BP's environmental irresponsibility pales in comparison to that of state-run oil companies

Consider this outpouring from a socialist organization known as the Internationalists:

> The reasons why capitalism cannot solve the environmental crisis are located in the nature of capitalist production itself, namely its need for continual growth.
>
> As long as capitalism exists as the global system of production it can never be in equilibrium with nature and degradation of the planet will result.
>
> The problems of climate change can only be solved within a more developed system of production, namely communism.
>
> Under communism production would be for need and not for profit. Hence the continual drive for growth could be eliminated. The demands of mankind could be balanced against the sustainability of the planet. Competition which drives capitalism to much waste production and degrades the planet could be replaced by cooperation. Centuries of environmental destruction, which will be the legacy of capitalism, can start to be reversed. Such a new society can only be achieved from the struggle against the present system.
>
> ... The choice facing the world on the environmental front as on the social front is one of the ruin of civilization or the construction of a communist world.[1]

These young socialists need a field trip to the Aral Sea—or what's left of it.

Planning Ecocide

The Aral Sea, which actually is a lake, once was one of the world's most magnificent bodies of water, covering more than 25,000 square miles of territory between Kazakhstan and Uzbekistan to form the Earth's fourth-largest lake. Fed by two rivers, the Syr-Daria and the Amu-Daria, the Aral Sea supported a host of industries, fishing most prominent among them, and was central to the surrounding people's way of life.

Then the central planners set their eyes on it. In 1920, Kazakhstan became a Soviet Socialist Republic, a component of the USSR, and Uzbekistan followed suit in 1924. The socialist economic doctrine of the USSR called for the centralization and systemization of agriculture as a prelude to the massive and rapid industrialization of the new socialist society. So the rivers feeding the Aral Sea were diverted, by order of the central planners, to be used for irrigating the new collectivized state farms—in this case, massive cotton plantations.

By the 1960s, work rechanneling the rivers had been completed, and the Aral Sea was devastated. Eventually the hundreds of small islands that dotted the sea would emerge as a continuous land mass and the Aral split into three separate lakes—which, combined, comprised about 10 percent of its former glory. One of those three lakes would subsequently disappear, and another, already little more than a shadow of the original Aral, would be reduced to a shadow of a shadow. Water equivalent to the combined volumes of Lake Erie and Lake Huron was lost.

Socialist management of the Uzbek and Kazakh water resources produced what some observers have referred to as "ecocide." Most agree that the Aral Sea catastrophe is one of the worst environmental disasters of human history.

Spot the Pattern

In 2009, *Time* magazine listed the world's ten most polluted cities. Every one of them was in a country with a socialist or formerly socialist government. The list:

- Linfen, China
- Tianying, China
- Sukinda, India
- Vapi, India
- La Oroya, Peru
- Dzerzhinsk, Russia
- Norilsk, Russia
- Chernobyl, Ukraine
- Sumgayit, Azerbaijan
- Kabwe, Zambia

The shocking thing is this: it was not an accident. The destruction of the Aral Sea was precisely what had been intended by the central planners, who saw the liquidation of the Aral and the destruction of the communities that depended upon it as just one more cost to be borne on the way to achieving a rational and just economy.

What remains of the Aral Sea is a pond of poison. After the rivers were diverted and the sea began to dry up, mineral salts and other toxins in the sediment turned to dust and were dispersed upon the land—and into people's lungs—by the wind. The water and the underlying sediments had long been contaminated by runoff from the surrounding agricultural projects, which were run in a chemically intensive manner, with excessive use of pesticides, herbicides, and fertilizers. Likewise, intensive industrial projects, mostly involving mining and metallurgy, had been empowered by governmental authorities to engage in massive discharges of pollution. Uranium plants stored radioactive waste in poorly constructed containment facilities, and the nearby Polygon nuclear weapons testing facility produced its share of toxins as well. The region's rapidly eroding and heavily salinated soil has contributed to the desertification of far-flung areas onto which it has blown. Those who have charged that capitalism is the worst thing ever to happen to the Earth's environment have not had a good look at socialism's environmental record.

Toward the end of the Soviet era, the central planners were still busily polluting the land, air, and water as far away as the Kola Peninsula and Norilsk in the Arctic. As the environmental analyst Philippe Rekacewicz reported in 2000, mining operations stripping nickel, copper, and phosphorous from the region, along with the huge pulp factories set up there, were producing untold amounts of pollution. Sulfur dioxide emissions alone amounted to 600,000 tons per year in the Kola Peninsula and 2 *million* tons per year in Norilsk. Thousands of square miles of formerly pristine Arctic wilderness and forest were clear cut or heavily devegetated. What the rapacious timbering operations left of the forests were ravaged by acid rain and chemical runoff from the industrial facilities. They even managed to poison the snow: high levels of heavy metals such as copper and zinc found their way into the precipitation and spread pollution wherever the snows fell. Nearby rivers are still full of ammonia and methanol, along with metal runoff from the mining operations.[2]

Mining is a nasty business in general. Even under the best environmental operating standards, the extraction industries impose significant environmental costs, as anybody who has seen a mountaintop-removal dig or a strip mine can testify. But unlike their capitalist counterparts, who are constrained not only by adversarial environmental regulators but also by the property rights of their neighbors, socialist mine managers are backed by the full power of the state.

While American miners were conducting environmental studies and spending billions of dollars on environmental-mitigation studies, their socialist counterparts were literally nuking their way to meeting their production goals. In the Soviet Arctic, at least twenty nuclear explosions were engineered from 1969 to 1988, Rekacewicz reports—not for weapons-testing purposes, but for mining operations. There were plenty of nuclear-weapons tests, too—more than 100, in fact—and the International Atomic Energy Agency has warned that the socialist-era nuclear-power station at Polyarnyy is a danger to the public and the environment.[3]

A dangerous nuclear-power plant run by socialist central-planning authorities—what could possibly go wrong?

The explosion at the Soviets' Chernobyl nuclear power plant in 1986 was one of the worst environmental catastrophes in world history. The mismanagement of the plant was shocking, as was the central planners utter disregard for the public they purported to serve—shocking, but categorically typical of socialism. The connection between this disregard for both man and environment on the one hand and the remorseless dictates of socialism on the other was not entirely lost on the Russian people, who at the time of the Chernobyl disaster had more intimate experience with the excesses of advanced industrial socialism than the people of any other nation. Chernobyl, in an important way, marked the beginning of the end of Soviet socialism. (Unfortunately, though, not the transition to capitalism: after a decade of lawlessness, what came next—Putin's socialist-corporatist hybrid—proved to be another in the long-suffering Russian people's long line of disastrous governments.)

It's important to keep in mind the environmental context in which the Chernobyl disaster occurred. Socialist mismanagement of the environment was not limited to the Aral Sea catastrophe or pollution in remote Arctic outposts. By the time the Soviet government collapsed, one-sixth of Russia's territory had been rendered uninhabitable because of pollution and other environmental devastation.[4] Water pollution, in particular, was extreme—far beyond anything in the capitalist world's experience—and such drinking water as was available was extravagantly squandered, a third of it lost to leakages in the distribution pipelines.

But socialists are immune to evidence. In the 2010 *Dissent* magazine symposium "Socialism Now?" significant attention was given to the prospects of further development of the red-green alliance. A similar forum on socialism published by the *Nation* a few years earlier likewise upheld the environmental movement as the likeliest channel for socialist advancement.

Do they have a point? It is easy to look at the damage inflicted on the Gulf of Mexico by BP (formerly British Petroleum, a state-run enterprise until the 1980s) and conclude that they do. Socialist critics of environmental policies in the capitalist world reliably call for greater regulation and more robust government oversight of environmental conditions and resources, none of which sounds unreasonable. But they fail to account for the fact that governments have economic incentives of their own to neglect or abuse the environment—and, in many cases, government planners will treat the environment with much greater disregard than will private interests.

Big (Socialist) Oil

One of the best examples of this is the world's state-run oil companies. The nationalization of heavy industries has been a hallmark of socialist regimes everywhere. In India, Iran, Mussolini's Italy, 1970s-era Britain, Libya, Mexico, Nigeria, and Venezuela, the oil companies were nationalized under socialist theories of economic planning. (The Arab oil emirates are a special case where it was more like the oil industry seized a country rather than the other way around.) In most of those cases, the coal industry and other sources of energy were nationalized as well.

What resulted was, in almost every case, extraordinarily high levels of pollution—with zero accountability. If BP spills oil in the Gulf of Mexico, the United States knows, in the words of President Obama, "whose ass to kick." But what if the oil were spilled by SinoPec, China's state-run oil producer. Kicking Beijing's ass over an oil spill is a whole different kettle of thermonuclear-armed fish. But at least in such an international dispute there would be a kind of balance of power, a set of countervailing interests that have to be taken into consideration.

Far worse are those cases in which a national government operates a pollution-heavy industry within its own borders, with no countervailing pressure and no oversight. It's one thing to have the government regulate the oil industry—but when the government *is* the oil industry, who regulates the regulators? Or, as the Roman poet Juvenal and fans of comic books put it: *Quis custodiet ipsos custodes*? ("Who watches the watchmen?") For the people of Mexico, that is more than a hypothetical question: Pemex, the behemoth state-run oil company, has been a full-steam pollution machine.

With a market capitalization of nearly a half-trillion dollars, Pemex is the second biggest company in the world—but its shares are mostly owned by the Mexican government, which completely controls the firm and its operations. The government derives significant revenue from

Pemex's oil operations, so it has little incentive to crack down on the firm for environmental or safety reasons. Its record on both has been lethal. In 1979, an explosion at Pemex's Ixtoc well in the Gulf of Mexico, off the Texas coast, caused what was, at the time, the largest oil spill in history. In 1984, a poorly managed Pemex storage facility at San Juan Ixhuatepec in Mexico City went up in flames, setting off a series of massive explosions that killed more than 500 people. Another 200 were killed in Pemex explosions in Guadalajara in 1992. Unguarded Pemex pipelines were attacked by Mexican terrorists in 2007, with more explosions and more leaks, and later that same year a Pemex-operated oil rig collided with a drilling platform, killing twenty-two workers.

Moreover, Pemex chemicals dumped into the Coatzacoalcos River have wiped out most of the fish population, bankrupting fishermen and devastating the ecology. "You cut the fish open and a smell like ammonia comes out," fisherman Eusebio Gonzalez told Joel Simon of oil-industry

See No Evil

"Until the rivers stank of raw sewage and the coal dust clogged the air, almost no one gave much thought to the negative influences of industrialization. My father, Liang Sicheng, a well-known architect and an expert on city planning, was one of the few exceptions. He strongly opposed developing heavy industry in Beijing—a view for which he was severely criticized by the Communist Party. Party officials maintained that environmental problems could not exist in socialist countries, since pollution was an 'evil inherent in capitalism.'"

Liang Congjiem, "Most Polluted City on Earth," *Time Asia*, 1998

watchdog Global Community Monitor. "If you eat it, your stomach swells like a balloon."[5] During the worst periods of pollution, the Coatzacoalcos River would catch fire every few months. The nearby groundwater is poisoned, leaving residents without clean drinking water and farmers without proper water for irritation—their crops already having been damaged by Pemex's poison runoff.

The Mexican locals have some hope for an environmental cleanup at sixty-one Pemex plants. While it is a touch-and-go proposition, Pemex has been exploring the possibility of privatizing these facilities, the first privatization of any part of Pemex's operations. That is to say, Mexico's only real hope for containing or reversing the environmental devastation wrought by its socialized oil industry is desocialization. "We're hopeful this will be an opportunity to develop a plan to deal with the hazardous waste,"[6] says Mexico City–based environmental activist Betty Ferber. Similarly, *Global Community Monitor* reports, "Some environmentalists are hoping the sale will pave the way for a major environmental cleanup of the plants by the new owners. Others fear Pemex will simply use the sale as an excuse to wash its hands of the environmental disasters it has left behind, in effect handing over an environmental time bomb before it explodes."[7]

It would hardly be the first time Pemex had ducked responsibility for causing an environmental disaster. In the 1979 Ixtoc disaster—now the fourth largest in world history—oil spewed for months into the Gulf of Mexico, polluting the Mexican and Texan coastal waters. At the beginning of the spill, 30,000 barrels of oil per day were flooding into the gulf. Pemex responded by pumping mud into the well, reducing the flow to 20,000 barrels of oil a day. Relief wells eventually were drilled, and the flow reduced to 10,000 barrels of oil a day—still catastrophic levels. Some 71,500 barrels of Pemex oil washed up on U.S. beaches, polluting 162 miles of waterfront. More than 10,000 cubic yards of oil-polluted material had to be collected and disposed of.

Among the hardest-hit specimens of sea life were the Kemp's Ridley sea turtles that were just laying their eggs at the beach at Rancho Nuevo, Mexico, when the oil washed ashore. It was decades before their numbers recovered.

Recall that within weeks of its oil spill, BP had set aside $20 billion to pay claims for future damages. In contrast, Pemex, being a state-run firm, simply invoked sovereign immunity and refused to pay for almost any damages—including the damage caused by the 30,000 tons of oil it left on Mexican beaches, the 4,000 tons of oil it left on Texas beaches, or the 120,000 tons of oil it let sink to the bottom of the Gulf of Mexico, wiping out crab populations, devastating coral islands, and doing incalculable damage to coastal flora and fauna.

Similar dramas have unfolded elsewhere. In the single-party state of Gabon, strongman Omar Bongo decided that his country was to become the "Costa Rica of Africa," a green haven for eco-tourism. Accordingly, he set aside a huge swath of the country as a national park, summarily evicting native people from their lands and uprooting their traditional way of life. As usual, central planners could not be bothered with such abstractions as people and their lives when there was a plan to implement. Western progressives cringed at the rough treatment of the locals, but they celebrated President Bongo's newfound commitment to the environmental cause—including, of course, the shepherding of economic resources in accordance with the green creed. But they'd overlooked a clause in the law creating the Gabonese Eden: "If oil or mineral riches are discovered in the protected areas they can be exploited for the economic and social benefit of the country."[8] Found they were, and "exploited" may be too weak a word for what happened next.

Gabon, being a fairly backward country thanks in no small part to the misrule of the Bongo dynasty (young Ali Bongo recently took over for the late Omar, his father), was ill-equipped to carry out its own petroleum-development work. But it discovered a partner in central-planning—the

People's Republic of China and its state-run oil company, SinoPec. So, in came the Chinese, prospecting for oil among the lowland gorillas and endangered manatees of Gabon's great green reserve—and they did it with dynamite. As *Wildlife Extra* reported:

> Conservationists have reacted with horror after oil company prospectors commenced drilling in one of Africa's most important wildlife reserves. Teams from Chinese state-owned oil company SinoPec moved into Gabon's Petit Loango national park last month, exploiting a loophole in the law to begin operations that threaten the habitats of dozens of rare and endangered species, including West Africa's highest concentration of lowland gorillas.
>
> Professor Christophe Boesch, a primatologist performing field work in the park, says the Chinese have ignored requests from Gabon's environment and parks administrations to cease operations until a legally required environmental impact study has been completed.
>
> "They were asked to leave on October the 6th, but since then over 100 explosions a day have been heard in the park," he said. The use of explosives in the Loango lagoon—one of the world's most important manatee breeding sites—is feared to have caused the deaths of several of the mammals.[9]

Capitalism has its problems, to be sure, and a cavalier attitude toward the environment is, from time to time, one of them. But the liberal political institutions supported by capitalism—property rights, contracts, arbitration—ensure that no single interest can so utterly dominate the political or economic sphere that they are tempted to, for instance, go marauding through a supposed environmental paradise with dynamite. For the most part, capitalist criminals at least have the decency to be ashamed of their crimes; not so the socialist, who claims to be creating a rational economic order and protecting the poor and the vulnerable—whether those vulnerable parties are human beings or endangered species.

Against all the evidence, well-meaning environmentalists have, for the most part, bought the argument that capitalism kills baby seals and socialism saves them. It is no surprise that the environmental movement is utterly dominated by socialists, former socialists, and crypto-socialists. But, given socialism's record on managing the Earth's resources in a responsible way, why on Earth would we ever think about putting them in charge?

It's All about the Plan

It is important to appreciate that the environmental problems experienced under the authoritarian socialism of the Soviet Union were very much like those experienced under the democratic socialism of Mexico. Socialism, not authoritarianism, is the problem, and that is because socialism is philosophically disinclined to appreciate the value of the environment. Under the Labor Theory of Value, resources as such have no real value, not until they are made the object of labor—which is to say, made the object of socialist economic planning.

This brings us to another problem: central planners discount environmental damage because they will not count costs they are not forced to count. Environmental externalities can be hidden—or, as in the case of Mexico and China, they can simply be denied. Whether the form of socialism in question is totalitarian or partial, authoritarian or democratic, the underlying philosophical commonalities that unite all expressions of socialism are an invitation to environmental catastrophe. As Villanova University Professor Joseph W. Dellapenna puts it in *Behind the Red Curtain*, there are several distinct reasons that socialism destroys the environment:

> First, Marxism carried forward the western tradition of treating nature solely as providing resources for human consumption.

Perhaps a Bit Overzealous

In contrast to the environmental nightmare that emerges under socialist governments, environmental regulations in capitalist countries often reach comic extremes. *Reason* magazine reported on one such regulation in 1994:

> By law, cities must remove at least 30 percent of organic waste from incoming sewage before treating it. This poses a problem for Anchorage because it has so little waste in its sewage. The Environmental Protection Agency won't give the city an exemption. So rather than build a new, state-of-the-art $135 million treatment facility capable of removing even traces of organic waste, the city has asked two local fish-processing plants to dump fish viscera into the water. The fish waste is then removed, and the federal regulation met.

As Vaclav Havel explained, Marxism saw humans as the "productive force" and nature as a "production tool," destroying the necessarily intimate relationship between the two. This concept was succinctly captured in the "labor theory of value" that denied economic value to natural resources as such when consumed in productive processes because no human labor was expended in creating the natural resources. A second feature of Marxism reinforced the effect of the labor theory of value— its denial of individual responsibility. As a result, no one felt responsibility for the natural environment, leading to reckless disregard of environmental consequences. Thirdly, the socialist goal of "transforming the world" led easily to "gigan-tomania"—a desire for the largest and most grandiose techno-logical feats. Gigantomania is also found in western countries, but structural features of Communism prevented effective counter-pressure that, at least sometimes, stopped some of the most substantial excesses in the west. . . . Finally, there was the importance of "fulfilling the plan." Success and promotion for officials—and all major economic decisions were made by offi-cials—came only from fulfilling the plan, which generally was measured solely through quantitative achievements, resulting in pervasive poor quality production. New construction is what the plan called for, not maintenance, while cost, in any rational sense, simply was not a factor. The result, as a friend in China commented to me while I was living there before the market reforms, is that "They build old buildings here." That comment could just as well be applied across Eastern Europe and the for-mer Soviet Union.[10]

They also build old dams. The Three Gorges Dam, still under construc-tion, is one of the world's great environmental catastrophes unfolding in slow motion. As with the Soviet irrigation project at the Aral Sea, the Three Gorges Dam is not only interrupting the natural flow of water, it is preventing the dispersal of the massive amounts of pollutants that Chi-nese state industry pours into the Yangtze River, contributing to toxic lev-els of water pollution, soil erosion, mudslides, the collapse of riverbanks, and the decimation of aquatic life. But not all aquatic life has been harmed by the project—otherworldly algae blooms now thrive where high concentrations of fertilizer runoff have built up in the waters.

Those kinds of environmental consequences could have been pre-dicted, and were. But there have also been other, largely unforeseen conse-quences. For instance, the concentration of new construction activity in the Yangtze watershed, combined with the disruption of the river's flow, has produced enormous islands of garbage—not just the kind of trash flotilla common on uncared-for rivers, but mountains of garbage so densely packed that men can stand on them. Reuters reports:

> Thousands of tons of garbage washed down by recent torrential rain are threatening to jam the locks of China's massive Three Gorges Dam, and is in places so thick people can stand on it, state media said on Monday. Chen Lei, a senior official at the China Three Gorges Corporation, told the *China Daily* that more than 3,000 tons of trash was being collected at the dam every day, but there was still not enough manpower to clean it all up.
>
> "The large amount of waste in the dam area could jam the miter gate of the Three Gorges Dam," Chen said, referring to the gates of the locks which allow shipping to pass through the Yangtze River. The river is a crucial commercial artery for the upstream city of Chongqing and other areas in China's less developed western interior provinces.
>
> Pictures showed a huge swathe of the waters by the dam crammed full of debris, with cranes brought in to fish out a tangled mess, including shoes, bottles, branches and Styrofoam.[11]

Recall what Professor Dellapenna's Chinese friend had told him: "They build old buildings here." It would be more accurate to say: they build things here with no concern for the people who will use them or have to live with them. Every Three Gorges Dam, Aral Sea catastrophe, or brutalist housing project in the Bronx is socialism in miniature; THE PLAN is elevated over everything, even over the people it was meant to benefit—*especially* over them, in fact. That dictum might as easily apply to an inner-city school in Philadelphia or a food-distribution center in Venezuela—or, as we shall see, the entire Venezuelan oil industry.

Chapter Ten

VENEZUELA:
ANATOMY OF A CRACKDOWN

For the purposes of our analysis here, there probably is no better example of contemporary socialism, its effects, and its pathologies than Venezuela under the government of Hugo Chávez, whose United Socialist Party of Venezuela has 5.7 million members, making it the largest socialist party in the Western Hemisphere. Most pertinent to Americans, Venezuela shows what happens when socialism is appended to a large country with a complex economy and society. Venezuela is neither a homogeneous northern European ethno-state insulated by its wealth and generations of accumulated social capital, nor a Third World hellhole ravaged by endless civil war, an unbroken history of autocratic, single-party rule, or the doctrinaire application of ultraorthodox Marxism-Leninism.

Venezuela has something like the kind of socialism that American socialists intend and admire. Its socialist regime came to power through democratic means (means which it has since sought to limit, lest they be used to restrict the power of the socialist regime, leaning toward, if not quite achieving, the usual socialist model of democracy: "one man, one vote, one time").

Moreover, the regime's centralization of power is of the sort that is essential under socialism; the state has tightened its control of petroleum and other vital industries as necessary for implementing the political discipline required to carry out President Chávez's central-planning agenda.

Chávez's crackdown on opposition media can even be dismissed as a small, regrettable excess in an otherwise democratic socialist agenda—even though such censorship is a routine part of socialist regimes, which cannot bear much scrutiny and will not bear much opposition. (It's no accident that one of the most dangerous occupations in Cuba is that of *librarian*.)

Unlike many of the socialist regimes that took power in Third World countries with scanty resources, the Chávez regime took over a relatively prosperous, stable, and civil country that had relatively strong institutions. In the early twentieth century, Venezuela had the largest economy in Latin America, one that was turbocharged by the discovery of massive oil reserves. But the influx of petrodollars turned out to be, as it often is, a mixed blessing. The government spent and borrowed lavishly, operating on the theory that oil prices would continue to rise forever. (You know, like housing prices in the United States.) But in the 1980s, oil prices collapsed—and the Venezuelan economy collapsed along with them.

What followed was the familiar pattern of a national fiscal crisis. Given a choice between formally defaulting on its debts or informally defaulting on them by devaluing its currency and paying off its creditors with debased money, Venezuela chose the latter. Inflation predictably skyrocketed, and real standards of living for Venezuelans fell dramatically. A relatively affluent country became a relatively poor one almost overnight, thanks to failed government economic planning.

The crisis created an opening for the former paratrooper Hugo Chávez, who had been jailed after attempting to stage a *coup d'etat* in 1992. The *nouveau pauvre* Venezuelans, feeling the sting of their economic setback, were ready for some hope and change, and Chávez promised it to them. Specifically, he promised to plunder the country's oil wealth on behalf of the lower classes. When he was elected president in 1998, tightening the state's grip on the oil and energy industries was at the top of his agenda.

He proceeded with a fury—but not without opposition. Angered by corruption and vote fraud in Chávez's re-election campaign and in an ensuing constitutional referendum, the opposition coalesced into a unified group called Coordinadora Democrática, which brought the Fedecamaras, the Venezuelan version of the chamber of commerce, together with the non-*Chávezista* labor unions represented by the Confederacion de Trabajadores de Venezuela. There were strikes and protests, but the opposition only made Chávez more militant. In 2000 he forced through the "*ley habiltante*," legislation that invested him with dictatorial powers—literally dictatorial powers, the ability to rule by decree—for one year. Thus aggrandized, Chávez decreed forty-nine additional laws that established his socialist vision as the law of the land for Venezuela.

The backlash against Chávez's dictatorial ambitions was severe and sustained. As the strikes and protests increased in intensity, in 2002 a group of military officers staged an abortive coup, charging that Chávez had no intention of truly surrendering the dictatorial powers he so plainly relished. Chávez survived the coup, but in December Coordinadora Democrática staged a crippling strike that shut down the oil industry. Managers at the major state-run oil company, Petróleos de Venezuela (PDVSA), walked off the job, and the captain of an oil tanker dropped anchor in the main shipping channel at Lake Maracaibo, refusing to budge and shutting down oil shipping.

The strikers were demanding that Chávez either leave office or amend the dictatorial decrees that established his socialist framework. Chávez refused, and within a few months Venezuela's oil production had fallen nearly 40 percent. Throughout the oil-rich country, motorists were left stranded without gasoline. Where fuel was available, drivers had to wait

But Don't Call Them Socialists

"Late last year, 16 U.S. congressmen voiced their approval for Venezuelan president Hugo Chavez. Representatives Barney Frank, John Conyers, Chaka Fattah, Jan Schakowsky, Jose Serrano, and others complained in a letter to President Bush that the United States was not adequately protecting Chavez against a groundswell of internal opposition to his increasingly authoritarian rule—an upsurge that might lead to his ouster. Elected to power in 1998, Lt. Col. Chavez has hijacked democracy in Venezuela and is openly moving the country toward totalitarianism. Beyond Venezuela's borders, he celebrates, protects, and does business with terrorists."

Weekly Standard, 2003

in serpentine lines encircling gas stations for hours before they could fill up. Domestic air travel shut down.

In spite of assistance from sympathetic governments in the region, the Venezuelan economy imploded. Not only was gasoline scarce, but soon food and other basic necessities were in short supply. The economy contracted 27 percent during the first quarter of 2003 and unemployment topped 20 percent. Conditions grew so bad that even the merchants and shopkeepers, normally the most apolitical of businessmen, went on strike against Chávez—at Christmas, no less, adopting the slogan, "2002 Without Christmas, 2003 Without Chávez."

The strikers had energy, but Chávez had the army, the police, and the tax authorities, the last of which he used to seize control of the media—television networks critical of Chávez suddenly found themselves facing huge assessments for back taxes. Eventually, the strike was crushed, and the

main leaders of Coordinadora Democrática—the presidents of Fedecamaras and the Confederacion de Trabajadores de Venezuela—were arrested.

Chávez Seizes the Oil...And Everything Else, Too

Crucially, after the strike was suppressed, some 18,000 PDVSA workers were fired, leaving Chávez with more direct control of the company
and its oil revenues. This was a development from which PDVSA has
never really recovered. Chávez does not know or care much about running an oil company. What he cares about is having a goose that lays
golden eggs from which he can whip up his socialist omelet. Overall
Venezuelan oil production has never returned to pre-strike levels. As analyst Peter DeShazo put it in a 2007 report for the Center for Strategic and
International Studies,

> Venezuela's hydrocarbons sector is shaped by Chávez's ideo-
> logical vision of a Bolivarian revolution and his strategy to put
> that in motion. That vision implies a politicized PDVSA with
> a social mandate that supersedes the production mandate.
> Resource nationalism drives the process of rolling back the
> effects of the aperture of the sector during the 1990s, when pri-
> vate investment was encouraged, to put in place a regime of
> state control.
>
> In the wake of the 2002–2003 strike/lockout and declining
> private and PDVSA investment, oil production in Venezuela
> has fallen from over 3 million barrels per day (mbd) to a figure
> of around 2.4 mbd (according to OPEC estimates) in 2007.
> PDVSA official production figures are 3.3 mbd.
>
> While PDVSA's business plans forecast strong growth in
> production to over 5 mbd by 2010, current levels of investment
> preclude any major rise in production.[1]

THE PLAN called for 5 million barrels per day in 2010. Venezuela's actual oil production in 2010 was less than half that figure, 2.3 million barrels per day—or 100,000 barrels a day less than it was in 2007. Other oil companies have been brought under stricter state control as well, as have dozens and dozens of smaller oil-services firms that had business with PDVSA.

The fundamental problem, of course, is that Chávez wants the golden eggs, but he does not want to feed the goose. (In some cases, those eggs are literally golden; Chávez has nationalized the country's major gold-mining operations.) A large oil operation will continue to produce millions of barrels of oil per day for a long time, even it if is allowed to fall into disorder and disrepair—which is precisely what is happening to PDVSA. With basically no new investment coming from foreign sources—which are afraid to do business with the capricious and nationalization-happy Chávez—or from domestic sources—which are completely under the thumb of Chávez, who would rather use the money to reward his political supporters—PDVSA is foundering.

As is the wider Venezuelan economy.

The problem, apologists for socialism invariably argue, is that these state-run enterprises are not run like proper businesses; either they are corrupt, too highly politicized, or incompetently managed. Of course, all that is true. Never mind, for the moment, that the best way to ensure that these enterprises act like businesses is to forgo converting them from private enterprises into public ones; one must keep in mind that solid business practices alone cannot impart to a socialist enterprise the discipline and market-generated knowledge enjoyed by capitalist businesses. Mises commented at length on the futility of socialist enterprises' attempts to adopt free-market business techniques such as improving technology, reducing duplication, and instituting business training:

It is not difficult to expose the fallacies inherent in such notions. The attributes of the business man cannot be divorced from the position of the entrepreneur in the capitalist order. "Business" is not in itself a quality innate in a person; only the qualities of mind and character essential to a business man can be inborn. Still less is it an accomplishment which can be acquired by study, though the knowledge and the accomplishments needed by a business man can be taught and learned. A man does not become a business man by passing some years in commercial training or in a commercial institute, nor by a knowledge of book-keeping and the jargon of commerce, nor by a skill in languages and typing and shorthand. These are things which the clerk requires. But the clerk is not a business man, even though in ordinary speech he may be called a "trained business man."

When these obvious truths became clear in the end the experiment was tried of making entrepreneurs, who had worked successfully for many years, the managers of public enterprises. The result was lamentable. They did no better than the others; furthermore they lacked the sense for formal routine which distinguishes the life-long official. The reason was obvious. An entrepreneur deprived of his characteristic role in economic life ceases to be a business man.[2]

There is corruption, inefficiency, and incompetence in every socialist enterprise, of course, just as there is corruption, inefficiency, and incompetence in a fair number of capitalist enterprises as well. (Enron? AIG? Lehman Bros? Should we keep going?) The critical difference is this: inefficient or incompetent capitalist enterprises eventually fail. Corrupt traders can be banned from the markets, corrupt executives put in jail. Investors will mercilessly punish venality and stupidity, and they have strong incentives to uncover it.

But here's the kicker: even without corruption, incompetence, or inefficiency, a socialist enterprise will still malfunction, because its managers cannot have access to the sort of information provided by price signals in the private marketplace. That, and not the petty corruption of Hugo Chávez, is what ails Venezuela's "social" sector.

Aside from the oil industry, the Chávez regime seized control of much of the rest of the economy as well. Chávez in effect nationalized the Venezuelan electricity industry when he pried ownership of the country's largest private generator from a U.S. company, AES Corp. (He paid them $740 million for it—not an entirely unreasonable price, most analysts thought, but it was a take-it-or-leave-it proposition, or, perhaps more accurate, a take-it-or-I'll-take-it-anyway proposition.) Likewise, Chávez redirected great streams of Venezuelan oil revenue to nationalize other firms, for example, acquiring control of the cement industry by buying out private operations run by Mexican, Swiss, and French companies.

The cement nationalizations were necessary under Chávez's economic plan; after the Venezuelan government began imposing price controls, cement producers found they could sell their product more profitably abroad than in Venezuela's increasingly state-smothered markets. Rather than concede the reality that his plan called for paying unrealistically low prices for cement (prices below market-clearing world prices), Chávez simply seized the industry by leveraging the one commodity he was happy to see sold at its full market value: Venezuelan oil.

Similar stories unfolded in the telecoms, steel, paper, and food-processing industries. Several large agricultural operations also were nationalized, including Venezuela's major coffee producers, and large swathes of land were expropriated from other private concerns. A food-processing facility owned by the U.S. firm Cargill, which produces rice in Venezuela, was seized when the firm reduced production in response to government price controls. This policy had the predictable result that formerly productive farmland today sits fallow or marginalized by government mismanagement, while Venezuelan domestic food production has tanked. When ceramics, steel, and plumbing-supply operations had problems with their labor unions, Chávez "solved" the problem by nationalizing the businesses.

Organized labor, of course, is one of the great sources of Chávez's power, and if he didn't quite nationalize the Venezuelan labor unions, he certainly has tried to Chávezize them. He had a law passed that empowers the government to monitor internal union elections, a move criticized by labor leaders around the world as undue government interference in internal union matters. When Chávez was unable to subdue Venezuela's version of the AFL-CIO, the Confederacion de Trabajadores de Venezuela, which had resisted some of his more authoritarian innovations, Chávez simply set up a rival umbrella union of his own, the Union Nacional de Trabajadores. As Chávez acolytes have infiltrated individual unions, those unions have switched their affiliation from the anti-Chávez ACT to the *chávista* UNT. Chávez has rewarded them by making the relatively small newcomer UNT Venezuela's representative to international labor conferences.

When he was asked about possible plans to nationalize German industry, the leader of the German National Socialist Workers' Party, Adolf Hitler, replied, "Why should I nationalize them? I shall nationalize *the people*."[3] Chávez has made every effort to nationalize his people, too. Why merely nationalize industry when you can nationalize *reality*? So Chávez habitually rigs the numbers in his favor. When the Venezuelan National Statistics Institute released figures showing that poverty was on the rise under Chávez's government, climbing as high as 53 percent in 2004 in spite of surging oil revenues, the president simply called for a different measurement of poverty, one that conveniently showed a much lower poverty rate. When the data have suggested that unemployment is rising, the Chávez regime has finessed the way it calculates unemployment.

In this, Chávez is replicating an old practice perfected by his mentor, Fidel Castro, whose impressive—and utterly fictitious—statistics documenting Cuba's literacy and childhood-health achievements have been endlessly trumpeted by those seeking to socialize American healthcare. (Indeed, the American left is so committed to the myth of Cuba's socialist success—see, for example, the paean to Cuban healthcare in Michael Moore's anti-capitalism "documentary" *Sicko*—that even Castro's recent confession that "the Cuban model doesn't even work for us anymore"[4] has hardly dampened their enthusiasm.)

All Socialism Is National Socialism

Note that these are relatively petty acts of dishonesty and data-massaging. Anybody can lie with statistics, and most politicians do. But there is a certain thoroughness to socialism that often is lacking in other kinds of systems, even in highly centralized and authoritarian ones. Because socialism relies on the mechanisms of the state to enforce the dictates of its central planners, and because those dictates are marketed as the efforts of the best and the brightest to establish a rational order on behalf of the people—who cannot do so themselves—it is politically necessary that the state and its leaders (in many socialist systems, THE LEADER) be strongly identified, in an almost religious way, with the people.

Though they were devout atheists, the Soviets frequently invoked religious–nationalist interpretations of Russian history, the recurring narrative that Russia is a chosen nation with a special missionary role to play in world affairs. In the traditional narrative, Holy Mother Russia is Christendom's bulwark against the Islamic and pagan East. In the Soviet gospel, Russia is chosen by History to show the way to the one true faith of socialism.

While socialism has in theory been presented as an internationalist creed, in fact practically all socialist enterprises in the world have been

Spicoli: Chávez Critics Are Bogus, Should Be Jailed

"During a brief segment on *Real Time With Bill Maher*, [actor Sean] Penn explained that the mainstream news media in the United States regularly lies about Chávez by designating him a dictator, and that 'truly, there should be a bar by which one goes to prison for these kinds of lies.' Such a sentiment is likely (or do I mean hopefully?) not Penn's measured view on matters of free expression, but it is eerily close to the kind of threat Chávez uses to intimidate members of the opposition and elicit self-censorship within the Venezuelan media."

Reason magazine, 2010

nationalist enterprises as well. The Soviets were nationalists when it came to Russia and internationalists when it came to the surrounding peoples they subjugated; the Chinese were and are as frankly nationalist a regime as exists in the world today. And it is not merely to score a cheap rhetorical point that critics of socialism feel obliged to remind the world that Adolf Hitler came to power as the champion of a particular kind of socialism and at the head of a socialist party. As historian John Lukacs writes,

> We are all national socialists now. Of course the proportions of the compound of nationalism and socialism vary from country to country; but the compound is there, and even where social democracy prevails, it is the national feeling of the people that ultimately matters. What was defeated in 1945, together with Hitler, was German National Socialism: a cruel

and extreme version of national socialism. Elsewhere nationalism and socialism were brought together, reconciled and then compounded, without violence and hatred and war.[5]

Chávez's implementation of his own version of national socialism has not resulted in a full-on war, though he's come close a few times with his provocative saber-rattling against Columbia. Still, it would be too generous to say that his work has thus far been accomplished without violence or hatred. But to understand Venezuelan socialism, it is essential to understand that it is a socialism that incorporates nationalism, just as Soviet socialism did, just as Maoism did, just as the Marxist-inspired postwar revolutionary liberationist movements of the Third World did. What Holy Mother Russia was to the Soviets, what the pride of the Middle Kingdom is to the Chinese, what the *volk* were to Hitler—all of that has a counterpart in Latin America, concentrated in the person and legacy of a single man: Simón José Antonio de la Santísima Trinidad Bolívar y Palacios, known variously as "El Libertador" and "the George Washington of South America."

It is often said of a great man that he would "roll over in his grave" if he could see what his epigones had done in his name. Well, Chávez helped Simón Bolívar roll over in his grave—literally. Writer and human-rights activist Thor Halvorssen told the story in 2010:

> Shortly after midnight on July 16, Venezuelan President Hugo Chávez reached back in time. He presided at the exhumation of the remains of Simón Bolívar—Latin America's greatest independence hero, who helped liberate the region from Spain in the 19th century, and the object of Chávez's personal and political obsession.
>
> The skeleton was pulled apart. Pieces were removed, such as teeth and bone fragments, for "testing." The rest was put in a new coffin with the Chávez government's seal. Chávez, who

also tweeted the proceedings, gave a rambling speech in which he asked Christ to repeat his Lazarus miracle and raise the dead once more. He also apparently conversed with Bolívar's bones.

"I had some doubts," Chávez told his nation, paraphrasing the poet Pablo Neruda, "but after seeing his remains, my heart said, 'Yes, it is me.' Father, is that you, or who are you? The answer: 'It is me, but I awaken every hundred years when the people awaken.' "[6]

Even before assuming official power in Venezuela, Chávez had long sought to identify himself with El Libertador, and thereby to unify, in the public mind, his own person, the state, and the people. As the Sun King had put it some centuries before, "*L'etat, c'est moi.*" ("I am the state.") After failing to achieve power through a military coup, Chávez immersed himself in electoral politics—along with plain old-fashioned mob politics—and he named his gang the Bolivarian movement. Upon assuming power, Chávez demanded that Venezuela change its name to the Bolivarian Republic of Venezuela. He insists that a chair be left open at cabinet meetings for the use of Bolivar's ghost, and he had Bolivar's sword pillaged from the national museum for his own use. (He has given away replicas as gifts to such deserving luminaries as Mahmoud Ahmedenejad, Moammar Gaddafi, Robert Mugabe, Alexander Lukashenko, Vladimir Putin, and Raúl Castro.)

To underline his image as the reincarnation of Bolivar, every news station in the country was required to broadcast footage of Chávez's exhumation of the great man's corpse and his conversation with it. As the Venezuelan national anthem played behind the footage, all of the nation's televisions broadcast historical images of Bolívar from famous paintings, then images of his skeleton, then images of Chávez.

"If you can imagine Washington, Jefferson, Madison and Lincoln rolled into one," Halvorssen writes, "you can appreciate Bolívar's historical power in much of Latin America, and why a 'Bolivarian' revolution is infinitely more legitimizing than a 'Chávez' revolution. Chávez's aggressive appropriation of Bolívar—first politically and now physically—is especially meaningful because it is an attempt to wipe away the most important opposition leader and philosophical nemesis Chávez could ever face: Bolívar himself."[7]

Notably, far from being a proto-socialist, Bolívar was a man who traveled with a copy of Adam Smith's *The Wealth of Nations*, a man who so admired Thomas Jefferson that he sent a favored nephew to study at the University of Virginia, which Jefferson had designed. The content of his thought, however, is not nearly so useful to Chávez as the contents of his crypt, and the nationalist emotions that they can be used to stir up to provide a distraction from the inevitable failings of socialism. "Simón Bolívar's cadaver is like any other cadaver, but his legacy is a great deal more worth stealing than that of Kim Il Sung," writes the iconoclastic socialist journalist Christopher Hitchens, who has spent a good deal of time in the company of President Chávez. Having developed a keen eye for the delusions of an authoritarian, Hitchens writes that Chávez

> is very close to the climactic moment when he will announce that he is a poached egg and that he requires a very large piece of buttered toast so that he can lie down and take a soothing nap. Even his macabre foraging in the coffin of Simón Bolívar was initially prompted by his theory that an autopsy would prove that The Liberator had been poisoned—most probably by dastardly Colombians. This would perhaps provide a posthumous license for Venezuela's continuing hospitality to the [Columbian] narco-criminal gang FARC, a cross-border activity that does little to foster regional brotherhood.[8]

Bolívar, in fact, was a product of the Enlightenment and an admirer of the American Revolution. In some ways, he was more committed to the implicit ideals of the United States than were the Founding Fathers themselves—among other things, he opposed slavery. His intellectual landmarks included Jefferson, Smith, and Montesquieu. Chávez, too, embraces the Enlightenment, in his way; he identifies with the Dark Prince of the Enlightenment, Jean-Jacques Rousseau, the anti-liberal who, living at what was then the apex of Western liberty, saw man only "everywhere in chains."[9] It was Rousseau who developed the distinction between the "popular will"—which might be expressed in democratic elections and the like—and the "general will," which had to be discerned by enlightened rulers, and which provides camouflage for every kind of authoritarian undertaking in the name of the common good.

"There is often a great deal of difference between the will of all and the general will," Rousseau writes. "The latter looks only to the common interest; the former considers private interest and is only a sum of private wills. But take away from these same wills the pluses and minuses that cancel each other out, and the remaining sum of the differences is the general will."[10] It is within this construction that the political theorist detected the roots of "totalitarian democracy." President Chávez, who describes himself as a "Bolivarian democrat" and a "Rousseauian democrat," has been occasionally democratic in his means and reliably totalitarian in his aspirations.

The Worst of Both Worlds

Like many anti-American autocrats, and practically all socialist autocrats, Chávez has not wanted for apologists in the West, particularly in the United States. It was no surprise to find apologia for Chávez and his regime being published by such organs of official opinion as the Center for Strategic and International Studies. What was surprising, however, was the extent to which Chávez's "Rousseauian" song-and-dance shtick went over with the smart set. CSIS's Howard Wiarda offered up the official talking points: "Chávez follows in the footsteps of Jean Jacques Rousseau and Simon Bolivar rather than Locke, Jefferson, and Madison. Rousseau was an advocate of direct democracy. We need to recognize that other forms of democracy are legitimate. Chávez is no threat to U.S. interests at the present time. The United States can try to influence Chávez, but should be prepared to wait him out."[11]

Say this for Rousseau: centuries later, the philosopher is still in the headlines. Identifying some comments by Chávez that could supposedly help us understand his overall program, Wiarda writes,

> Two comments in particular stand out. When Chávez on one occasion declared, "I am a Rousseauian Democrat" and on another said, "I am a Bolivarian Democrat," it drove the U.S. Embassy in Caracas crazy because (1) the embassy had no idea what those terms meant and (2) it is inconceivable to U.S. citizens that there could be any form of democracy besides our own Lockean, Jeffersonian, Madisonian kind.
>
> ... Rousseau was an advocate of the leadership principle, like Plato's "philosopher-kings." He believed that great heroic charismatic leaders—presumably like Chávez's image of himself— could lead their people in innovative, revolutionary new directions, without the careful preparation in self-government or gradual development of institutions that the more prosaic (and boring) writers like Locke, Madison, and de Tocqueville understood as the base of democracy. . . . It follows from Rousseau's analysis that the separation of powers or check and balances is not needed because those institutions would only get in the way of a heroic leader's ability to act on the general will. Rousseau, like Marx one hundred years later, would also be against the intermediaries or what we now call "civil society"

because that would also hinder a leader's ability to carry out the general will, which he presumably knows intuitively.[12]

Intuition? That's one way to get around the Hayekian knowledge problem. But is it a good one? The outcome in Venezuela suggests it is not. In any case, the intuition of a man who produces public policy after communing with the corpse of his political hero may be suspect.

Socialism always presents itself as a rational system. Marx called his vision "scientific," but the lesser socialists are no less prone to argue that they are engaging in rational management and rational planning of the economy or of particular sectors. One obvious example is the gang that wants to reshape American healthcare in the name of such an econometric abstraction as the ratio of healthcare spending to GDP, as though there were a Golden Proportion that applies to national medical expenditures.

Now, American socialists are not quite so crude as Chávez; they did not dig up FDR's grave, but they did invoke his name, his image, and his legacy at every turn. It would be too much to say that all instances of socialism ultimately are identical, but there almost always is a family resemblance. And very often that resemblance takes the form of a brutal crackdown, which is precisely what has happened in Venezuela as it has become clear that THE PLAN is not going to be fulfilled—not now, not in the near future, not in the distant future, not ever.

Chávez's popularity plunged along with Venezuela's economic prospects. In light of the country's crumbling infrastructure, chronic food and water shortages, massive unemployment, 35 percent inflation, scarce basic consumer goods, and a failing electricity system, it's no surprise that Venezuelans have turned against their president. In early 2010, Chávez's approval ratings were down to 40 percent—but, in truth, they probably were far lower. Venezuelans are afraid to criticize the president in public, much less with a stranger taking a phone survey. And they have good reason to be; Chávez has shown that when it comes to those who criticize his regime—those who criticize THE PLAN—he can take down the high and mighty, to say nothing of a regular citizen.

Raul Baduel, for example, once was one of the most powerful men in Venezuela. He was a general who helped to defeat the anti-Chávez coup of 2002. He was, for a time, a close associate of the president, but like many others, he became disillusioned with Chávez's consistent policy failures and his increasingly authoritarian ways. When Chávez stripped him of his post as minister of defense, Baduel was liberated to become an open critic of the regime.

In 2007, Baduel helped hand Chávez one of his few political defeats when the president was forced to accept the outcome of a referendum

Socialism: Turning an Energy Giant into an Energy Pygmy

"[Venezuela] may be an energy colossus, with the largest conventional oil reserves outside the Middle East and one of the world's mightiest hydroelectric systems, but that has not prevented it from enduring serious electricity and water shortages that seem only to be getting worse.

"President Hugo Chávez has been facing a public outcry in recent weeks over power failures that, after six nationwide blackouts in the last two years, are cutting electricity for hours each day in rural areas and in industrial cities like Valencia and Ciudad Guayana. Now, water rationing has been introduced here in the capital.

"The deterioration of services is perplexing to many here, especially because the country had grown used to cheap, plentiful electricity and water in recent decades. But even as the oil boom was enriching his government and Mr. Chávez asserted greater control over utilities and other industries in this decade, public services seemed only to decay, adding to residents' frustrations."

New York Times, 2009

that blocked one of his moves to augment his power. Chávez had been trying to find a way to set aside the outcome of the vote, but Baduel and a group of fellow officers persuaded him that he would be wise to accept the judgment of the electorate. Soon afterward, military police took Baduel into custody on charges of having mismanaged his budget while minister of defense. He was quickly sentenced to eight years in prison.

Chávez had little to fear from making an example of his former minister of defense. As a former soldier himself, Chávez is deeply familiar with the politics of the Venezuelan military, and he had long since purged his critics and enemies from the officer corps and key defense ministry roles. Beyond that, his friend Fidel Castro has lent him a team of Cuban counterintelligence operatives who monitor the allegiances of top military personnel—a little gift from one socialist to another.

But it is difficult to keep a lid on a large and energetic country such as Venezuela—even with teams of Cuban spies at one's disposal. In response to the crackdown on Chávez's critics, General Alberto Mueller Rojas, the vice president of Chávez's party, quit his post in March 2010. Chávez's various ministries put out dishonest press releases claiming that Mueller had asked to be relieved of his duties because of failing health. But Mueller, not one to be cowed, made it clear in public that it was not his health, but Chávez's revolution that is failing.

Chávez's critics seem to habitually develop "health problems," along with legal problems, career problems, tax problems, and regulatory problems. Globovision owner Guillermo Zuloaga, whose TV network is the leading critic of Chávez's regime and an advocate for free-speech rights, is also the owner of a chain of car dealerships. After delivering a blistering attack on Chávez's stifling campaign against the free press, he found himself arrested on charges of usury and price-fixing, accusations stemming from his car business. Likewise, a large Globovision shareholder who also owned a large bank had his bank seized.

Globovision, incidentally, is the outfit that broke the story about all that food rotting in government warehouses. That is to say, Globovision's owner and investors are going to jail and having their property seized for exposing the inefficiencies and corruption of Venezuela's socialist system. Another television station, RCTV International, met a similar fate, along with five cable outlets. About forty independent radio stations have been shut down as well, and a new law will allow Chávez to imprison reporters, editors, or publishers who share "information that harms the interest of the state."

The clampdown has economic aspects as well as political aspects. Indeed, one of the difficult tasks in analyzing a socialist economy is separating mere economic incompetence from intentional economic abuses committed with malice aforethought. For instance, when the Chávez regime's failed central-planning efforts produced massive shortages of food and household goods, it tried to exert direct management of the grocery stores. The supermarket chain Exito was seized by the government, and another chain, Cada, was made a takeover target.

But such nationalizations failed to make THE PLAN work, so the government's next step was to try to control the import and, especially, the export of food and consumer goods. It is a well-established law of economics that price-fixing leads inevitably to shortages, which is precisely what Chávez's program of price controls did. When that failed, he tried to increase his control of the import-export economy by interfering with the exchange rate of Venezuela's currency, which is named, inevitably, the *bolivar*. By setting an artificially high rate of exchange for bolivares, Chávez had intended to buck up the buying power of Venezuelans and thereby help strengthen the economy. What he actually did—what any competent analyst of state economic planning could have told him he was doing—was to create a giant black market for currency, making criminals out of practically every importer, exporter, and traveler in

Venezuela. The real rate of exchange for bolivares in the free market—which is, in this case, the black market—set the currency's strength at about half the official rate.

What followed next was pure comedy. Chávez decided that Venezuela needed two exchange rates, one for the purchase of essential goods and another rate for the purchase of non-essential goods. Venezuelans exchanging bolivares to purchase essential goods could do so at 2.6 to the dollar, while those buying inessential goods had to exchange at 4.3 to the dollar. (The real rate, on the black market, hit about 7 bolivars to the dollar around the same time.) The result was, of course, economic chaos. Inflation jumped from an already catastrophic 30 percent to a truly ruinous 35 percent. The price of oil began to weaken shortly thereafter, leaving the Chávez regime strapped for the cash it needed to continue Boss Hugo's campaign of stockpiling Russian weapons and military matériel while selling his countrymen's oil at a steep discount to allies such as Castro.

Naturally, this economic, social, and political displacement has been accompanied by the decay of public institutions—particularly law and order. Caracas is, as of this writing, the most dangerous capital city in the Americas, a place where ransom kidnapping is out of control. The Chávez regime's response, so far, has been quintessential central planning—to require the reporting of kidnapping cases (victims' families often have not bothered, since the police, when they are not actively involved in crime themselves, are ineffective), and, when cases are reported, to freeze the bank accounts of the victims' families—thereby preventing the payment of ransoms. The result, of course, is the death and disfigurement of kidnapping victims whose families have no recourse and who cannot rely upon the police to rescue their loved ones. Thus Venezuela endures the worst of both worlds: a police state that cannot control crime.

Lights Out

There is a famous picture of the Koreas that demonstrates, in the most dramatic way imaginable, the differences between a socialist economy and a capitalist economy. Taken by satellite at night, the photo shows South Korea's roads and cities flooded with light. The light stops abruptly at the border, with North Korea shrouded in darkness except for a dim glow around the official precincts of Pyongyang.

Darkness is falling on Venezuela, too.

In spite of being one of the world's energy powerhouses, Venezuela cannot produce enough power to meet its own citizens' needs. There are many reasons for this: chronic underinvestment in the state-run oil firms is one; chronic underinvestment in the state-run electricity firms is another. The Chávez government, unable to ignore the rolling blackouts that, along with food shortages, have set so many Venezuelans against him, did what socialists do—he unveiled a five-year plan. In 2010, the first year of the plan, Venezuela was to add 5,900 megawatts of power. It managed just over 20 percent of that goal.

Why would a country that produces a large share of the world's petroleum be unable to power its own cities and factories? One of the reasons is that Venezuela has, in recent years, resisted building oil-based electricity plants, relying instead on hydropower, which makes generation vulnerable to changes in weather. Chávez, of course, wants to use as little of his country's oil at home as possible; with his currency controls and other regulation having thoroughly disrupted the export-import markets, and the economy in shambles because of his broader socialist agenda, Venezuelan oil sold on the international markets is the government's main source of hard currency—mostly those hated Yankee dollars—that it needs to provide for its own operations, to pay its apparatchiks' salaries and gratuities, to fund its shenanigans abroad (such as its support of FARC terrorists in neighboring Colombia), and to pay Fidel Castro the rent on his spies. Thus are Venezuelans not only starved of the things they need to import from abroad, but also starved of the one thing that they ought to have in abundance: energy.

The darkness that is falling on Venezuela is the same darkness that can be seen over North Korea at night. It is familiar, and it is predictable. We have seen it creep across country after country. And we can see it creeping across our own.

Chapter Eleven

SOCIALISM AND NATIONALISM: ALLIES, NOT RIVALS

I n a 2000 essay in the *International Socialist Review*, writer Tom Lewis argues that real socialism is lexically internationalist. "Socialists are internationalists," he writes. "Whereas nationalists believe that the world is divided primarily into different nationalities, socialists consider social class to be the primary divide. For socialists, class struggle—not national identity—is the motor of history. And capitalism creates an international working class that must fight back against an international capitalist class."[1]

Lewis knows whereof he speaks—unfortunately, he seems to know only that. It is true that socialists in the United States tend to be highly internationalist. This is largely a function of the fact that they have been safely contained in intellectual ghettos for decades upon decades, venturing out from time to time to teach a graduate seminar in the thought of Julia Kristeva or to do a little phone-banking for the Dennis Kucinich campaign.

American socialists tend to be internationalists because they tend to be anti-American; in fact, it seems to be more often the case that their anti-Americanism leads them to socialism rather than socialism leading them to anti-Americanism. Until quite recently, American socialists were kept safely away from power—and their internationalism is in no small

Guess What?

★ Despite their supposed internationalism, most socialist leaders are nationalists

★ International free trade is incompatible with socialism

★ Socialism provokes nationalist conflicts by creating shortages of natural resources

part a function of that fact. In the rest of the world, when socialists approach power they almost always do so as nationalists.

That was especially true of the most self-consciously "internationalist" of the socialist regimes, that of the USSR. While Marx's international socialism quickly transformed into the patriotic campaign for "socialism in one country" under Stalin, the Russian socialists consistently talked out of both sides of their mouths about nationalism. Operationally, they were internationalists when it came to the satellite states Russia absorbed into the USSR and to their various factota and puppets around the world, but they were robustly nationalistic when it came to Russia herself. Naturally, this sub rosa nationalism was accompanied by the suppression of ethnic minorities, such as Chechens and ethnic Germans. According to the *Russian History Encyclopedia*,

> In the official Soviet ideology there appeared the term "unreliable" nationalities. Accused nationalities were the subject of deportation and collective punishment, based on allegations of collaboration with the Nazis. As the result of this policy, the Volga Germans, Chechens, Crimean Tartars and dozens of smaller nationalities were deported from their homelands to Central Asia and Kazakhstan. Under Stalin, fifty-six nationalities, involving about 3.5 million people, were deported to Siberia and Central Asia.
>
> First Secretary of the Communist Party Nikita Khrushchev rehabilitated the repressed nationalities and allowed most of them to return to their original homes. The main exceptions were the Crimean Tartars and Volga Germans, because their lands had been taken over by Russians and Ukrainians.
>
> . . . Soviet leaders had a double standard toward Russian nationalism versus the nationalism of the other nations of the

Soviet Union. Thus the expression of Russian superiority over other nations was permitted. Movies, paintings, and novels were created about the heroic Russian past. The official Soviet ideology called the Russian nation the "older brother" of all nationalities of the Soviet Union.

Meanwhile expressions of national feelings by the non-Russian nations were suppressed. Even demonstrations of respect for some distinguished national figures from the past were forbidden. Thus Soviet authorities forbade gatherings near the monument of the distinguished nineteenth-century Ukrainian poet Taras Shevchenko .... Ukrainian nationalism was considered by the Soviet rulers as one of the most serious threats to national unity and was severely suppressed.[2]

Soviet socialism was nationalist socialism. This may sound odd to the American ear, which is used to thinking of Soviet socialism as the arch-enemy of national socialism—Nazism, as it was known in Germany—but what mostly transpired between Russia and Germany during World War II was a conflict in nationalisms among two governments that largely agreed on the socialism.

One can oversell that shared socialism, of course; Soviet socialism was in many ways a very different economic system from German national socialism. But the two systems were much more similar to one another than either was to Anglo-European liberalism. My *National Review* colleague Jonah Goldberg has been the target of a lot of left-wingers' hooting for the provocative thesis of his excellent book, *Liberal Fascism*, but it is a fact that the international socialist Benito Mussolini did not have to radically alter his economic agenda when he became the fascist duce Benito Mussolini. The anti-capitalism was already in place, the statism, the central planning—Mussolini's fascism in Italy was very

The River's Source

"The only doctrine of which I had practical experience was that of socialism, from until the winter of 1914—nearly a decade. My experience was that both of a follower and a leader, but it was not doctrinal experience. My doctrine during that period had been the doctrine of action. A uniform, universally accepted doctrine of socialism had not existed since 1905, when the revisionist movement, headed by Bernstein, arose in Germany, countered by the formation, in the see-saw of tendencies, of a left revolutionary movement which in Italy never quitted the field of phrases, whereas, in the case of Russian socialism, it became the prelude to Bolshevism.

"Reformism, revolutionism, centrism, the very echo of that terminology is dead, while in the great river of Fascism one can trace currents which had their source in Sorel, Peguy, Lagardelle of the Movement Socialists, and in the cohort of Italian syndicalists who from 1904 to 1914 brought a new note into the Italian socialist environment."

Benito Mussolini, *Doctrine of Fascism*, 1923

much of a piece with Stalin's "socialism in one country." Hitler's fanciful projects for the Germany economy were, if anything, in the long run more grandiosely socialist than were Lenin's aspirations.

But Soviet central planning failed, much as German central planning had failed before it. And, inevitably, the central planners began to seek an enemy on which to blame their failures. Those Tartars and ethnic Germans were handy as "unreliable" nationalities, but of course the Soviet socialists eventually followed their German counterparts and began to target the Jews. From the *Russian History Encyclopedia*:

After World War II the Jewish intelligentsia was persecuted during the political campaign of struggle against "cosmopolitanism." Almost all those who were accused of cosmopolitanism and pro-Western orientation were Jewish. This accusation was followed by loss of employment and by imprisonment. In 1952 the elite of the Jewish intelligentsia, including prominent scientists and Yiddish writers and poets, were secretly tried, convicted, and executed. The anti-Jewish campaign reached its height in the Soviet Union in 1952 with the investigation of the "Jewish doctors' plot." Jewish doctors were accused of intentionally providing incorrect treatments and poisoning the leaders of the Communist Party. These political campaigns provoked mass hysteria and the rise of anti-Semitism among the local population. The growing anti-Semitism was supposed to be a prelude to the planned deportation all Soviet Jews to Birobidzhan in the Far East. Only the death of Stalin on March 5, 1953, saved the Jewish population from deportation.[3]

That is to say, the world's most developed socialist system was actively plotting the dispossession of its entire Jewish population only a few years after the Nazi Holocaust. It is something to keep in mind when one considers the role that the Stalinist organization International ANSWER—an alliance of hardcore socialists and Mideastern anti-Semites—played in the 2001–08 antiwar movement, which helped to put into office Barack Obama, the most robustly socialistic president the United States has endured since Woodrow Wilson. More on that later.

Workers of the World, Attack Each Other!

Jews are a favorite target of authoritarian regimes, wherever there are Jews. (And in some places where there are no Jews.) But it is a big, complex world, and the hunt for enemies is a longstanding socialist obsession; it is an important part of what binds socialism to nationalism in the real world, as opposed to the intellectuals' imaginary world of international socialism.

There is probably no better example of that today than the case of China. One longtime China watcher, having returned from a sojourn in the Middle Kingdom, told me, "I returned from China convinced that there was nothing to worry about from their ideology. I don't think any of them really believe in communism any more. But I was terrified of their nationalism." My *National Review* colleague John Derbyshire, who himself resided in China for some time, identifies a blend of frank racism and national romanticism in the Chinese outlook. Many Sinologists argue that very little other than nationalism holds China together as its top-down socialism necessitates ever-greater expansions of Beijing's police state.

Fortunately for the Chinese Politburo—but unfortunately for the Chinese people—history has supplied the Chinese socialists with a ready enemy in the form of Japan, the once-masterful imperial power that raped and repressed China mercilessly throughout long stretches of its history. Japan, of course, has become a modern, capitalist nation; such nationalism as there is in Japan is largely the stuff of political eccentricity, and there is far too little of it to present much of a threat to anybody. Not so Chinese nationalism, which gives Japan very good reason to worry about its national sovereignty and its national defense in the coming decades. The tenor of anti-Japanese rhetoric in nationalist China can be shocking. Peter Gries, an expert on the subject, describes one raging anti-Japanese protest:

> "The Chinese people are very angry; there will be serious consequences!" read a long banner held aloft by a dozen marching demonstrators. It was Saturday, Apr. 16, 2005, and

thousands of mostly college students were protesting through downtown Shanghai. Another banner revealed the object of their anger: "Oppose Japanese imperialism!" Other signs displayed a variety of specific grievances: "Oppose Japan entering the Security Council!" "Boycott Japanese goods, revitalize China!" "Oppose Japan's history textbooks!" "Protect our Diaoyu Islands!" Other students expressed their protests individually, holding high a wide variety of handmade placards and posters.

The most persistent messages focused on a proposed May 2005 boycott: "Boycott Japanese goods for a month and Japan will suffer for a whole year." "Boycotting Japanese goods will castrate Japan!" The two most striking visual images were of weapons and Japan's Prime Minister Junichiro Koizumi. Pictures of butcher knives, swords and arrows were painted to pierce the rising sun of Japan's national flag. Yet it was the image of Koizumi that received the most attention from the young demonstrators. One protestor gave him a mustache to make him look like Adolph Hitler, and others went further, dehumanizing Koizumi. One placard placed his head on a pig's body and declared him to be a "little pig." Another painted a pig's snout and ears onto his face and declared in large characters, "Death to Koizumi the pig!"

But the most ominous images evoked a dead Koizumi, with tombstones bearing his name, and a photo of a funeral with Koizumi's picture at the center. In addition to peacefully waving the flag of the People's Republic of China (PRC), singing the *Internationale*, and chanting anti-Japanese slogans, the demonstrators also engaged in a number of activities of a less benign nature. On their way to the Japanese consulate, they smashed the windows of Japanese stores and restaurants, over-turned Japanese cars, and burned Japanese flags and photos as well as placards of Koizumi. When they arrived at the consulate, they hurled eggs and pelted it with paint bombs.[4]

Notice the largely *economic* character of that rhetoric. "Boycott Japanese goods, revitalize China!"—as though Japan's prosperity were the reason for China's often uneven economic ascent. The image of a boycott as an act of castration is particularly chilling—and particularly emblematic of the crude economic thinking that underlies nationalist socialism in practically all its manifestations.

Spanish economist Faustino Ballvé (1887–1959) understood that socialism was entirely incompatible with a sophisticated understanding of economics—particularly international economics—years ago, writing,

> The slogan, "Buy what the fatherland produces; produce what the fatherland needs," has not been and cannot be of any avail at all, because whoever is in want of a commodity buys it however and wherever he finds it. This, indeed, is the very essence of man's innate faculty of economic judgment and choice. On the other hand, for a country to produce what it needs, natural conditions have to be favorable, and there must be a sufficient demand to make production profitable, for no one will undertake to produce a commodity, no matter how much the country may need it, that economic calculation shows to be unprofitable and incapable of competing on the world market.[5]

The extreme form of this line of thinking is *autarky*, the condition in which a nation attempts to live exclusively on its own produce, as North Korea has endeavored to do from time to time.

Ballve's analysis, like that of Hayek and Mises, suggests that national economic planning is not so much unwieldy as impossible:

No less illusory is the myth of the economic solidarity of the citizens of one country as opposed to the inhabitants of other countries. From what we have already observed of the economic interdependence of all people everywhere, it becomes manifest that it is absurd and impossible for a country to attempt to live in *autarky* exclusively on its own resources. No country, however extensive and diversified it may be, not even Russia or the United States, has at its disposal all the natural resources needed for its production and consumption. All countries have to import, and not on a small scale, food and raw materials as well as manufactured goods, if they are not prepared to content themselves with a miserable subsistence dearly paid for, because there are branches of industry that can produce at low cost only on a large scale or under especially favorable conditions. (As we know from the law of comparative cost and the law of returns, few countries are in a position to produce economically heavy machinery, automobiles, etc.) They need to export in order to pay for their imports.

For this reason, the only really integral economic whole is the international, or rather, the worldwide, market, because, in fact, trade takes place, not between nations, but among men and across national frontiers. This universal economic community can be realized only when every entrepreneur buys and sells in the markets of the whole world.[6]

The international nature of free-market capitalism has lethal ramifications for the would-be central planner. What the central planner cannot do within a single country (or even within a single industry), the markets do across industries, nations, continents—even across time. That is to say, markets coordinate the incomprehensibly complex means of production, ranging from physical capital to financial capital to credit, labor, intellectual property, organizational capital, and the other subtle inputs that make modern material life possible—and national central planning impossible. Hugo Chávez can try to set the price of rice in Venezuela, but so long as rice can cross borders, his regime does not have the last say on the question.

Putting the Socialism in National Socialism

"We are enemies, deadly enemies, of today's capitalist economic system with its exploitation of the economically weak, its unfair wage system, its immoral way of judging the worth of human beings in terms of their wealth and their money."

Gregor Strasser, Nazi ideologue

"The State shall make it its primary duty to provide a livelihood for its citizens...the abolition of all incomes unearned by work...the ruthless confiscation of all war profits...the nationalization of all businesses that have been formed into corporations...profit-sharing in large enterprises...extensive development of insurance for old-age...land reform suitable to our national requirements."

Nazi Party platform, 1920

"We are socialists, we are enemies of today's capitalistic economic system for the exploitation of the economically weak, with its unfair salaries, with its unseemly evaluation of a human being according to wealth and property instead of responsibility and performance, and we are determined to destroy this system under all conditions."

Adolf Hitler, 1927

Resource Nationalism: Another Socialist Specialty

The American socialist writer Dan Jakopovich (whose work we will closely consider later in this book) is not alone among the so-called international socialists in praising this strategy of "resource nationalism." It has a long history but remains as fresh as the morning headlines: as Russian collective agriculture failed and productivity plunged, the Soviet economic planners responded by banning the export of what Lenin called "the currency of currencies"—grain. Although the collapse of communism allowed Russian agriculture to recover enough for the country to resume grain exports, in 2010 the outwardly nationalist Vladimir Putin once again banned grain exports, citing poor harvests.

Food is of course a particularly sensitive area—failing electricity grids are bad, but hunger is much worse. Because socialist countries tend to engage in relatively little trade, or in highly restricted trade, they have been historically vulnerable to food shortages. While many of the softer socialist regimes have learned to accommodate themselves to the realities of trade (you just can't get good home-grown oranges in December in Sweden), the most robustly socialist regimes have not, and they remain extraordinarily at risk of disruptions in their food supplies.

Indeed, most governments engage in a fair amount of attempted central planning when it comes to food, and, inevitably, they do so ham-handedly. The world markets have seen some very disruptive developments in food trade in recent years, something that has caught the attention of executives at Cargill, the world's largest food business. Cargill senior vice president Paul Conway offers a Hayekian analysis of the problem: politics distorts or blocks price signals. As the *Sunday Times* of London reports,

> These intermittent crises provoke what Cargill believes are bad policy decisions—stockpiling, hoarding and export curbs.

Whether it was EU butter mountains or the international agencies set up in the early 1980s to manage markets in commodities, such as cocoa and sugar, all came into disrepute, Mr Conway says.

The reason they failed is that governments forgot the role of farmers. "When governments have held a lot of stock, such as in the Soviet Union, [price] signals did not get through to farmers. Last year, the Argentinian Government increased export tariffs, which meant there was no point in planting. You had grain rotting in some countries last year because governments banned exports."

Instead of trying to manage food output, governments need to invest, he suggests, in infrastructure, irrigation, ports and, counterintuitively, he says that developing countries should sponsor futures markets.

"To blame futures markets for causing problems is nonsense. What they do is give clear price signals. We are a great believer in giving price signals to farmers. A futures market is a tool, a bit like biotechnology. If there is a crisis, blaming the tool is not . . . wise."

It's a message that many don't want to hear—that futures markets are the answer, not the problem.[7]

Of course, socialist regimes are likely to take precisely the opposite role. Rather than engage with the markets and thereby provide useful information to farmers, packagers, and other producers, socialist governments have attempted to use such clumsy tools as import-export controls to impose THE PLAN, even when the economics say otherwise. In many cases, those moves are accompanied by politically motivated seizures and nationalizations.

Socialist governments have a particularly bleak history concerning the redistribution of land. The collectivization of farming in Soviet Russia and Maoist China were unmitigated disasters, but one need not look that far back into history for an example. The socialist president of Zimbabwe, Robert Mugabe, managed in the course of a few short years to transform the nation once known as "the breadbasket of Africa" from a major food exporter into a starving shell of itself—from breadbasket to basketcase. He accomplished that by enacting a "spread the wealth around" program for the country's farmland, which had for generations been owned mostly by white Zimbabweans resented by black Zimbabweans. After just a few years of attempting to politically manage Zimbabwe's agricultural economy, Mugabe left 45 percent of his countrymen malnourished and agricultural production lower than it has been in generations. Production of some crops has fallen by nearly 80 percent. Production of maize, Zimbabwe's staple food, fell some 75 percent. When prices soared in response to falling production, Mugabe enacted price controls. The result was that farmers switched from price-controlled crops such as maize to uncontrolled crops such as tobacco and paprika, driving production down even further and driving real prices—which is to say, black-market prices—even higher.

Zimbabwe's plight is no mystery. Socialism needs nationalism, and such "resource nationalism" as exhibited by the Mugabe regime is to be expected. The real mystery is: why would the United States want to recreate Zimbabwe's failures in its oil industry?

Chapter Twelve

U.S. "ENERGY INDEPENDENCE" AND CENTRAL PLANNING

Guess What?

★ Attempts to plan the U.S. energy sector are classic cases of socialism

★ American advocates of socialist energy resort to crude nationalist appeals

★ The green agenda serves the interests of Big Business

Why would the United States seek to apply the Zimbabwe model to energy, one of its most important industries? Although it sounds unbelievable, the American crusade for "energy independence"—a centrally planned economic exercise if ever there were one—promises exactly that.

Resource nationalism is a prominent feature of the oil industry. In fact, most of the world's major oil companies are arms of national governments. "The 13 largest energy companies on Earth, measured by the reserves they control, are now owned and operated by governments," the *Wall Street Journal* reports. "Saudi Aramco, Gazprom (Russia), China National Petroleum Corp., National Iranian Oil Co., Petróleos de Venezuela, Petrobras (Brazil) and Petronas (Malaysia) are all larger than ExxonMobil, the largest of the multinationals. Collectively, multinational oil companies produce just 10% of the world's oil and gas reserves. State-owned companies now control more than 75% of all crude oil production. The power of the state is back."[1]

The U.S. government is nearly alone among the world's oil producing nations in not owning or having owned a large oil corporation. But even in relatively free-market countries such as the United States, the state is deeply involved in the energy industry. And in the emerging capitalist powers, oil often is the exception to the rule of free-market reform. Ian Bremmer reports in *Foreign Policy*,

> Brazil's emergence as an investor-friendly, free market democracy has been one of the world's most encouraging stories of the past several years. As Venezuela's Hugo Chávez perfects his Castro impersonation, Ecuador and Bolivia follow Chávez's example, and Argentina's economy flounders, Brazil's President Luiz Inacio Lula da Silva has maintained responsible macroeconomic policies—while redistributing wealth to narrow the still-considerable gap between the country's rich and poor. But as he begins his final year in office, a huge off-shore oil find has emboldened his government to deepen state control of the energy sector, clouding the investment picture. Lula now looks likely to win a legislative battle over the future of Brazil's oil sector. State-owned oil company Petrobras will then hold exclusive rights to operate all new exploration and production in off-shore fields that are believed to contain one of the world's largest deposits of crude oil discovered in recent years. Brazil's government will then control all activity in the new fields, making the big decisions on project operation and management. Over time, Petrobras will become a much larger but less profitable and less efficiently run enterprise.[2]

President Lula does not in most ways resemble Hugo Chávez, nor does he wish to. But the Brazilian liberal and the Venezuelan thug are alike in that they each run an oil company or two. Their American counterparts—would-be energy socialists who may be found in both parties—will not attempt to directly take over Exxon or any other U.S. oil company. Instead, they intend to direct the entire American energy industry from Washington, D.C.

In some ways, America's oil socialists are more audacious in the scope and depth of their plans than are their South American, Middle Eastern, and Far Eastern brethren. Hugo Chávez simply wants to control Venezuela's oil companies in order to produce more oil, sell it in the international markets, and use the proceeds to fund his police state at home and his adventuring abroad. In contrast, the American oil socialists believe they can reshape the entire U.S. energy sector—which means reshaping the entire U.S. economy, to say nothing of the global energy markets—so that it produces a cheap, plentiful, non-polluting source of energy that operates in accord with their political interests. It's the sort of project that would have made Trotsky blush and Hayek's head explode in frustration, though it enjoys wide support from both the American people and from mainstream politicians of both parties.

Here it's worth reiterating a point made early in this book: socialism is not principally about redistributing wealth or income from the rich to the poor. Socialism is about politicians planning the economy. Politicization of the economy, not redistribution, is the hallmark of socialism. Redistribution, while an economically complex and morally fraught issue, is a normal part of practically every modern welfare state.

Socialism, properly understood, is something quite different. And while a high degree of redistribution necessarily accompanies socialist planning efforts, that redistribution often channels wealth and income from the poor and middle classes to the wealthy—particularly those who are either members of the political-planning class or who can exploit connections to that class for their own benefit. It's worth keeping in mind that the erratically socialistic management of the U.S. agriculture industry mainly benefits individuals with a net worth of more than $1 million and giant agribusiness conglomerates such as Archer Daniels Midland and Cargill. In the case of oil socialism, those looking for a place at the planners' feeding trough include Oklahoma oil billionaire T. Boone Pickens,

Environmentalism for Profit

"Al Gore, the former US vice president, could become the world's first carbon billionaire after investing heavily in green energy companies."

The Telegraph, 2007

as well as Al Gore and his business partner David Blood, who are heavily invested in "alternative energy" operations that stand to benefit from (and which are only economically viable when accompanied by) massive government subsidies.

A Plan for American Energy Socialism

Like the various socialisms of South America and the Third World, American oil socialism is characterized by resource nationalism, fiercely nationalistic rhetoric, politicized central planning, and political mandates that entirely ignore the mind-boggling complexity of the economic and production issues at hand. Its supporters call it "ending America's addiction to foreign oil." Its critics call it, rightly, socialist poppycock.

The *Das Kapital* of American oil socialism is U.S. senator Jeff Merkley's remarkably vapid proposal titled "America Over a Barrel: Solving Our Oil Vulnerability." Senator Merkley, a left-wing Democrat from Oregon, is about the 642nd American politician to make an "over a barrel" joke on the subject of oil, but his proposal is far from funny.

Given what we have seen of the normal, predictable trajectory of socialist enterprises, it promises to impose hundreds of billions of dollars—perhaps trillions of dollars—in unnecessary costs on the U.S. economy, to inflict deep structural damage to the energy industry in the United States and abroad, and to entrench government central planners in every imaginable aspect of the American economy, from obvious ones such as car and road design to less obvious ones such as logistics engineering, the design of office chairs, immigrant-farmworker programs, and more. A look at "America Over a Barrel" shows just how far gone into central-planning fantasies an American politician can get when left unsupervised.

Merkley begins with the common and preposterous notion that American oil imports present some sort of special national-security risk. His commercials on the subject have, ironically, emphasized images of Hugo Chávez and Mahmoud Ahmedenejad, two oil socialists who very much share Merkley's views on how to manage the energy industry. This is pure, dishonest pandering, of course; the senator is not otherwise notable for his interest in national-security issues, nor for the robustness of his national-security positions. (He has been an advocate of surrender in both Iraq and Afghanistan, supports closing our terrorist detention center at Guantanamo Bay, accuses U.S. forces willy-nilly of engaging in torture—you know the type.)

He writes that America is "dangerously dependent on foreign oil imported from the Middle East."[3] Notice the rhetoric there, the unnecessary repetition of *foreign*, *imported*, and *Middle East*—in case you've missed the point, Merkley will keep making it. In truth, America imports more of its oil from Canada than from any other country, with Mexico in second place. But it's hard to make people fear Canada, a country whose last act of national aggression was committed in a hockey rink. The Saudis are a real menace to the world, and Hugo Chávez is an annoyance, but we buy comparatively little oil from them. And even if we did not buy a single drop of oil from them, oil is a fungible commodity in high demand on world markets. If the Saudis had to send their tankers east instead of west, it would be no skin off the emir's nose.

But that kind of saber-rattling, even from a saberless sap like Merkley, is essential for selling oil socialism—it distracts Americans from the fact that Merkley & Co. are attempting to do for the oil sector what Chávez has done for Venezuela's oil industry, what Mugabe has done for Zimbabwe's farms, and what generations of political management have done for U.S. public schools.

America is no more "dangerously dependent" on Middle Eastern oil than we are "dangerously dependent" on Far Eastern steel, Taiwanese computer chips, Vietnamese textiles, or Indian call-center operators. It is true that our economy would shut down without oil and that energy is critical to our national defense. But steel is also critical, as is concrete and information technology. Not to mention that all of that, when it comes to government purchases, is heavily dependent upon the goodwill of the foreign central banks that do so much to finance our national debt—a real source of national vulnerability that Merkley and his ilk have long ignored. Something to keep in mind for perspective . . .

The senator's case for oil autarky depends, as so many similar ideas do, on the myth of the national economy. "In total, the United States sends $1 billion a day overseas to fuel our oil habit," he writes.[4] That is not true, unless one believes that "the United States" is synonymous with Valero and Conoco Philips, the two largest refiners of crude oil in the country. Refiners buy a lot of crude, and they import a lot of the crude they buy. They do that for the same reason that Dell puts Korean- or Taiwanese-made components in the computers it assembles in Texas: because companies source their materials from the cheapest places they can, which keeps prices low and profits high. In practically every business, this is understood as a normal and desirable fact of life; it makes the economy efficient, which contributes to creating wealth, jobs, and a higher standard of living for Americans (and the rest of the world, too, a fact that should not be treated as unimportant).

But when it comes to oil, the normal rules of economics do not seem to apply, at least so far as the politicians are concerned. Of course, they will learn—the hard way—that there is no getting around the realities of supply and demand. Not that they will not try.

On top of the phony national-security argument, Merkley and the oil socialists pile on arguments about environmental concerns, which are significant in the energy industry. Both oil and coal impose real environmental costs, in extracting them and in burning them. But if Merkley wants to stop importing oil, that's going to mean a lot more oil rigs operating in U.S. waters and in U.S. territories, meaning that the United States will bear *more* of the cost of oil's environmental repercussions, rather than less.

His answer to this, of course, is a five-year plan, one that will see the United States suddenly using considerably less oil—a country in which, today, nearly 100 percent of the transportation energy comes from oil and in which practically the entire electricity supply comes from hydrocarbons (coal and natural gas). That is to say, his plan amounts to: magic! Maybe Hugo Chávez can show Merkley how to pull a national power grid out of his hat.

Merkley calls his version of the Soviet five-year plan a "comprehensive and diversified strategy to reduce our dependence on oil outright, with a goal of eliminating the need for any oil imported from outside of North America."[5] You'll notice he's leaving himself a little wiggle room there—no imported oil, except from the countries that already are our largest oil suppliers. The oil socialists show a real talent for that sort of rhetorical sleight-of-hand; one influential faction, Energy Independence Now, published a widely cited report in which it boasted that the new heavy-duty truck standards it has been pushing would save "the equivalent of more oil than we imported last year from Saudi Arabia, Venezuela, Mexico, Kuwait, Nigeria, Brazil, Iraq, and Angola combined."[6] And that is true—over the lifetime of the trucks, which could run more than a decade. Comparing one year's worth of oil imports to the lifetime fuel consumption of America's entire heavy-duty truck fleet distorts by many orders of magnitude the scale of those "savings." (Not to mention that the laundry list of oil exporters excludes the biggest one: Canada.)

That sort of dishonesty is the stock in trade of oil socialists, or as we could call them, the Committee for Energy Autarky.

Of course, no single-issue socialist worth his red socks could present THE PLAN without *der commissars*, and the senator proposes the creation of a "National Energy Security Council" to serve that role.[7] Again, the rhetoric is worth noticing: not a National Energy Council but a National Energy *Security* Council, making fuel-efficiency standards and subsidies for corn-farmers' ethanol operations the moral equivalent of *war*. (Note how American socialism is almost always national socialism.) And those central planners at the National Energy Security Council would have a second-tier commission to back them up, the Energy Information Administration (which already exists).

The creation of the central-planning authority is, in Merkley's argument, strictly political. It exists because similar pushes for energy autarky have come to naught when, as he writes, "the nation's focus turned elsewhere or the political winds shifted."[8] In other words, if the people's elected representatives fail to produce the policy outcome desired by Merkley and his central planners, then those plans must be made impervious to the "political winds"—which is to say, to democracy. Creating a central bureau to protect THE PLAN from the "political winds" of democracy has long been a concern of central planners; Lenin called his approach *democratic centralism*—"Lenin's deliberate misnomer for mindless obedience," as former secretary of state Zbigniew Brzezenski put it.

Merkley proposes that actions taken in 2010 and 2011 should come to fruition in 2016. Naturally, like most five-year plans, this one relies largely on numbers that have been plucked out of thin air. The Obama administration, for instance, has proposed tightening fuel-economy standards for passenger vehicles by 4 percent a year through 2016. That 4 percent is a questionable enough number—it seems calculated only to judge the standards just over 35 miles per gallon by 2016, a meaningless political target. But even those 4 percent standards, impractical and counter-

Green and Red

"Their 'New Socialism' doesn't need to capture property. It is content to control the economy through taxation and regulation and the attitudes of our citizens by the establishment of a culture through the power institutions of our society: the media, the education establishment, and powerful business interests. Moreover, the 'New Socialism' seeks to create a conventional wisdom that discredits all alternative thought.

"The liberal focus on 'green energy' and 'green jobs' are another means of taking control, for there is no free market involved, only government controlled 'green energy' and government-created 'green jobs.' And 'cap and trade' programs are put forward to control our economy in a way never before seen."

Jim Gilmore, *Human Events*, 2009

productive as they may be, are not enough for Merkley—he proposes 6 to 7 percent a year as a "reasonable goal."[9]

Interestingly, Merkley, like an errant fifth-grader, feels no need to show his work. Where did that 6 to 7 percent number come from? It's a total mystery. Actually, it's not a mystery—it didn't come from anywhere. It was made up, arbitrarily, as so many central-planning goals are. It is rooted in nothing other than politics.

The senator has studied nothing other than politics his entire life (bachelor's in international relations, master's in public policy) and has nowhere near the knowledge or expertise—probably not even the quantitative skills—to evaluate whether those goals are in fact "reasonable." Nor does he have the expertise to judge whether the staff he has hired and the experts he has consulted to formulate his plan (assuming he did so, rather than just making it up as he went along), have produced a reasonable plan. Much less does he have the ability to foresee what unintended consequences such an agenda might impose on the U.S. economy.

But not to worry; he writes that his plan will only call for the incorporation of "technologies that pay for themselves."[10] It would be fair to note that Congress historically has not excelled at identifying initiatives that "pay for themselves."

Lest you think that Merkley has limited himself to trucks and cars, know that he also has "non-road" vehicles in his sights; in other words, he's targeting planes, trains, and automobiles. Actually, make that planes, trains, and automobiles, and bulldozers, and lawnmowers (really, he has a plan for revolutionizing the lawnmower industry; wonder if he's ever mowed a lawn?), and ships, and boats. Also streetcars, light rail, and bicycles. (If you're walking, he has some thoughts on that, too.) Let's hope he does a good job with the bulldozers—America will need a good one to push this plan out the door of Congress.

At times, Merkley is refreshingly candid about his central-planning ambitions. He calls for "transportation planning requirements," he writes about expanding the capacity of this industry, reducing the capacity of that industry, "smart commuter planning programs," creating a central-planning council to help "the President coordinate the government's work to meet the nation's . . . energy goals," and he imagines "programs and authorities" that will—I kid you not—"create value for agricultural waste" through "local, regional, and national planning efforts."[11]

The senator, in fact, seems to realize that his energy autarky calls for his central planners to intervene in practically every aspect of American life. He wants to interfere in businesses' personnel decisions to encourage telecommuting; he wants more walkable communities, meaning that existing communities will have to be redesigned; and in order to make neighborhoods safe for walking, he seeks to deploy additional law-enforcement resources—*in the name of "energy independence."*

That is a magical idea, "energy independence"; you'd think that using the police to make neighborhoods safe enough to walk through would be a priority independent of its far-removed impact on America's consumption of Middle Eastern oil. But these central-planning mandates have a way of becoming all-encompassing. If energy autarky gives a senator a license to tell you whether to come into the office or work from home, it's a license for anything—which is why politicians like it.

Energy Autarky *(self sufficiency)*: A Boon for Supplicants of Government

Similar to Merkley's argument, Energy Independence Now emphasizes that we must have "national policies in place" to enforce energy autarky. "We cannot get to this zero emissions future without enacting strong policies," they insist.[12] Amping up the nationalistic rhetoric, they write that it will take a nation devoted to the cause, a nation that demands a sustainable path forward and refuses to let industry interests dictate our future. In reality, of course, those "industry interests" largely support the green agenda; when you're taking hundreds of billions of dollars in grants, incentives, tax breaks, and other political favors to the table, you can be sure that the business lobbies will show up—especially lobbies for industries like ethanol, wind power, and solar power, whose goods and services would mostly fail if the government stopped propping them up with massive subsidies and intrusive mandates.

In the case of energy autarky, lurking in the background is the powerful figure of Oklahoma oilman-*cum*-alternative-energy-prophet T. Boone Pickens. In 2010, I had the unique pleasure of sitting down with Mr. Pickens to discuss his plan for mandating, through an act of Congress, that 18-wheel tractor-trailer trucks operating in the United States switch from using gasoline to using compressed natural gas. Under the Pickens plan, Congress would force the trucks to be retrofitted and force new trucks to run on natural gas, too. It would also dip deep into taxpayers' pockets to subsidize that transformation; the subsidy would run to $65,000 per truck—considerably more than the average household income of the United States.

Five minutes into our conversation, my skepticism having become apparent, Pickens declared, "Well, you must be in favor of foreign oil. You must be in favor of the Saudis." His opening gambit, when challenged, was precisely the same as Senator Merkley's: frame this unwieldy central-planning campaign as America vs. bin Laden. And like the environmentalists (and central-planning advocates of all sorts), Pickens is willing to use some questionable data and analysis in his argument. One of his favorite factoids (and a favorite of the environmentalists) is this: "America uses a lot of oil. Every day 85 million barrels of oil are produced around the world. And 21 million of those are used here in the United States. That's 25% of the world's oil demand. Used by just 4% of the world's population."[13]

It is true that the 4 percent of the world's population who live in the United States consume 25 percent of the world's oil. They also produce 25 percent of the world's annual economic output. When one compares energy inputs to economic outputs, there is a close symmetry between consumption and production in the United States. What is remarkable about the United States is not that so few people consume so much, but that so few people produce so much of the world's wealth. States with central-planning regimes, or those with a legacy of central-planning regimes, do tend to consume much less energy (and much less of everything else) on a per capita basis than do Americans. There is a word for that: *poverty*. China's 2009 per capita GDP was about $6,600—less than the typical New York City resident earned in three weeks (and those num-

I Have a Scheme

"[T. Boone] Pickens controls Mesa Energy, which plans to spend up to $10 billion building a gargantuan wind farm in rural Texas whose value would be greatly enhanced amid the national effort that 80-year-old Pickens is proposing. His BP Capital hedge fund is heavily invested in natural gas as well as oil.

"It's amazing how many of the hundreds of news articles written about the proposal in the past two days have failed to mention Pickens' vested interests, while the Associated Press quoted him as making the following preposterous statement about his plan: 'I don't have any profit motive in this. I'm doing it for America.' Back in April he was more candid when speaking to the *Guardian* about his wind farm investment: 'Don't get the idea that I've turned green. My business is making money, and I think this is going to make a lot of money.'"

Phil Mattera, "Pickens' Self-Serving Energy Plan," 2008

bers come from 2009, after the financial crisis had sent New York wages down by a whopping 23 percent).

So the truth is not that Americans are energy hogs. It's that Americans are the engine of the world's economy, producing more wealth annually than any other nation on Earth—in fact, producing three times as much wealth as the No. 2 or No. 3 producers, China and Japan.

T. Boone Pickens is hardly a revolutionary leftist. And neither are most of the partisans of American oil socialism. So, why would they support the Sovietization of a major sector of the U.S. economy? You can be sure that Pickens did not favor the nationalization of healthcare or the banks.

Senator Merkley, as a member in good standing of the party of Big Government, clearly stands to gain tremendous amounts of power and prestige from the socialization of the energy industry. And Mr. Pickens? He just happens to own a whole bunch of natural-gas operations, with a major sideline in wind-generated power. Funny he should have chosen natural gas, and not some other flavor of unicorn-juice, to be at the center of his plan to remake the U.S. energy industry along lines amenable to his own financial interests.

"Gas holdings?" he queried, when a reporter asked him about the issue during a conversation I attended. "Sure, I've got interest in gas companies. What else can I say. Yeah, that's my business. I mean, that's what I know. I'm a geologist, and gas and oil is it.... I do not want to be identified as a wind man or a gas man. I much prefer to be called an oilman." *Of course* he does not want to be identified as a wind-and-gas man; to do so would reveal his self-serving arguments for oil autarky as the political flatulence they are. You can count on American energy socialism to achieve some real redistribution of wealth—to T. Boone Pickens, among others.

Another thing you'll notice about the Committee for Energy Autarky: to a man, they argue for shifting American freight traffic from long-haul trucks to railroads. But, of course, we once used rail for shipping practically all of our long-distance freight. Why? When it comes to rail shipping, as with so much else in the transportation sector, what the Committee for Energy Autarky hopes to do is to *undo* what we did in our last great national foray into central planning of the transportation system: the construction of the federal highway system.

Practically every item on the Pickens-Merkley agenda—encouraging mass transit, discouraging long commutes, encouraging denser development to produce walkable communities, discouraging highway-bound trucking, encouraging reliance on efficient railroads—is a response to a problem that was created in no small part by the creation of the federal highway system, a gigantic, city-killing, community-undermining, expensive national boondoggle that was sold to the country—just like "energy independence"—as a national-security program. Indeed, the official name of our national highway system is the Dwight D. Eisenhower National System of Interstate and *Defense* Highways—the idea being that if the Russkies landed in Tucumcari, New Mexico, we'd have eight lanes of blacktop running out of Amarillo on which to meet them. (Or something like that.)

Transportation systems are often thought of as a definitive public good, but they are no such thing; the first paved highway in this country and the first turnpike were built by private enterprise. So were the railroads. Even the New York City subway system has its origins in private enterprise: Charles Harvey's West Side and Yonkers Patent Railroad Co. built the first mass-transit train in the city, and other competitors soon followed suit. (Hong Kong's subway is to this day privately run, at a profit, and it makes New York City's rat-infested metro look like something from the nineteenth century—which it is.)

The U.S. federal highway system is a perfect example of what a politician with a Big Plan and Big Power is capable of inflicting on a country in the name of intelligent economic planning. By subsidizing the suburbanization of the United States, the federal highways effected a massive devaluation of urban and inner-city real estate, the effects of which are plain as day to anybody taking the time and exhibiting the gumption to drive through North Philadelphia or central Detroit.

The interstate highway running through practically any city in the country (other than the very special case of New York City) is a Berlin Wall of social and economic segregation. It was the taxpayer-subsidized creation of this system that allowed real-estate developers to build in ever-more-remote locations without forcing them—and through them, suburban and ex-urban home-buyers—to bear the actual costs they impose, which range from congestion and pollution to wear-and-tear on the roads, as well as social costs (such as higher rates of crime) in the newly depopulated city centers.

Of course, the highway system has its champions. Consider this report from the fortieth anniversary of the system's establishment by David Field at *Inside the News*:

> When President Dwight D. Eisenhower signed the Federal-Aid Highway Act in June 1956, the landmark legislation set in motion one of the greatest public-works projects in history. "The interstate system changed the way we live and the way we work," says FHWA Administrator Rodney Slater.... The 44,546 miles of interstate highways turned a two-month transcontinental journey into a four-day road trip.[14]

You bet it changed the way we live and work—that's what central planning is for. The question is: did it change them for the better?

> The interstates became an engine of development, making possible the postwar suburban expansion and transforming the nation's retail economy by creating shopping malls and spurring travel. In 1955, people drove 603 billion miles on U.S. highways; last year, they logged 2.3 trillion miles.
>
> Construction of the system cost taxpayers about $329 billion in 1996 dollars, according to transportation consultants Wendell Cox and Jean Love, or the equivalent of $58.5 billion in 1957 dollars—not far from the original estimate of $41 billion. Repair of the nation's roads and bridges will require $315 billion, says Darbelnet, citing federal estimates. The highway agency also says the government would have to spend about $72 billion a year during the next five years to upgrade roads and bridges—about $37 billion more than presently is spent on highway construction by federal, state, and local governments.

But critics say those figures are inaccurate. "The American people have paid about $130 billion for the interstate system," counting taxes on gasoline and diesel fuel, argues Fay. Motorists pay 18.3 cents in federal tax on every gallon of gas, of which all but 4.3 cents goes into something called the federal Highway Trust Fund dedicated to maintenance and repair. Truckers pay 43.33 cents a gallon, with a similar 4.3 cents set aside for deficit reduction.

To mask the true size of the federal deficit, however, every president since Richard Nixon has held highway spending below the level the trust fund would support. "Where there is a user fee that will generate $30 billion in 1996 alone, there is no excuse for not dedicating those funds to safer roads and bridges," says Fay.[15]

In short: it's an expensive misallocation of transportation resources—one that's used to help hide the federal budget deficit, to boot. It is a perfect example of the unintended consequences of attempts at central planning; if Eisenhower could have foreseen the massive costs that his highway system would have imposed on the United States—the direct economic costs of building and maintenance, the indirect economic costs born by American cities and the people who live there, the social costs associated with the billions and billions of dollars in sprawl subsidies paid out through the highway system, the ecological costs, the scarring of the American landscape—would he have done things differently? He probably would have: he did not do so much to save his country from the Germans only to give it a kick in the national shins when he got home.

We got it wrong—massively wrong—the last time we tried transportation socialism. What reason is there to believe that advocates of "energy independence"—with their shaky facts, their dodgy data, their tired and familiar rhetoric about "national security"—will get it right?

T. Boone Pickens has drilled a lot of dry wells in his day, but he did that with his own capital. How likely is it that a man who has gotten so much wrong in his own business is going to get it right—exactly right—when it comes to the incomprehensibly complex business of the entire nation? That's the problem with central planning. That's the problem with socialism.

Chapter Thirteen

EUGENE V. DEBS AND WOODROW WILSON: SOCIALIST WORDS, SOCIALIST ACTIONS

Eugene V. Debs—five-time presidential candidate for the Socialist Democratic Party of America, labor radical and Pullman strike veteran, International Workers of the World founder—began his career as a minor-league terrorist and ended it as a martyr to the stupidity of Woodrow Wilson. *Contra* Marx, some stories are farce the first time around.

Born in Indiana in 1855, Debs was a child of privilege, the son of a prosperous family of French immigrants. His father owned a textile mill and a grocery business. Debs himself gave in to his romantic strain early, leaving home at the age of fourteen and going to work for the railroad, first as a painter and later as a boiler man. Having exhausted that career and completed business school, he returned home to work in the grocery business and to dabble in labor radicalism, helping to found a local railroad union and becoming editor of its journal. He would use his newfound prominence as a labor activist and editor to get himself elected to the state legislature (as a Democrat) in 1884, serving a single term. All in all, it was not an unusual career for a progressive of his time.

It was the bitter battle of the Pullman strike that would make a minor historical figure of Debs. When railroad profits plunged following the Panic of 1893, railroad operators responded by cutting wages, inspiring a wildcat strike that began in Pullman, Illinois. Debs originally resisted

Guess What?

★ President Woodrow Wilson presided over a socialist coup

★ The imposition of socialism in America, as elsewhere, was accompanied by war and domestic repression

★ Wilson's economic policies proved a total failure

the proposal for a mass action against the Pullman railroad car manufacturer—the company was strong, the unions were weak and disunited, and the prospects of success were slim. Further, Pullman cars carried the U.S. mail, and President Grover Cleveland was no fan of the burgeoning labor movement.

Debs counseled prudence, but the restive radicals who ran the labor movement were not inclined to listen. Like any good politician, Debs realized he had lost the argument and quickly calculated that if there was going to be a strike, he'd do well to get in front of the parade. Debs became the public face of the Pullman strike—and the campaign he had counseled against became known as "Debs' Rebellion."

President Cleveland, citing the disruption of the mail, ordered an end to the strike, but the strikers refused. Cleveland sent in the Army to enforce the federal injunction, and the ensuing clash resulted in the deaths of thirteen strikers. Hauled up on federal charges of contempt of court for failing to heed the injunction, Debs was shipped off to prison. At trial he was represented by Clarence Darrow, a like-minded progressive with an enormous talent for self-promotion. Thus is history made.

Owning It

"From the crown of my head to the soles of my feet I am Bolshevik, and proud of it."

Eugene Debs, 1919

Debs, the socialist historian Howard Zinn writes with a good deal of glee, was "met with the full force of the capitalist state" in 1894 during his campaign against the Pullman Palace Car Company. In reality, Debs had been torching railroad cars—and punishing arson and the destruction of property is hardly an innovation of the "capitalist state," dating back, as it does, to Hammurabi at least. But socialists, as I have argued, are romantics; they will never let an inconvenient fact get in the way of a good rollicking denunciation.

Debs' imprisonment was not exactly the stuff of romantic martyrdom. In an 1895 letter to his father, Debs showed himself full of self-righteous sentiment and utterly immune to irony. Even as the panic and the strike resulted in death, displacement, and massive economic suffering, Debs remained the coddled teapot radical, writing, "I have immense satisfaction in knowing that you and mother, notwithstanding your years, are as proud, heroic, and defiant as the rest of us. . . . No disgrace attaches to the family. You need not blush." As for the conditions of his imprisonment: "My jail quarters are large, airy, clean and comfortable and I am perfectly at home with the sheriff's family whose residence adjoins the jail. Sunday, Charley Gould was here and we spent the afternoon in the Sheriff's parlors, regaling ourselves (after a good dinner of stuffed roast chicken) with a musical concert. Saturday Governor Waite of Colorado was with us from 11 till 2, taking dinner with us."

Debs thought of himself as a political prisoner—and, self-consciously, as a hero. "You and mother must carry yourselves like the Spartans of old. This is not the time for sighs of tears but for heroic fortitude which does not waver, not matter how trying [the] ordeal. If the night is dark the dawn is near. Our day is coming."[1] It was, of course, not to be Debs' last experience of prison—President Wilson, with his contempt for civil liberties and his mania for centralizing both political and economic power, would see to that.

Woodrow Wilson's Socialist Coup

Outside of left-wing circles, Debs is now mostly forgotten, and it is certain that his obscurity would be even deeper than it is today if not for the fact that Woodrow Wilson persecuted him under the Espionage Act for his antiwar activities, providing Debs with the opportunity of enacting a great drama, running his final presidential campaign from behind the prison's walls. As revolutionary careers go, it was not a great showing, but Debs remains the uncontested patron saint of American socialism, and his influence today remains lively in that camp. *Dissent* magazine's 2010 symposium on the future of socialism begins with a paean to Debs written by Michael Kazin.

> "The Socialist movement is as wide as the world," Eugene V. Debs told the large crowds that came to hear him all over the United States, "...its mission is to win the world, the whole world, from animalism, and consecrate it to humanity. What a tremendous task, and what a royal privilege to share in it." The history of the twentieth century made such confidence quite impossible. Yet socialism still has meaning, even if that meaning probably has never been as murky as it is today. Conservatives brand Barack Obama a socialist for signing a national health care plan that Richard Nixon would have viewed as timid; the rulers of the most populous country on earth say their booming capitalist economy is somehow building "socialism with Chinese characteristics"; while the socialist parties of Europe struggle to prove they can spur economic growth while keeping their welfare states from going bankrupt.[2]

Kazin has a number of excellent points here—about Nixon, about China, and about Europe's socialist parties—though they are not the points he thinks. But before we examine that, note the extraordinarily sharp contrast between Debs' language and Kazin's. Though Kazin passes over it uncritically, Debs' words must sound, to the modern ear, a bit tinny and slightly saccharine. It is also Manichean: he offers the audience a choice between "animalism" and his creed, which is "consecrated to humanity" (whatever that may hope to mean). Kazin's language, on the other hand, is jaded, cynical, and skeptical: "Socialism?" he all but asks. "You call this socialism? By those standards, Nixon was a socialist!"

(As, indeed, he was, to a greater extent than either he or his admirers probably understood.)

Kazin's pose is part of a deliberate rhetorical strategy used by the Left, in essence holding that anything short of Molotov cocktails in the street cannot possibly be regarded as real socialism. *Richard Nixon would have done it! How could it possibly be socialist?* Similar examples abound; shortly after the passage of Senator Christopher Dodd's cumbrous financial-reform bill, the *Nation* published a story under the headline, "Is Dodd Bill Socialist? Don't Make Socialists Laugh."[3]

Mockery, of course, is a cheap substitute for argument. Mikhail Gorbachev, the last leader of the Soviet Union, was unquestionably a true-believing socialist—we have his word and his record on that. But Gorbachev decontrolled wages and many prices; Richard Nixon enacted wage-and-price controls, attempting to micromanage the U.S. economy from Washington. China, for all its export-driven private fortunes and its *nouveaux riche* tycoons in their shiny new Buicks, remains very much a command-and-control economy, with government central planners in charge of both the commanding heights of the economy and street-level bureaucracy. The European socialist parties, encumbered as they are by economic realities, still work consistently for greater consolidation of economic power in political hands—as indeed does the European Union. Kazin scoffs at these things as weak-tea examples of socialism.

That is because he has paid too much heed to the words of Eugene Debs but not enough to the actions of Debs' nemesis, Woodrow Wilson. Debs gave great speeches about socialism; Wilson set about building the machinery of American socialism. Debs did not get on the outs with Wilson because Debs was anti-capitalism; Wilson put Debs in prison because Debs campaigned against the war that Wilson required to build his central-planning regime: the "war socialism" that accompanied American entry into World War I.

It may be a genuine ideological lacunae, or it may be simple willfulness, but the American Left cannot bring itself to identify a socialist unless he first identifies himself as a socialist. (And even then, they may demur: Kazin apparently believes that the politburo of the People's Republic of China, and the highest echelons of China's Communist Party, do not qualify as socialists, their own protestations to the contrary.) But socialism rarely comes in the form of peasants with pitchforks—and it certainly never stays there. Most of the very committed socialist regimes that the world has experienced have come to power either through civil wars or wars of nationalism, and the belligerents' aims were typically not explicitly socialist.

Where socialism has been imposed through democratic and quasi-democratic means, the process has been still less dramatic. The socialists of Western Europe, for example, have had little of Eugene Debs about them, preferring technocratic jargon to his messianic rhetoric; it is difficult to imagine a Mitterand exclaiming that he "was to be baptized in socialism in the roar of conflict ... In the gleam of every bayonet and the flash of every rifle the class struggle was revealed!" That's the stuff of adolescent rebellion and sophomore themes about the Abraham Lincoln Brigades. Socialism in the United States is a romantic phenomenon and a reactionary one as well; so focused are American progressives on romantic figures such as Debs that they fail to see the socialists in front of their faces—central planners like Wilson and Nixon.

Of course, there are few political movements that would be eager to claim Nixon, understandably; Wilson, to the extent that his legacy is embraced by neo-conservatives, is admired for the energy of his foreign policy and not for his centralizing ambitions at home. (It is a conservative blind spot that many on the Right fail to see how those two policies are linked.) Wilson was president of the United States, and a wartime president at that—hardly the sort of thing that appeals to an American Left that is more Berkeley than Bolshevik. Debs, on the other hand, was a martyr to free speech. (A rare American martyr to free speech—if American progressives desire more such martyrs, the socialist world has provided millions of examples, many of them buried in unmarked mass graves.)

Debs talked about socialism. Wilson put it into action. As Robert Higgs documents in his magisterial *Crisis and Leviathan,* the war saw rapid growth and consolidation of federal power, along with the political suppression that inevitably follows. Eugene Debs was hardly the only victim of the Wilson administration:

> Despite expansion during Woodrow Wilson's first term as president, the federal government on the eve of World War I remained small. In 1914, federal spending totaled less than two percent of GNP. The top rate of the recently enacted federal individual-income tax was seven percent, on income over $500,000, and 99 percent of the population owed no income tax. The 402,000 federal civilian employees, most of whom worked for the Post Office, constituted about one percent of the labor force.
>
> ...With U.S. entry into the Great War, the federal government expanded enormously in size, scope, and power. It virtually nationalized the ocean shipping industry. It did nationalize the railroad, telephone, domestic telegraph, and international telegraphic cable industries. It became deeply engaged in manipulating labor-management relations, securities sales, agricultural production and marketing, the distribution of coal and oil, international commerce, and markets for raw materials and manufactured products. Its Liberty Bond drives dominated the financial capital markets. It turned the newly created Federal Reserve System into a powerful engine of monetary inflation to help satisfy the government's voracious

appetite for money and credit. In view of the more than 5,000 mobilization agencies of various sorts—boards, committees, corporations, administrations—contemporaries who described the 1918 government as "war socialism" were well justified.[4]

Wilson, in short, enacted a socialist coup, one with very little bloodshed (but by no means none at all). Of course such projects are monstrously expensive: taxes were increased enormously, and federal revenue rose fourfold in two years. Debt exploded as well, as Higgs reports, with the national debt swelling from just over $1 billion to more than $25 billion. Complaining about the new taxes—or anything else, for that matter—was robustly discouraged. According to Higgs,

To ensure that the conscription-based mobilization could proceed without obstruction, critics had to be silenced. The Espionage Act of June 15, 1917, penalized those convicted of willfully obstructing the enlistment services by fines up to $10,000 and imprisonment as long as 20 years. An amendment, the Sedition Act of May 16, 1918, went much further, imposing the same severe criminal penalties on all forms of expression in any way critical of the government, its symbols, or its mobilization of resources for the war. Those suppressions of free speech, subsequently upheld by the Supreme Court, established dangerous precedents that derogated from the rights previously enjoyed by citizens under the First Amendment.

★★★★★★★★
I'm Sensing a Theme Here

"Men are as clay in the hands of the consummate leader."

Woodrow Wilson

"The world is not looking for servants, there are plenty of these, but for masters, men who form their purposes and then carry them out, let the consequences be what they may."

Woodrow Wilson

The government further subverted the Bill of Rights by censoring all printed materials, peremptorily deporting hundreds ✓ of aliens without due process of law, and conducting—and encouraging state and local governments and vigilante groups to conduct—warrantless searches and seizures, blanket arrests of suspected draft evaders, and other outrages too numerous to catalog here. In California the police arrested Upton Sinclair for reading the Bill of Rights at a rally. In New Jersey the police arrested Roger Baldwin for publicly reading the Constitution. The government also employed a massive propaganda machine to whip up what can only be described as public hysteria. The result was countless incidents of intimidation, physical abuse, and even lynching of persons suspected of disloyalty or insufficient enthusiasm for the war. People of German ancestry suffered disproportionately.[5]

"I am an advocate of peace," Wilson wrote, "but there are some splendid things that come to a nation through the discipline of war."[6] The pattern would, inevitably, be repeated during the next great war. President Franklin D. Roosevelt, in the early days of fascism, expressed his admiration for Mussolini and his system. He would also cite Wilson's war ✓ socialism as a model for his response to the Great Depression and the economic regimentation that took place during World War II. With his court-packing scheme and his general contempt for constitutional limits on executive power, Roosevelt is a problematic figure. But Wilson stands alone and uncontested as being the nearest thing to a Lenin or a Mussolini that the United States has yet endured.

Predictably, Wilson's campaign to bring regimentation and central planning to the U.S. economy resulted in massive failure. And, just as Stalin and Mao would do in their time, and Castro and Chávez in theirs, Wilson blamed his failures on defeatists, traitors, and saboteurs in our midst. Dozens of newspapers and magazines were shut down by the federal government, critics were thrown in jail under the sedition act, and mobs mobilized to intimidate and assault particularly unwelcome critics. Wilson paid particular interest to immigrants, whom he distrusted as insufficiently loyal to the United States. "The gravest threats against our national peace and safety have been uttered within our own borders," Wilson told a congressional audience. "There are citizens of the United States, I blush to admit, born under other flags, who have poured the poison of disloyalty into the very arteries of our national life; who have sought to bring the authority and good name of our Government into contempt, to destroy our industries wherever they thought it effective for their vindictive purposes."[7]

Wilson's propaganda and intimidation campaign would reach its zenith when he turned to a bona fide socialist, journalist George Creel, to run his Gestapo-like operations. As Fred Siegel documents,

> Wilson placed George Creel, a journalist, socialist, and strong supporter of child labor laws and women's suffrage, in charge of ensuring home-front morale through the Committee for Public Information. But the Committee, which Creel described as "the world's greatest adventure in advertising," wildly overshot its mark, encouraging the banning of everything German, from Beethoven to sauerkraut to teaching the German language. The Justice Department and the attorney general, Thomas Gregory, encouraged local vigilantism against Germans, giving the American Protective League, a quarter-of-a-million-strong nativist organization, semi-official status to spy on those suspected of disloyalty. The League went out of its way to break up labor strikes as well, while branding its critics Reds.
>
> Responding to the League's excesses, Wilson declared that he'd "rather the blamed place should be blown up than per-

secute innocent people." But in the next breath he said, "Woe be to the man or group of men that seeks to stand in our way." Despite his misgivings, Wilson deferred to Gregory's judgment and refrained from taking action against extremists. Only after the armistice ended the war in November 1918 did Wilson, heeding the advice of incoming attorney general A. Mitchell Palmer, move to end government cooperation with the League. But by now, the disparity between Wilson's call for extending liberty abroad and the suppression of liberty at home had become a running sore for disenchanted progressives.[8]

With its hostility toward foreigners, its distrust of private enterprise, its centralizing ambitions, and its allegedly "rational" managerial style, Wilson's war socialism long survived the Great War and its immediate aftermath—it was always intended to. The socialist philosopher Otto Neurath, a contemporary of Hayek's and Mises', was at the time of Wilson's ascent making a study of war socialism and considering the prospects for extending its rigors once the war ended. As Bruce Caldwell reports in his invaluable *Hayek and Socialism*,

> Before World War I [Neurath] began to make a reputation as a proponent of a new academic subfield, "war economy." He also participated, along with Mises, in Eugen von Böhm-Bawerk's famous economics seminar. Among the other seminar participants were Joseph Schumpeter, Otto Bauer, who would lead the Austrian Socialist Democratic party in the 1920s, and Rudolf Hilferding, one of the leading Marxian theoreticians of the 20th century.
>
> According to Neurath, during peace time, production in market economies is driven by the search for profits, but this leads to recurrent periods of overproduction and unemployment. In wartime, by contrast, production is no longer driven

by profit-seeking, and the war effort ensures that productive capacity is always fully utilized. Another characteristic of the war economy is the suppression of the price system, which is replaced by extensive planning of materials management from the center. This is all to the good, because for Neurath the monetary system, the search for profits, and the disorderliness of capitalist production all go hand in hand. Neurath argued that the central planning that emerges within war economies should continue in peacetime. He proposed that a "natural accounting center" be set up to run the economy as if it were one giant enterprise.[9]

Or, as Mussolini put it, "Everything in the State, nothing outside the State."

The Rotten Fruits of War Socialism

That line of thinking will, by this point, be entirely familiar. The notion that profits (and costs associated with them, such as marketing budgets and high levels of executive compensation) represent waste still is very much with us; it has been a cornerstone of the socialists' argument in the healthcare reform debate, as well as in the financial-industry reform debate. The writers at *Dissent*, for example, call for the construction of a "public-utility finance system" on the assumption that the lack of profits and a profit motive will make the system more efficient—despite generations' worth of experience that such systems are *less* efficient. Likewise, the low overhead of the Medicare system was used to argue that a government-run healthcare system will be more efficient than a privately run system, taking little or no account for the explicit and implicit subsidies enjoyed by Medicare—not the least of which is that it uses the IRS as its bill collector.

"One big factory" was Lenin's description of the ideal socialist economy, just as "one big union" was the IWW's ideal. And if the economy is one big factory with one big work force, then there is, in fact, no need for money and all that goes along with it: goods may be distributed directly to consumers on an as-needed basis. Neurath foresaw that development, as well, Caldwell reports:

> Most controversially, he insisted that money would be unnecessary in the new planned order: because production would be driven by objectively determined needs rather than by the search for profits, all calculation regarding the appropriate levels of inputs and output could be handled in "natural" physical terms. In Neurath's opinion, attempts to employ monetary calculations within a planned society would render impossible scientific economic management, which had to be conducted in terms of "real" physical quantities.[10]

"Objectively determined needs, rather than the search for profits." There's a reason that may sound familiar from the U.S. healthcare reform debate. It might also be restated: from each according to his ability, to each according to his needs (as objectively determined by the appropriate planner). President Obama and his secretary of health and human services regularly denounced the healthcare industry's profits—particularly insurance profits—during the debate over reform. (Clumsily, in a major speech on the issue, Obama also blamed high healthcare costs on excessive profits at a number of firms he apparently had not been informed are nonprofit.)

This is an old complaint, and yet one that is as fresh as today's headlines: "In the United States health care is a big business commodity with a big price tag, comprising 14% of the US GNP. Removing profit from the Wall Street-controlled health industry can fully fund a system that puts health before profit." That's from the 2010 party program of

Not a Good Legacy

"The blunt fact is that when [under Wilson] America was introduced to the War State in 1917, it was introduced also to what would later be known as the total, or totalitarian, state."

Robert Nisbet, 1988

the Communist Party of the United States of America, whose vision we will revisit later, but it could as easily have come from the mouth of Barack Obama or Nancy Pelosi.

For our current purposes, it is sufficient to note that all the central planners—from Marx himself to Lenin to Wilson's rationalizers to the CPUSA to the healthcare crusaders—see profit as something extraneous and exogenous to the economy, by which we mean the process by which goods and services are created, developed, and delivered. Profit, under all these models, inhibits efficiency and the rational distribution of goods, services, and capital.

The truth is precisely the opposite: the search for profit and the competition it leads to are what create efficiency and police the rational deployment of resources. Wilson's war planners bragged that they had outlawed 250 types of plows and 755 types of drills in their campaign to "strip from trade and industry the lumber of futile custom and the encrustation of useless variety"—as though one plow were the right plow for every field, as though one drill were the right drill for every hole. The welter of choices produced by capitalism—900 kinds of shampoo in your local Wal-Mart—are not waste; they are the price paid for innovation.

But the one-drill-size-fits-all mentality is natural to the central planner, who mistakes standardization for rational order and who sees the nearly infinite variety of goods produced by capitalism as frivolous. This mania for uniformity—and political conformity—defined the corporate culture of Wilson's War Industries Board, the main central-planning agency implementing his regimentation of the economy. The WIB held sway over virtually the entire U.S. economy. (An important exception to WIB domination was the food industry, which was governed by the one-man autocracy—"autocrat" was, in fact, the term employed—of Herbert Hoover, who ran the Food Administration. Hoover, inaccurately characterized by the FDR political machine, and subsequently by historians, as a laissez-faire market fundamentalist, never lost the taste for governmental macroeconomic management, and his interventionist policies, incubated in Wilson's war socialism, helped to deepen the Depression years later.)

The WIB's executives sought ever more dictatorial powers for themselves: Judge Elbert Gary, president of U.S. Steel, was given the portfolio of national steel czar, and demanded that he and his steel-industry cronies be given plenipotentiary power "if necessary to commandeer" the resources of recalcitrant steel producers, including the smaller and more nimble competitors of U.S. Steel.

But, for the most part, no such dictatorial powers were required. Just as the Obama administration bought off the health-insurance industry, assuaging their resistance to the quasi-nationalization of American healthcare with a mandate that every American buy what the insurance industry is selling, Wilson's WIB "rationalized" American industry by promising to lock in what were, at the time, high profits. Production, wages, prices, and profits were to be coordinated by the leaders of industry themselves, acting under the auspices of the government. In other words, Wilson's war socialism allowed the captains of industry to do what they had wanted to do all along—to collude against their smaller competitors—but had been prohibited from doing by antitrust laws.

It was not for nothing that Adam Smith wrote that "people of the same trade seldom meet together, even for merriment and diversion, but the conversation ends in a conspiracy against the public, or in some contrivance to raise prices." The romantic notion of politics holds that Big Business is synonymous with capitalism and the archenemy of socialism. In fact, Big Business is reliably against most of what must go into any modern definition of capitalism: free trade, free enterprise, free markets, and the impartial rule of law. Big Business reliably seeks to use the state to seek advantages in trade and to crush smaller (and often more innovative) competitors.

Big Business loved Wilson's war socialism, just as ensconced industrial interests would back the national socialisms of Mussolini and Hitler. If Russia had had much of an industrial economy, it is likely that its industrialists would have sought to reach an accommodation with the central planners, just as China's industrialists today are the most perfervid supporters of single-party autocratic rule under the Communists.

But if you're going to be Mussolini, you have to make the trains run on time. How did Wilson's war socialism perform?

In one important way, it performed much like Soviet socialism: the Soviet Union did not achieve much in the way of long-term material improvements for the Russian people (or their vanquished neighbors), but it did achieve massive, radical industrialization at unprecedented speed. Wilson's war socialism had a similar outcome and employed similar (though not identical) techniques. Lenin and Stalin had their campaigns of forced collectivization and massive internal displacements; Wilson had the draft, which expanded the pre-war army of 174,000 to a force that eventually sent nearly 5 million Americans to war as active soldiers. Furthermore, through the WIB he drafted the entire economy into what Dwight D. Eisenhower would later describe, ominously, as the "military-industrial complex," a term of which Wilson and his central planners certainly would have approved.

In the end, war socialism proved itself a terrible investment. Although U.S. industrial production grew 39 percent between 1916 and 1918—a remarkable feat—it came at a huge cost: federal spending skyrocketed from $1.3 billion in 1916 to $15.5 billion in 1918. Even as the war wound down, federal spending remained high: $12.4 billion in 1919, $5.7 billion in 1920 (figures in constant 1916 dollars). Inflation was rapid and brutal. Setting aside the horrific human toll of the war—which was a domestic cultural catastrophe as well, ratifying the reach of a limitless federal Leviathan—those economic gains amounted to nowhere near the real economic costs of the war. Modern warfare is usually a net economic loss to all players, but that was especially obvious in the case of the Great War and American war socialism.

Such gains as there were proved transitory, in spite of the central planners' bare-knuckled campaign to hold onto their temporary war powers after the war ended—"to make wartime necessity a matter of peacetime advantage," as one contemporary observer put it.[11] By 1920, industrial output had radically contracted, returning close to its 1916 levels. Federal revenues continued to set records, but federal spending (unbelievably, to the modern reader) was cut by more than half in a sober effort to pay down the war debts, a burden made somewhat easier by the fact that

This Ends Badly

"With pride and joy we watch each advancing step of our comrades in Socialism in all other lands. Our hearts are with them in their varying fortunes as the battle proceeds, and we applaud each telling blow delivered and cheer each victory achieved."

Eugene Debs, 1900, mourning the death of German communist leader Wilhelm Liebknecht the United States, by financing much of the Allied war effort, emerged from the conflict a net creditor nation. The real GNP of the United States grew from $46 billion in 1916 to $49.6 billion at the height of the war, but by 1920 it fell back to nearly its pre-war level, declining to $47 billion—all that spending, killing, and regimentation had bought the country, under the most charitable interpretation of the economic data, an extra $1 billion in GNP, at a cost equivalent to $7 *trillion* in 2010 dollars.

There is a good deal of controversy about whether America's entry into that war served the national interest, but there is no question that the war and Wilson's war socialism were an enormous net economic loss. And the massive misallocation of capital created by Wilson's policies created deep economic imbalances that would make themselves painfully manifest in the Great Depression a decade and a half later.

Most important, Wilson's war socialism also failed on its own terms. Those gross industrial production numbers are indeed impressive, but a closer look at the data suggests that production was unreliable and erratic. Well into the war—a war in which America was involved for only nineteen months—U.S. troops still were going into battle with French artillery, because the American munitions industry—the *ne plus ultra* of war socialism—could not provide our soldiers with sufficient weaponry.

And the losses, of course, were not limited to war expenditures. The real cost of Wilsonian war socialism must include the opportunity costs of all the gains that were forgone by the WIB's mismanagement of the economy, by its encouragement of cartelization and price-fixing among major industrial interests, and by setting a precedent for radical federal intervention in the private economy—a precedent that would come back to repeatedly haunt the United States: in the Great Depression, in World War II, during the Nixon-Carter years, and during the financial crisis of 2008.

Chapter Fourteen

SOCIALIST INTERNATIONALISM AND THE UNITED STATES

Wilson's war socialism is not what the reds had in mind, at least in terms of its rhetorical content and its reliance upon industrial barons rather than the dictatorship of the proletariat. (Forget, if you can, that practically every socialist regime the world has ever seen has far more closely resembled Wilson's version than Marx's.) One of the reasons that socialists fail to recognize the socialism in Wilson is that Wilson was a nationalist—a frank one who made his mark on the world by making war on America's enemies.

Socialism, as envisioned by Marx and his immediate acolytes, was to be an international affair. For the modern academic Marxists, it still is. But internationalist socialism is almost exclusively an intellectual affair, a theoretical exercise for tenured radicals and their epigones. There is an easily identifiable academic flavor to be found in the publications of the major academic journals of socialism. One does not imagine that Hugo Chávez or Kim Jong Il spends a lot of time reading them.

But we should revisit the internationalist tendency, if only briefly, because it tells us something about the kind of socialism we have in the United States, where the sort of socialism that grows amid Harvard ivy— as opposed to the socialism that grows up out of actual revolutionary movements, i.e., the socialism that grows from the barrel of a gun—has influence comparable to, if not greater than, the kind of socialism that

Guess What?

★ International socialists believe President Obama is opening a window to socialism

★ To bring about socialism, American socialists work with everyone from environmentalists to Islamic extremists

★ The Left does not reject the prospect of violent socialist revolution

comes down through the American tradition of labor radicalism and populist movements.

Intellectual internationalist socialism offers the sort of theoretical structure that proves irresistible to Western academics. It is easy to lampoon—in fact, it lampoons itself. Consider this recent essay by socialist writer Dan Jakopovich, titled, "In the Belly of the Beast: Challenging U.S. Imperialism and the Politics of the Offensive." He begins,

> This work is an exploration of the required strategic path of anti-capitalist and anti-imperialist struggle in the United States, considered both in relation to the specific domestic circumstances and the global role and function of the U.S. and its capitalist socio-economic forces. I investigate how the achievement of international socialist change might depend on the state of U.S. imperialism, and how anti-imperialist resistance in the U.S. might have to strategically engage with the realities of the U.S. political system and social and economic situation.
>
> I will begin by identifying certain possible political implications of the "superstructural" element (stressed by Schumpeter for instance) in the interpretation of variations in the nature of imperialisms, as applied to the United States.
>
> In the next section, I briefly examine the differing strategic argumentation of Marx and Engels, Lenin and Samir Amin regarding the "spatialization" of anti-systemic change, the potential and presumed role of simultaneous anti-systemic victories across the capitalist center, and the opposite concepts of the (peripheral and semi-peripheral) "weakest links in the imperialist chain" and "delinking."
>
> Lastly, largely on the basis of a Gramscian theoretical instrumentarium, I try to adapt the notions of the "national-popular," "self-emancipation," and a "system of alliances" to the U.S.

situation. I will attempt to concretize the dialectical interrelationship between united and popular frontist approaches in U.S. circumstances, and the main subjects of anti-imperialist change. This will necessitate an evaluation of some of the central strategic dilemmas and differences among the American Left, which I attempt to reconcile through a modified new strategic synthesis.[1]

Just so. Hugo Chávez simply seizes factories and whole industries when it suits THE PLAN, having no obvious need of a Gramscian theoretical instrumentarium, or an instrumentarium of the non-Gramscian sort, for that matter, and his spatialization seems to take care of itself. I doubt Chávez has read a word of Schumpeter. Mao just shot people, and that seemed to work for him.

Jakopovich's first section is titled "Imperialist Subjectivity," in which he sneers at lowbrow "vulgar Marxism." But if you can get past the pretentious cant, Jakopovich does have some useful observations to make about how the supposedly internationalist creed of socialism got mixed up with nationalism in Russia, China, Korea, Vietnam, Venezuela, Iraq, Cuba, Iran—which is to say, virtually every place socialism has been seriously explored outside of university classrooms and nearby cafes. The problem, which Lenin immediately confronted after leading the first successful communist revolution, is that Marx's vision of a simultaneous worldwide revolution among workers—whose countries exist at radically different levels of development and economic sophistication—is an extraordinarily unlikely thing. Jakopovich writes,

> Lenin revised [the internationalist] thesis through his theory
> of the "weakest link in the imperialist chain." He stressed that
> "the development of capitalism proceeds extremely unevenly
> in different countries. It cannot be otherwise under commod-
> ity production. From this it follows irrefutably that socialism

cannot achieve victory simultaneously in all countries. It will achieve victory first in one or several countries, while the others will for some time remain bourgeois or pre-bourgeois. This is bound to create not only friction, but a direct attempt on the part of the bourgeoisie of other countries to crush the socialist state's victorious proletariat."

Despite his often greatly mistaken application of this principle, Lenin was right in attempting to dialectically integrate complex, context-specific tactics and strategies into a common strategic framework. "The mechanistic rigidity... cannot understand... how the Communist International does not for a moment abandon the world revolution, striving to use every means at its disposal to prepare and organize it, while the Russian workers' state simultaneously tries to promote peace with the imperialist powers and the maximum participation of imperialist capitalism in Russia's economic construction.... The mechanistic rigidity of undialectical thought is incapable of understanding that these contradictions are the objective, essential contradictions of the present period."

... Only the failure of revolutions in the West fully raised the problem of delinking for Lenin and his party.[2]

This is an elaborate way of writing that socialism is, by its nature, opportunistic, and that, as a political philosophy, it provides its own rationale for its opportunism. If you can't have a worldwide revolution, you can have national revolutions in Russia, China, and Venezuela. If you can't have a national revolution, you can have socialism implemented bit-by-bit, *a la* Chávez. If you can't have a real nationwide socialist program, you can still implement bits of socialism in the parts of the political economy that Lenin would have identified as the "weakest links." In the United States, that means having a socialist education system and an increasingly socialist healthcare system, taking advantage of the fact that a misapplied body of moral reasoning holds that the most vulnerable—children, the sick—cannot be left to the devices of amoral capitalism. (In truth, it is the vulnerable who most need the plentiful resources provided by free-market economies.)

American conservatives have from time to time—and especially since the election of Barack Obama—described the progressive project in the United States as "socialism" and their opponents as "socialists." This rhetorical gambit is largely met with scorn and derision on the part of the Democratic party, the Left at large, the traditional media (which is indistinguishable from the first two), and most of polite society, including much of conservative polite society. But there are some political analysts who take that argument seriously, and they are not part of the Right—quite the opposite in fact: they are the international socialists themselves.

When it comes to the United States, "the battle against the militaristic Right . . . is a central component of an integrated international strategy for systemic change in our analysis," Jakopovich writes. He offers up a laundry list of U.S. policies, foreign and domestic, that he believes should be the subject of close attention from the internationalist socialist movement:

In Plain Sight

A subsection of the Obama "movement" website "Organizing for America" is titled, "Marxists/Socialists/Communists for Obama." In case you don't get the picture, they explain, "This group is for self-proclaimed Marxists/Communists/Socialists for the election of Barack Obama to the Presidency. . . . We support Barack Obama because he knows what is best for the people!"

foreign policy in Latin America, military spending, trade policy, internal economic policy, etc. And lest you think that a revolutionary socialist would view both of the two major U.S. political parties with near-equal disdain, consider that, when it comes to questions of U.S. foreign policy initiatives that irritate the international socialists, "Obama's presidency has already managed to largely reverse the escalation of these trends," he writes.[3]

Opening the Window to Socialism

The idea that the American progressive agenda, and the agenda of the Obama administration in particular, is part and parcel of a coordinated, worldwide socialist program is a joke—to everybody but the socialists themselves. Jakopovich identifies U.S. policy as a top concern for South American socialist movements, insisting, "The non-revolutionary priority of confronting the far Right in the U.S. is a direct result of the non-revolutionary U.S. context. Yet this strategy can be clearly connected with Left strategies in countries where anti-capitalists are largely already in power, namely Venezuela and Bolivia." He continues,

> Venezuela's, Bolivia's and Ecuador's resource nationalism (or the assertion of energy sovereignty), as well as different forms of Latin American integration (like the proposed Bank of the South, Petrosur plan for a joint South American state-owned petroleum industry venture, Mercosur, and especially the ALBA—Bolivarian Alternative for the Americas—initiative for regional economic and social integration based on mutual aid, outside of neoliberal coordinates) all might require a degree of peace and stability in order to be able to carve out a space for a certain developmental "autocentricity," outside of confines imposed by the ruling neo-liberal dogma.

The current differences in the approach of U.S. policy-makers to state clientelism, manifested by the disagreements regarding Bush's proposed trade agreement with Colombia (for instance), are not irrelevant, as further confirmed by the nervousness of the far Right elite on this issue.

... The recent aggressive doctrine of preemption is particularly dangerous for the Left's prospects in Latin America. Socialists cannot leave these popular regimes and movements alone in the face of the ferocity of militaristic violence.[4]

It is important to note that the socialists' call for cooperation against the capitalist Yankees extend beyond defensive fears that the United States will work to undermine—or even to overthrow—socialist governments in the Americas. Notice the high priority Jakopovich pays to questions of banking and state-owned enterprises—and, above all, to the pending U.S.-Colombia free-trade agreement. Free trade, as we have seen, is anathema to socialists of both the international and nationalist variety. (And, indeed, the two factions have learned to play together nicely since the 1930s. Note that the professed international socialist Jakopovich praises the "resource nationalism" of the Chávez regime.)

Turning to domestic U.S. politics, Jakopovich cites the progressive mobilization against the Bush administration—particularly the anti-war movement—as "a window to socialism." Advancing the socialist agenda, he writes, is difficult when working in coalition with the Democratic party—because the Democratic party is, whatever its other faults, not a revolutionary Marxist front—but it is not impossible. The main shortcoming is that the Democrats' piecemeal approach "conditions the principles on which socialist engagement with the Democratic Party should be based." Thus, while he accepts the need for cooperating with Democrats against the Right, Jakpovich cautions socialists against being exploited as "embellishment for neoliberal and 'realist' foreign and domestic policies."

The focus, he says, "should remain on developing solidaristic structural reforms, as a 'window to socialism.' "[5]

What does that "window to socialism" in U.S. politics look like for the internationalist socialists? According to Jakopovich, it looks a lot like Jesse Jackson. Jackson's "Rainbow Coalition" strategy—the formation of a group too weak to take over the Democratic Party but strong enough to cost Democrats elections and political power—appeals to American socialists, who lack both raw numbers and sufficient ready allies to enact their agenda or achieve electoral power on their own. (It's worth remembering that in their literature, socialists incessantly denounce democracy *per se*. "Real democracy," as they define it, is socialism. Democracy that produces outcomes other than socialism is not, in the socialists' understanding, real democracy.) What Jakopovich hopes to create is a Rainbow Coalition for socialists:

> Transitional politics could preserve their full meaning only if approached within this longer-term programmatic context. Some new "Rainbow Coalition" is probably unlikely at the moment (though it should remain a medium-term objective), but the current engagement with the Democratic Party (especially its "outer layers") might serve as an important springboard for reviving mass social movements as an indispensable leverage for progressive electoral initiative. Jesse Jackson's progressive-populist Rainbow Coalition, an opposition movement or "party within the party," illustrated the serious potential of this strategy. For instance, it successfully mobilized over such issues like Reagan's Supreme Court nomination of rightist Robert Bork. But it achieved much more than that. "As millions of Americans saw when Jackson spoke at the Democratic Convention in Atlanta last summer, the appeal of class... tapped emotions and released energies as no other politician

in memory has been able to do.... At the end of the long sea-
son of primaries ... Jackson had won elections or caucuses in
almost every important city in the country (including New
York, Chicago, Philadelphia, Houston and Los Angeles), a
majority of the states in Deep South, as well as Michigan,
Maine, Vermont, Alaska and other Northern states where a
winning black candidacy had been thought impossible. He had
mobilized millions of voters on a platform of "economic justice," racial justice, and the realignment of America's relations
with the Third World. In Atlanta, his forces raised previous
taboo subjects, such as Palestinian rights, "soak-the-rich" taxation and significant restraint in military projects and expenditures.... So impressive was the Jackson presence that
Dukakis was forced to negotiate an "Atlanta Pact" promising
the Jackson forces a prominent role in the campaign and in the
administration if Dukakis won, plus support for Jackson on a
number of special items on the Rainbow agenda.[6]

If you are wondering how a self-professed communist such as Van
Jones ended up in Obama's White House, why so many people affiliated
with explicitly socialist and communist organizations have ended up
with prominent roles (as well as behind-the-scenes roles) in the Obama
administration, this should shed some light on the question. Obama was
made president of the United States by the anti-war movement, and the
anti-war movement, in the United States, was explicitly and unquestionably a creature of socialism. The most prominent of the anti-war rallies
were staged by International ANSWER, an offshoot of the Stalinist World
Workers' Party. ANSWER's steering committee is practically a socialist
international in miniature. As Ryan O'Donnell reported at the time,

> ANSWER's steering committee reads like a "Who's Who" of
> radical political organizations. The most influential member

of ANSWER's steering committee, Ramsey Clark's pet project known as the International Action Center (IAC), is considered by many observers to be little more than a communist front organization for an obscure Stalinist organization known as the World Workers Party (WWP). Yet, the IAC is not the only member of ANSWER's steering committee committed to extremist causes. The Korean Truth Commission and Pastors for Peace are staunch allies of Kim Jong Il and Fidel Castro, respectively, and both groups continue to support these murderous regimes' violation of International law. In addition to its role as a front for the support of totalitarian/communist governments in North Korea and Cuba, members of ANSWER's steering committee such as the Muslim Student Association and the Free Palestine Alliance continue to provide ideological, logistical and financial support for organizations devoted to the destruction of the state of Israel, including the terrorist group, Hamas. A comprehensive investigation of the members of ANSWER's steering committee make it clear that the organization is in actuality one of Peace's greatest enemies.

...ANSWER's organizers, many of whom are documented members of the WWP, have frequently refused to let devoted political leftists and peace advocates speak at rallies if they hold a pro-Israel position. The most celebrated of these incidents occurred when Rabbi Michael Lerner was barred from speaking at a recent IAC anti-war rally in San Francisco. Yet, at its January march in Washington, ANSWER "handed a microphone to Abdul Malim Musa, a Muslim cleric who on October 31, 2001 appeared at a news conference at the National Press Club with other Muslim activists and members of the New Black Panther Party, 'where speakers asserted that Israel had launched the 9/11 attacks and that thousands of

Jews had been warned that day not to go to work at the World Trade Center.' At that press conference, Musa blasted the 'Zionists in Hollywood, the Zionists in New York, and the Zionists in D.C.' who 'all collaborate' to put down blacks and Muslims.'"[7]

No Socialism to See Here . . .

Among the groups that marched in the October 2010 One Nation Working Together rally in Washington, D.C., hosted by MSNBC Democratic commentator and Obama enthusiast Ed Schultz:

- The Service Employees International Union, Barack Obama's single largest campaign supporter
- Coffee Party Progressives, a group formed in reaction to the Tea Party movement

Okay, so those are the usual suspects. And they were joined by:

- Socialist Party U.S.A. (an official sponsor)
- Communist Party U.S.A (an official sponsor)
- Committee of Correspondence for Democracy and Socialism
- Democratic Socialists of Ohio
- Democratic Socialists of America
- Socialist Alternative
- Socialist Worker Party
- Organizacion Marxista-Leninista de los Estados Unidos
- Party for Socialism and Liberation
- New York City Democratic Socialists of America
- Ex-Offenders Association of Pennsylvania

At least the felons were *ex*-offenders.

Many of the Obama administration's white suburban supporters—particularly its white, suburban, Jewish supporters—have been mystified by the administration's hostility toward Israel, a dramatic break with longstanding U.S. foreign policy toward a critical ally. Many Democratic strategists have said in private they were equally perplexed by the administration's controversial decision not to prosecute the New Black Panthers Party voter-intimidation case in Philadelphia, a case that saw a uniformed, jackbooted member of that explicitly racist organization menacing would-be voters with a nightstick. But if you understand the socialists' "Rainbow Coalition" strategy—making common cause with environmentalists (Jakopovich goes out of his way to praise Iceland's "Green-Left Movement," which he ranks with the radical SYRIZA leftists in Greece as the great signs of international hope and change), Islamists, secular Palestinian militants, left-wing nationalists like Hugo Chávez, the anti-war movement, and anti-American movements of any serviceable type—then Obama's hostility toward Israel and his administration's solicitousness toward the New Black Panthers is understandable.

Barack Obama is a talented politician, and he understands the *Realpolitik* of the Left. He knows that it was the anti-war movement that helped him to defeat Hillary Clinton and ensured his victory over John McCain. And, since President Obama has no plans to make any sudden moves out of Iraq or Afghanistan, he has to court that socialist Rainbow Coalition in other ways. Jackson's original Rainbow Coalition won him and his supporters a place at the table in a Democratic party still dominated by the likes of Michael Dukakis. The socialists' new Rainbow Coalition is aimed at the same thing: winning them a place at the table in a party in which the Wall Street Democrats (Rahm Emmanuel, Peter Orzsag, Robert Rubin) are locked in a contest for power with the "community-organizing" gang (ACORN, the NAACP, the Democratic machines in New York, the District of Columbia, Chicago, Los Angeles, and Philadelphia, etc.)

It does not matter much whether President Obama and the members of his administration see themselves as part of an international socialist vanguard (and, for the most part, they almost certainly do not see themselves that way). The international socialists themselves see the Obama administration as a part of their "window to socialism." For the Obama administration and the Democratic Party at large, it's enough that they know how to count votes. The most puritanical socialists are, of course, hesitant about getting all the way into bed with a party that courts corporate interests at least as vigorously as do the Republicans, and Wall Street interests even more so. Jakopovich, for example, advocates establishing local "Democratic clubs," to be dominated by socialists, with the goal of taking over particular party organizations—from state parties to national groups such as the Progressive Democrats of America—one piece at a time, "pushing the boundaries of existing political space."

The Dream That Never Dies

I've relied heavily upon Jakopovich's analysis here because he is one of the more lucid—and more open—of the self-professed socialists to have written on the subject specifically in the context of the waning Bush administration and the rising Obama administration. But one finds similar sentiments—and similar mixes of ideological and operational concerns—across the socialist spectrum.

It is worth bearing in mind that today's socialists, for all their democratic rhetoric, do not disavow violence, either in rhetoric or in practice. Writing in a 2010 issue of the *New Left Review*, Slavoj Žižek, arguably the most influential leftist intellectual alive, calls explicitly for the use of violence—as he has in the past—and excuses—as he has in the past—the atrocities perpetrated by socialists in the name of socialism. In the same article, he explicitly disavows reliance upon democratic institutions for advancing the socialist cause. He refers to these twin proposals as the "de-fetishization of democratic institutions" and the "de-fetishization of violence."[8]

It would be difficult to exaggerate the inhumanity of Žižek's politics. "What was wrong with 20th-century Communism," he writes, "was not its resort to violence *per se*—the seizure of state power, the Civil War to maintain it—but the larger mode of functioning, which made this kind of resort to violence inevitable and legitimized: the Party as the instrument of historical necessity, and so on." Noting that U.S. policymakers have sought to use economic pressure to isolate and marginalize the brutal socialist regime in Venezuela—a government that suppresses free speech and engages in wanton political violence—he asks, "Are not defensive counter-measures in order?" He approvingly quotes one of Mao's many mottos—"Everything under heaven is in utter chaos; the situation is excellent!"—and goes on to argue that in a world without socialism, violence is always by definition legitimate:

> From the standpoint of the subordinated and oppressed, the very existence of the state, as an apparatus of class domination, is a fact of violence. Similarly, Robespierre argued that regicide is not justified by proving the King had committed any specific crime: the very existence of the King is a crime, an offense against the freedom of the people. In this strict sense, the use of force by the oppressed against the ruling class and its state is always ultimately "defensive." If we do not concede this point, we *volens nolens* "normalize" the state and accept its violence as merely a matter of contingent excesses. The standard liberal motto—that it is sometimes necessary to resort to violence, but it is never legitimate—is not sufficient.[9]

The point here is not that there exist fat and coddled European intellectuals with risible ideas about the use of violence; the point is that the

Utopias by the Dozen

"*'On ne saurait faire une omelette sans casser des oeufs.'* Translation: 'One cannot expect to make an omelet without breaking eggs.'

"With those words in 1790, Maximilian Robespierre welcomed the horrific French Revolution that had begun the year before. A firm believer in using government to plan the lives of others, he would become the architect of the Revolution's bloodiest phase—'The Reign of Terror' of 1793–94. Robespierre and his guillotine broke 'eggs' by the thousands in a vain effort to impose a centrally planned, utopian, 'omelet' society....

"Every collectivist experiment of the twentieth century was heralded by socialists as the Promised Land. 'I have seen the future and it works,' the intellectual Lincoln Steffens said after a visit to Stalin's Soviet Union. In *The New Yorker* in 1984, John Kenneth Galbraith argued that the Soviet Union was making great economic progress in part because the socialist system made 'full use' of its manpower, in contrast to the less efficient, capitalist West. But an 846-page authoritative study published in 1997, *The Black Book of Communism*, estimated that the communist ideology claimed 20 million lives in the 'workers' paradise.' Millions more died in places like China, Cambodia, and North Korea."

Lawrence W. Reed, *Where Are the Omelets?* 2005

Left still harkens to the call of Mao and Lenin, and that its calls for democratic approaches to socialist reform do not preclude other approaches to socialism, including its imposition through violence. The dictatorship of the proletariat is not a dream that dies easily. Žižek is not merely some crackpot radical ranting at a Parisian café; he is the toast of intellectual society in the United States and abroad, celebrated in the most rarified circles, lecturing and debating at the most elite venues, publishing in the most prestigious journals. His anti-establishment pose is amusing, but the more sobering fact is that he *is* the left-wing establishment, and he is still calling for the *violent* imposition of socialism by any means necessary.

When considering the American leftists who fall along the more moderate wing of the socialist spectrum, it is essential to keep in mind what that spectrum includes. As Adam Shaw put it in an *American Thinker* essay, "There are as many exact definitions of socialism as there are socialists. Yet they do have common characteristics. Love of big government, nationalization of industry, massive taxation, wealth redistribution, etc. all point towards socialism. Someone like [President Obama] would not even have to say he was a socialist in Western Europe; it would be assumed quite normally, without any fuss or conspiracy."[10]

In fact, there are key aspects of Obama's agenda that are socialist in all but name. But we have to understand that what the American Left has in mind is not red banners and workers' committees. It is a top-down, managerial, Ivy League flavor of socialism, one that works its way through the "commanding heights" of the economy one sector at a time; having long controlled education and labor, they are looking to such issues as trade, finance, and energy. They have been emboldened by a major victory won for them by the Obama administration: the partial socialization of American healthcare.

This clearly is the way Žižek sees things. "I am a Leninist," he said in a 2009 interview with *The New Statesman*. "Lenin wasn't afraid to dirty his hands. If you can get power, grab it. Do whatever is possible. This is why I support Obama. I think the battle he is fighting now over healthcare is extremely important, because it concerns the very core of the ruling ideology."[11]

Chapter Fifteen

YES, OBAMACARE IS SOCIALISM

O f course ObamaCare is socialism. It has been designed along explicitly socialist lines—which is to say, on the central-planning model—
and it features such secondary features of socialistic enterprise as
income-redistribution, economic leveling, the co-opting and nationalization of private enterprises, and the elevation of an elite planning class
that is not subject to the rules it will draw up for the rest of the country.

That much of Obama's agenda is socialist is hardly the subject of serious debate. Writing in the socialist journal *Dissent*, Robin Blackburn considered the government's response to the financial crisis of 2008 (a
response whose nationalizing orientation was apparent during the last
days of the Bush administration, to say nothing of the opening days of the
Obama administration). "In the weeks and months after September
2008," she writes, "capitalism as we know it was saved from a near-death
experience by massive state intervention that left the U.S. federal authorities with major assets that included a huge stake in Citigroup, the country's largest bank; in AIG, the largest insurer; and in GM, the world's
largest automobile concern. Fannie Mae, the mortgage giant, was returned
to public hands. Although it is ridiculous to label these desperate—and
temporary—measures 'socialism,' it would be equally absurd not to see
that public ownership on this scale presented an element of a distinctly

Guess What?

★ ObamaCare will
institute central
planning in
healthcare

★ One of ObamaCare's
key architects is a
fervent supporter of
socialist healthcare

★ The first steps
toward socialist
healthcare in Britain
were policies similar
to ObamaCare

socialist approach."[1] In other words, it's a distinctly *socialist* approach, just don't call it *socialism.*

And that goes double for healthcare.

The most fundamental fact at issue in the healthcare debate—the datum most cited by supporters of healthcare nationalization—should have given away the game early and easily: the United States spends about 15 percent of GDP on healthcare, while other countries such as Canada and Germany spend about 10 percent. Obama revisited that fact consistently in his speeches on healthcare: "We spend one and a half times more per person on healthcare than any other country," he told joint session of Congress, "but we aren't any healthier for it."[2]

Set aside the second part of that claim (Americans do, in fact, enjoy significant returns on their healthcare spending) and concentrate on the first. It is true, unquestionably, that the United States spends more as a share of its economy on healthcare than do most other countries. Why is that inherently problematic? The United States spends more on lots of goods and services than do other countries, and spends a lot less on some, too. Relatively speaking, the United States spends much more of its collective income on information technology, and much less on food, than do Haiti, Rwanda, or the alleged economic powerhouse that is the People's Republic of China, for that matter.

Does that mean the Haitians and the Rwandans are getting a much better deal on their laptops and Internet routers than we are? Does it mean that Chinese peasants are eating better? Probably not. The truth is that, as societies become wealthier, it takes much less of their income to cover things like food and shelter; with much more disposable income to dispose of (and Americans, with our low savings rate, *do* dispose of our disposable income), wealthy societies will tend to consume more entertainment, travel, education, professional services, and the like. Healthcare is a service that is in very high demand—when you need it, you need it. Americans' high level of healthcare spending is not evidence that we are getting ripped off; it's evidence that we are a rich country.

Why would there be some metaphysically "correct" portion of GDP to spend on healthcare? The answer, of course, is that there isn't, just as there is no metaphysically correct level of spending on food, clothing, shelter, entertainment, bubblegum, campaign commercials, or any other item of consumption that might come to the interest of the powers in Washington.

One might as easily point out that the United States spends far more on education than do most other countries—significantly more than do Japan or Korea. And it would be difficult to argue convincingly that we are getting better results than the Japanese or the Koreans. But when it comes to education spending, the argument is precisely the opposite of that made for healthcare reform; no amount of spending on education ever is considered too much. It is impossible to imagine Barack Obama telling a joint session of Congress that we, as a nation, spend too much of our GDP on education, and that we should prune ourselves back to the level of spending seen in Singapore, which gets a very good education bang for its buck.

Why the discrepancy? The politics is obvious: U.S. education consists of expropriating money from the private sector and transferring it to the public—since almost all education in the United States is public education. For healthcare the cashflow vector is reversed: even before ObamaCare, more than half of all U.S. healthcare spending was done by the government, but the parties cashing the checks are mostly private businesses: doctors, hospitals, pharmaceutical medical-device manufacturers, and the like. President Obama is not going to tell the teachers' unions that America is spending too much money on them, but he's happy to tell that to doctors and medicine-makers.

ObamaCare: It Looks Like Socialism Because It Is Socialism

Abstracting spending on a particular sector as a share of GDP is a classical symptom of central planning. Advocates of healthcare socialization mistake the measurement for the thing measured—they mistake the map for the territory. Why should it be a problem that the United States spends 15 percent of GDP on healthcare? Why would 14 percent be inherently preferable? Why would 10 percent be preferable? If lower is better, why wouldn't 1 percent be preferable?

These abstractions are about as meaningful as Stalin's plan to double the wheat harvest every five years—they do not tell us anything at all about the underlying activity, which is far too complex to be captured in simple measurements. Likewise, the relative comparisons between countries are nearly meaningless. The United States is the third most populous country on the planet, behind China and India. Its population is mind-bogglingly diverse, its economy incomprehensibly complex. It is full of immigrants from all over the world, legal and illegal. It is ethnically, religiously, culturally, and demographically one of the least homogenous places on Earth. Comparing Americans' healthcare outcomes with those of Swedes is foolish. (Although it is worth noting that Swedish-Americans end up with healthcare outcomes very similar to those of Swedes in Sweden. Similarly, people of Okinawan origin tend to be extraordinarily long-lived wherever they are in the world.)

Understood properly, ObamaCare is an obvious exercise in socialistic central planning. It is not what we would recognize as full socialism—it is not Canada's government medical monopoly, or Soviet Russia's government medical monopoly, for that matter—but it does not have to be. Venezuela's oil industry is no less socialistic for its having more than one firm involved—all the firms are dominated by Hugo Chávez, by THE PLAN, and by politics. The United States under ObamaCare may very well end up with dozens of insurance companies—but every one of them will be offering a product designed in Washington, D.C., rather than one produced by the marketplace.

Like so much American central planning, the socialization of healthcare is being enacted indirectly, through the socialization of a particular kind of finance. Much as Fannie Mae and Freddie Mac, the Federal Housing Administration, tax policy, and even the highway system were used by Washington to reshape the housing market according to political *diktats* (the result of which was the financial crisis of 2008, which itself was used as an excuse for the further socialization of finance), healthcare has been federalized through the socialization of insurance.

This did not, incidentally, begin with ObamaCare. Before the Democrats' healthcare bill was even considered, the U.S. government already spent 50 percent of all healthcare dollars, dominating the marketplace through Medicare, Medicaid, and other federal programs. Using the crude tools of politics, Washington decided that the fundamental problem with U.S. healthcare was not access to quality medical services and products, but access to healthcare insurance—which, as rigorous empirical analysis has shown, is only tangentially related to access to healthcare.

But well-insured voters are reasonably docile on healthcare concerns, even though there is much in U.S. healthcare that cries out for reform. Insurance coverage acts as a political sedative, so Obama & Co. came up with a solution that was every bit as ham-handed as Hugo Chávez's decision to fight ransom kidnapping by seizing the bank accounts of victims' families. Their plan was to pass a law requiring every American to buy insurance. One would think that Americans who 1. wanted insurance and 2. could afford to buy insurance would 3. already have insurance, but the Obama administration didn't see it that way.

This oversight was, of course, a case of willful blindness. Once the federal mandate to buy insurance was in place, the government had a

National Healthcare in Practice

Leftists often champion the Cuban healthcare system as a model of the efficiencies of socialized medicine. While touting the Castro regime's falsified statistics, they deny the nightmarish reality of the system. For example, the *National Post*'s Larry Solomon recounted how the Cuban regime reacted to a 1997 outbreak of dengue fever: fearing news of the disease would hurt Castro's reputation and lessen the influx of tourist dollars, health authorities simply denied the affliction's existence. When a Cuban doctor, Dr. Dessy Mendoza Rivero, circumvented the official cover-up by informing a Miami radio station about the outbreak, he was arrested and sentenced to eight years in prison. Later, the government admitted the disease was dengue fever.

Solomon notes the wider pattern:

> Anecdotes abound of the government cooking the books to prove the glories of the Revolution to the world, with many academics distrusting the official government figures. A demographer from the National Academies of Sciences found that the Cuban government's own data was at odds with official overall statistics for child mortality: If anything, it indicated a growing, not a falling, infant mortality rate, a suspicion supported by other statistics from the Cuban Ministry of Health which showed high rates of several childhood diseases that generally correlate with high infant mortality. Other scientists doubt the claims made over HIV, noting the many Cubans who had served in African wars, the many African students in Cuba, the rampant sex trade in Cuba, and the high rate of HIV among Cubans who escaped from the island. A secret 1987 Cuban Communist Party survey of 10,756 respondents showed 88% of the public in one province to be disappointed with their health-care system. When the Cuban suicide rate skyrocketed—it's now twice the typical rate in Latin American countries—the Cuban government stopped reporting suicide statistics in a way that allowed international comparisons.

moral and political excuse to intervene, deeply and wantonly, in the structure, pricing, and delivery of insurance. Having long experience with socialism-by-finance, the Fannie Mae and Treasury department veterans in the Obama administration could hardly have hit upon a solution more attuned to their own worldview and interests—or less attuned to the political and economic realities of healthcare.

Northwestern University professor David Dranove, author of *The Economic Evolution of American Healthcare*, notes that few if any of those building ObamaCare would identify themselves as socialists, but socialism is what they are building nonetheless. (He does not mention that Medicare czar Donald Berwick, one of the most influential architects of ObamaCare, is blisteringly anti-capitalist in his rhetoric, denouncing the "darkness of private enterprise," or that his preferred model is the explicitly socialist National Health Service in the United Kingdom. Perhaps this is an oversight, perhaps mere professional courtesy.) Whatever their political motivations, their error is identical to Hayek's "fatal conceit"—the belief that the best and the brightest, given sufficient political power, can rationally plan human affairs. Describing the Ivy League academics who are being tapped to implement ObamaCare, Professor Dranove writes,

> My Cambridge colleagues are mostly economists and know a lot about how markets do and do not work. They have learned from economic theory and practical observation that free market health insurance is imperfect. Fearing adverse selection, unregulated insurers take steps that leave some individuals uninsured, while other individuals choose not to buy insurance and free ride off of taxpayer subsidized charity. Most economists (myself included) agree with this diagnosis of the problem with insurance markets.
>
> ...But this solution does not end with a government takeover of health insurance. There isn't a public or private health insurer anywhere in the world that doesn't directly

intervene in the delivery of medical care. Socialized insurance necessarily leads to socialized medicine, and if the government controls well over half of the insurance sector through Medicare and Medicaid, and tightly regulates the rest, it is only inevitable that it will also seek to control how healthcare is bought and sold. And I don't think it will make much difference whether it is Democrats or Republicans in control. The temptation to set the rules for 17 percent of the GDP is too great.

The Obama administration has hired an army of academics to implement the new reforms. They bring with them the finest Cambridge pedigrees and promising ideas. They will write the first draft of the rules and academics everywhere will nod in approval at the cleverness of our colleagues. (Some of us may even enjoy seeing our own pet ideas turn into policy.) But in the fullness of time, the rules and regulations that will govern our healthcare system will bear the imprint of politicians more than academics. It is the nature of the beast.

My Cambridge colleagues do not favor socialized medicine. But I fear that the regulatory behemoth they have been entrusted to manage is too big for them, despite their talents. Ten years from now, we will look back at these days as the beginning of the end of market-based medicine in America. And my colleagues will only be able to look back, shake their heads, and say "it wasn't supposed to turn out this way."[3]

Translation: *it wasn't the socialism we dreamed of!*

But it *will* be the socialism the bureaucrats asked for. Personnel is policy, at the federal level no less than at the local school board. The Center for Medicare and Medicaid Services (CMS), once an obscure federal backwater, will be at the center of the federal takeover of U.S. medicine, generating policy, imposing rules, and creating protocols. In appointing

Dr. Berwick to head that organization, President Obama was sending a strong message about what kind of system his administration intended to build. Speaker of the House Nancy Pelosi famously opined that Congress had to pass the healthcare bill to find out what's in it—but the political reality is that the largely unread bill's main thrust is to create gigantic new federal administrative body that will generate its own rules and pro- cedures, and that those will be profoundly influenced by Dr. Berwick and his colleagues. What do they have in mind?

"An Example for the Whole World"

Let us consult Dr. Berwick himself for an answer to that question: "I am romantic about the NHS," he said, referring to Britain's National Health Service. "I love it. All I need to do to rediscover the romance is to look at healthcare in my own country."[4] The NHS, he said, is "an exam- ple for the whole world—an example . . . that the United States needs now more than most other countries do."[5] Lest you think that he has exceeded the limits of fulsomeness in praise, he goes on: "The NHS is not just a national treasure; it is a global treasure."[6]

Dr. Berwick is resolutely anti-capitalist. In addition to denouncing pri- vate enterprise as "immoral," he advised would-be reformers in Britain, many of whom are unhappy with the results of their own exercise in med- ical socialism, "Please don't put your faith in market forces."[7] Market forces, of course, are all that stand between would-be central planners and the rationally planned economic order they imagine. In an article on healthcare reform, Dr. Berwick argued, "In the United States, competition is a major reason for our duplicative, supply-driven, fragmented care sys- tem."[8] Sounding every inch the socialist, he referred to "collective action overriding some individual self-interest" as the "Holy Grail" of healthcare.[9]

The smart set scoffed at Sarah Palin's talk of "death panels," but Dr. Berwick has this to say: "The decision is not whether or not we will ration care—the decision is whether we will ration with our eyes open."[10] Specifically, he argues that we must use the force of government to "reduce the use of unwanted and ineffective medical procedures at the end of life."[11] Unwanted is one thing; if you do not wish to receive medical care, it takes no Herculean effort to avoid it. But who shall decide what is "ineffective"? The answer, of course, is Dr. Berwick and the other central planners.

Single-sector socialism of the sort suffered by British healthcare consumers or American public-school families depends upon context and local conditions, of course—there are, after all, a few excellent public schools in the United States, and no doubt some Britons receive high-quality healthcare. But we can watch those systems over time and analyze the results, especially since enterprises such as the NHS produce a lot of data. It's worth taking a look at some of it to get a foretaste of what the socialized U.S. system will look like.

The NHS is very strongly parallel to the U.S. education system in one important regard: the class of people from which the central-planning staffers are drawn do not rely upon it. Just as the very wealthiest Americans still send their own children to private schools (as, indeed, do many of the non-wealthy who can afford to do so, including a majority of Chicago's public-school teachers—itself a telling fact) about 8 percent of Brits maintain private insurance and thereby access to healthcare outside of the national system. This is, in many cases, a matter of some urgency; NHS routinely denies services to sick people on purely financial grounds. Like Dr. Berwick, they know they must ration, and they choose to do so "with their eyes open" and their green eyeshades on.

As the BBC reported in 1999, "Patients are suffering and some have died as a result of rationing in the NHS, doctors have claimed. A survey of almost 3,000 doctors by *Doctor and Hospital Doctor* newspapers found that one in five doctors know patients who have suffered harm as a result of rationing. More than 5% of GPs surveyed also said they knew of patients who had died as a result of being denied treatment on the NHS."[12] The results of such rationing are not always obvious. Because the NHS does a relatively poor job providing care for elderly patients with chronic conditions—because such care is expensive and because the "return on investment" is calculated to be low in the case of the old and sick—many elderly Britons with conditions such as Parkinson's or dementia are cared for mainly by family members, especially by spouses.

Furthermore, a denial of care to a caregiving family member can have a cascading effect, as the BBC discovered. "Among those doctors was Sidcup GP Dr. Richard Money, who reported the case of a 70-year-old man who was awaiting surgery while acting as the sole carer for his wife, who had developed Alzheimer's Disease. Dr. Money said the patient was referred for surgery in 1997. Despite the fact that he had a poor outlook without surgery, he was kept on the waiting list for more than six months. Eventually, his condition deteriorated, and he died after about a year after the initial referral while he was still awaiting surgery."[13]

Such stories are depressingly common in Britain and in other countries with similarly politicized systems. Unsurprisingly, U.S. hospitals and clinics are routinely treated as medical havens by Canadians denied care by their "free" socialist system. One of the main problems is that central planners take their political mandates to be realities; they cannot bear to speak about rationing, so they pretend it does not exist. Doctors and hospital administrators, of course, know otherwise. "Nearly half—45%—of GPs who responded to the survey said they were aware of patients whose treatment had been delayed on grounds of cost," the BBC reported. "Ministers have repeatedly argued that rationing is not necessary in the NHS. But doctors claim that, with finite resources, rationing is inevitable."[14]

To patients denied care, it will not much matter whether that rationing was conducted with eyes closed or, as Dr. Berwick prefers, with eyes open.

The NHS, created in 1946, was already mired in scandal, politicization, accusations of favoritism, and financial mismanagement by the 1960s. A study of complaints against Ely Hospital in Cardiff turned up abuses out of a Dickens novel: nurses even assaulted patients, cracking their heads open and then suturing up their split scalps without medical supervision. A litany of similar abuses was catalogued. Incredibly, the NHS tried to put as non-scandalous a spin as possible in its report, a sampling of which reads:

> The middle-aged patient Housman (on Ward 21) was on one occasion handled with undue roughness by Charge Nurse "M" and Staff Nurse "N" and mismanaged so as to be wounded in the scalp. The wound was sutured by Charge Nurse "M" and the patient treated with paraldehyde without any medical supervision and was not seen by a doctor until the following day. This incident was caused not by malice but by the acceptance of old-fashioned, unduly rough and undesirably low standards of nursing care; and of a system whereby members of the nursing staff were permitted to suture wounds and administer drugs without any or sufficient reference to or supervision by medical staff (Paragraphs 89 to 96).
>
> (c) The elderly patient Addison (on Ward 17A) was struck in the face on at least one occasion in course of an unduly clumsy and rough attempt to control his movements. The incident was caused by lack of skill and some lack of sympathy in handling a difficult patient and probably not by malice. We were unable to identify with certainty the male nurse responsible for this incident (Paragraphs 30 to 37).
>
> (d) The young epileptic patient Masefield (on Ward 23) who had aggravating and difficult habits, was slapped on the face on more than one occasion by Charge Nurse "A" and Staff

Nurse "R". This conduct was not caused by malice but was due to the acceptance of old-fashioned and unsophisticated techniques for controlling a difficult patient (Paragraphs 109 to 113).

(e) We were unable to pursue the allegation that Charge Nurse "A" used a hose on certain naked patients in a yard. XY did not claim to have been an eye witness of this incident; and the witness to whom he attributes the story was unwilling to give evidence before us.[15]

A lack of skill and some lack of sympathy—for *nurses beating elderly patients so badly they required stitches*. Notably, the authorities were not even able to identify which staff members were responsible for the abuse, which of course bespeaks negligent oversight and a bureaucratic culture of self-protection, features that will by now be familiar from our studies of socialism around the world. For all that "darkness of private enterprise," it is impossible to imagine American medical practitioners hosing down naked patients in a hospital yard.

Various attempts were made at reform in the 1960s and the 1970s, but they were largely ineffective. This era was, it is worth noting, the very height of British socialism. In the years preceding the election of Margaret Thatcher, Britain had been transformed into a democratic socialist state, and thereby had been brought to its knees by rapacious public-sector workers, recalcitrant union bosses protected by the central-planning elites, and gross misallocations of capital and distortions of investment decisions. The intellectual failure of British socialism was nowhere more obvious than in British healthcare, but healthcare socialism is a particularly nefarious variant. Even as heavy industry was re-privatized during Thatcherite rule, the NHS survived unscathed.

It is remarkable that it did so, given its performance. Central planners can and will attempt to ignore economic realities, but incentives will continue to act in accord with the laws of supply and demand, which are as

It's Called Overselling

"The NHS, [former UK deputy prime minister John Prescott] says, is Britain's 'greatest creation'. Really? Greater than parliamentary democracy? Greater than penicillin? Greater than the discovery of DNA, or the abolition of slavery, or the common law? John, the NHS produces some of the worst health outcomes in the industrialised world. Britain is the Western state where you'd least want to have cancer or a stroke or heart disease. Ours is now a country where thousands of people are killed in hospitals for reasons unrelated to their original condition. If this is our 'greatest creation', Heaven help us."

Daniel Hannan, British Conservative MEP, 2009

non-negotiable as the laws of gravity. Just as the Obama administration in 2008 to 2010 was very concerned with final prices paid for healthcare, the NHS bureaucrats necessarily set upon hospitals' profits and doctors' relatively high salaries as inefficiencies to be weeded out in the new, rational order. The result was, inevitably, a shortage of doctors. Again, the results were so extreme as to be unimaginable to most Americans, who could expect to enjoy better healthcare in prison than many Britons received in their hospitals.

By the middle 1970s—the high-water mark of British socialism—conditions in many British hospitals had reverted to pre-Victorian standards. This was especially true for those treating the mentally ill—which is to say, for those British subjects with the least political power. In 1975, there was one—one!—doctor in NHS hospitals for every 660 mentally ill patients. In his 1975 study *Rationing Health Care*, Michael Cooper wrote,

"It is possible to find wards in mental hospitals where patients sleep, eat, excrete, live and die in one large room." Cooper's work is referenced in a lengthy study of the NHS by University of Dallas professor John Goodman, "National Healthcare in Great Britain," which contains page after page of horrifying revelations: "Mentally ill patients, who fill 45 percent of all occupied beds, receive an average attendance of one hour per year from hospital doctors. As one commentator observed, 'it would be extraordinary indeed if patients did not suffer from delays in prescribing, in motoring side effects, in over-treatment, and in discharge following recovery' under these conditions."[16]

Given that doctors were investing in these patients a grand total of *one hour per year* of medical attention, it is much easier to see how nurses could get away with beating their patients bloody and then stitching them up without medical supervision.

Desperate for warm bodies to fill available physicians' slots, the Brits began to import enormous numbers of doctors from abroad, most of them trained at foreign medical schools that did not, to put it mildly, necessarily live up to Western standards. As Professor Goodman notes, by 1975 some 85 percent of the new doctors in geriatrics and 86 percent of the new doctors in mental health were foreign-trained.

There is nothing inherently wrong with foreign-trained physicians, of course, and overseas medical training has made great advances since the 1970s. These figures are simply cited to indicate that with the advent of NHS, suddenly nobody in Britain wanted to be a doctor, especially a doctor treating the elderly or the mentally infirm, i.e., those most likely to need intensive medical care and least likely to be able to agitate politically to secure their own interests. The results were, as the data make clear, nothing short of horrific.

Bear in mind, this was not some Third World backwater, and this was not 100 years ago. This was England—civilized England!—only a few years ago.

There have been additional attempts at reform, of course, and the most recent of them have attempted to allow more Britons to avail themselves of the capacities of the country's tiny surviving private healthcare system. In other words, while the Obama administration has been inspired by the socialist NHS, the NHS itself is looking to de-socialize itself, at least in baby steps. Needless to say, the introduction of market-oriented reforms has been met with opposition from the central-planning elites that is absolutely red in tooth and claw.

Evolution of a Tragedy

Will socialized healthcare in the United States more closely resemble 1970s-era Britain, as its critics fear, or 2010 Sweden, as its enthusiasts hope? The Patient Protection and Affordable Care Act, known colloquially as ObamaCare, does not, after all, establish a single-payer system, as the most socialistic advocates of healthcare reform had hoped. It does not make doctors employees of the state (though many already are functionally that when it comes to Medicaid and Medicare patients, which is one reason why so few doctors accept new patients under those programs). Why should we assume—what reason do we have to believe, other than history, experience, prudence, economics, and a passing familiarity with political realities—that ObamaCare will give us the socialism Britain suffered, rather than "the socialism we dreamed of"?

To answer that question, bear in mind that Britain did not start with a single-payer system. It began with a system very much like the American one pre-ObamaCare: the provision of direct medical services for the very poor under a system rather like our Medicaid, later supplemented by a national health-insurance program that, like Medicare and Medicaid, accounted for about half of all healthcare spending. In fact, the timeline of Britain's transformation from an almost entirely private system of healthcare to an almost entirely socialist one will prove strikingly familiar to the observer of the contemporary American scene.

Professor Goodman's study provides an invaluable history of the evolution of British healthcare; writing in the 1970s, he could hardly have predicted the extent to which he was describing America's future while chronicling Britain's past, but it's all there: the individual mandate, buying off the insurance companies, means-testing and rationing, the replacement of decentralized systems with central planning, and ultimately, the imposition of socialism on the whole mess.

Britain had long taken an official interest in the plight of the poor, and particularly in their healthcare. Indeed, throughout much of British history, poverty has been treated as a matter of public hygiene, with the government's anti-poverty programs owing as much to early epidemiology as to economics. The Act for the Reliefe of the Poore, a.k.a. the Poor Law, was enacted in 1601 under the reign of Queen Elizabeth I. As Professor Goodman notes, it remained the fundamental framework for public-health and anti-poverty programs in Britain until the establishment of the NHS.

Unlike their later colonial cousins, the British maintained an established church, and the Poor Law empowered local Church of England parishes to levy taxes for the support of their impoverished parishioners. Some of their programs, such as the rather austere poorhouses and workhouses, will seem practically medieval to the modern reader, but then, this was not long after the end of the Middle Ages, so there's a good reason for that. Compared with much of the rest of Europe, to say nothing of the rest of the world, the British system was the most progressive thing going. A commercial society, Britain was highly attuned to the issue of economic incentives, and so those dependent upon public relief were maintained at an economic level below what they would earn as laborers, thus helping to ensure that services were only consumed by those who had few or no other options. This was an early version of what today we'd call "means testing" and the rationing of government benefits.

But the working classes had other options available as well. Charitable undertakings, mostly run by religious groups, made available various kinds of relief services, including medical care, even to those poor who were not eligible for the poorhouse. And as the national home of the world's first insurance market, Lloyd's of London, Britain was, predictably, an innovator in the world of private health insurance. Mutual-aid organizations, known as "friendly societies," provided sick pay, disability benefits, and death benefits to their members in exchange for a weekly premium. Many of these societies grew to be extremely financially sophisticated; indeed, it is a tragedy of history that they did not have access to modern actuarial techniques. If they had, Britain and the rest of the English-speaking world might have been spared both the indignities of socialist medicine and the cruel buffoonery of the modern insurance industry.

Between the primitive insurance business and the public-relief system, the British underclass enjoyed what was for the period a remarkably advanced social-security network. "Overall, the poor-law system was quite successful in providing food and shelter for millions of poverty-stricken individuals," Professor Goodman notes. "Medical care of some sort existed in the public relief houses, and by the end of the eighteenth century most parishes provided some medical services for the poor in their own homes." But the system would soon be transformed in a way familiar to those who have studied *Crisis and Leviathan*: a public emergency would erupt, inspiring "reformers" to take steps far beyond what would have been necessary to head off similar catastrophes in the future.

In the case of British healthcare, the Leviathan-enabling crisis was the cholera epidemic of 1866, after which the hygienic conditions of the poorhouses became a *cause célèbre*. The reformers first pressured local parishes to set up a network of hospitals, including isolation wards for those with contagious diseases and asylums for the insane. These existed alongside charity hospitals that had long been maintained by religious orders and local churches. At the same time, the friendly societies were beginning to experience financial difficulties—largely, as Professor Goodman notes, as a consequence of the fact that British workers were living longer as their healthcare, nutrition, and work conditions rapidly improved. With the existing system facing economic pressures and the memory of the 1866 epidemic fresh on the minds of reformers, the stage was set for the creation of a national health system.

The real opening salvo in the socialization of British healthcare—as in the socialization of American healthcare—was the socialization and nationalization of the insurance market. David Lloyd George, at the time chancellor of the exchequer, was the author of the national health-insurance system. Much like the planners of ObamaCare, Lloyd George viewed healthcare principally as an economic abstraction, and his benefits-and-battleships socialism was not terribly unlike that of war socialist Woodrow Wilson. And, like Wilson, he was partly inspired by the example of Otto von Bismarck, who had established an individual mandate for industrial workers in the late nineteenth century, which would later be expanded to cover almost all German workers in the buildup to World War I.

For Lloyd George as for Bismarck, healthcare was mainly an economic question. As Professor Goodman writes, he was "primarily concerned with sickness as a cause of poverty, not for its own sake. His proposal sought to provide medical care for the breadwinner—but not his family—so that he could return to work." Accepting public benefits was for generations known as "going on the Lloyd George."

Like the U.S. Social Security/Medicare/Medicaid system, the Lloyd George program was funded by a combination of payroll taxes levied on workers, a second payroll tax levied on employers, and a government contribution paid out of general tax revenues. It does not take a great deal of economic sophistication to appreciate that all three of those taxes ultimately are paid by the same party: the worker himself.

But economic sophistication was not then in great supply. "The Lloyd George scheme was sold to the public on the cry of 'ninepence for fourpence,'" Professor Goodman writes.

> In other words, low-income workers were told that they were being offered benefits whose value was more than twice the value of their weekly fourpenny contribution. The facts were otherwise. Both economic theory and empirical evidence suggest that employment taxes are not actually borne by employers. The threepence employer contribution was simply part of the cost of hiring a worker for one week. Employers had no financial reason to care whether the "contribution" went to an insurance scheme or to workers in the form of wages. So most economists believe that the burden of such taxes ultimately falls on the workers themselves. In the absence of the tax, the worker's wage would have been threepence higher. In addition, part of the burden of general taxes undoubtedly fell on low-income workers. So the twopence contribution from the state partly came out of the pockets of workers as well. The siren song of something for nothing, then, was largely a hoax.[17]

It is a hoax familiar to contemporary Americans. While the Obama administration has promised not to raise taxes on any but the wealthiest Americans, it plans to raise taxes on Americans' employers, as though those expenses will not be passed on to the workers themselves. Additionally, payroll taxes will be raised for a minority of U.S. households under the program. As Dr. Berwick, Obama's man at CMS, put it, "We must—must!—redistribute wealth" through the national healthcare program.[18] Similarly, the law will raise taxes and fines on many businesses—

which will have the inevitable result of driving many (probably most) Americans out of market-based systems into "free" or subsidized government programs.

Never mind that those "free" programs come at a price of trillions of dollars. That something-for-nothing approach is a critical component of central planners' political platform. Alleging to rationally plan these industries, they argue that they can squeeze waste, fraud, and abuse out

Redistributing Wealth—and Human Rights

One insidious aspect of socialist governments' wealth redistribution policies is that they allow for the redistribution of political rights. Because property rights are fundamental to any liberal society, the disruption of those bedrock rights invites the truncation of many other political rights. Zimbabwe's land-redistribution plan under the socialist government of Robert Mugabe is one dramatic example. Another is the case of Albania's post-World War II "agrarian reform" program, which was used as a pretext to attack organized religion, a sector that harbored significant opposition to the socialist regime. As Raymond Zickel and Walter R. Iwaskiw reported in a federal research project for the Library of Congress, the aim was to destroy organized religion in Albania by confiscating and even burning down houses of worship and other religious property.

If land reform can be used as a pretext to burn down monasteries, health-care reform can be used as an excuse to repress unpopular political speech, as already is happening in the United States, with the Obama administration threatening to close down any insurance company that publicly links rising health-insurance costs to the passage of ObamaCare.

of the system; misunderstanding the role of competition and profits, they claim that by eliminating those negative elements, they can achieve savings—the magical formula of better care at lower costs.

This is why much of the healthcare debate is so abstract, dominated by meaningless questions such as what portion of GDP represents the optimum for healthcare spending. Predictably, much of this discourse is dishonest—and incompatible with well-established facts. As the *New England Journal of Medicine* puts it, "Barack Obama has argued that 'too little is spent on prevention and public health.'...Our findings suggest that the broad generalizations made by many presidential candidates can be misleading. These statements convey the message that substantial resources can be saved through prevention. Although some preventive measures do save money, the vast majority reviewed in the health economics literature do not."[19]

Lloyd George argued that his program would, in the long run, save Britain untold sums of money by preventing the impoverishment of working-class families. Get the breadwinner back in working trim, the argument went, and we'll save a lot of money down the road by not having to put his widow and children on the dole. It hasn't worked out that way, of course.

Like Barack Obama, David Lloyd George faced one major obstacle to enacting his program: opposition from the insurance lobby. And like Obama, he was able to overcome that obstacle through the second-oldest tool in the political arsenal: bribery. (The oldest tool, if you're wondering, is a large rock to the head.) The friendly societies of Lloyd George's day were, like their modern counterparts, hostile to the socialization of their industry, and for much the same reason: they stood to lose money. The British Liberals responded by creating a program that would work through the existing insurance industry, requiring the working class to purchase insurance coverage and providing subsidies to enable that purchase.

American Democrats would take precisely the same route a century later, with the "individual mandate" for health insurance and the array of subsidies that enabled it. Like their later American counterparts, the British insurers were very much pacified by having the government pass a law requiring that practically every family purchase its products. The friendly societies made another calculation that would later inform their American epigones: by establishing themselves at the intersection of government, finance, and medicine, they—not the doctors, not the patients, not the hospital owners—would be in charge of the system.

In other words, ObamaCare will place the United States in much the same position in which the United Kingdom found itself in the wake of David Lloyd George's reforms: with a system dominated by profit-seeking insurance companies, but one that is at the same time financed mostly through the government, with all of the clumsiness and lack of accountability that entails. The economics are quite similar, and so are the politics: Lloyd George's reform package was sold in part as a measure for mitigating a restive working class that might otherwise be tempted into demanding more radical measures to secure its interest. ObamaCare has been sold as the moderate alternative to an NHS-style single-payer system.

Moreover, Lloyd George's system was met with mixed feelings by Britain's Fabian socialists, who believed that it did not go far enough but who also insisted that the working classes were not competent to see to their own affairs without oversight from the Oxford and Cambridge men who dominated the political class. The American Left has greeted ObamaCare as a distasteful compromise with the private sector but celebrate the insurance mandate on the theory that the American working class is too stupid to secure its own interests without being forced to do so by federal statute.

You will notice, though, that Britain did not stand still after the Lloyd George insurance reformers. Neither will America after the establishment of ObamaCare. In fact, it took Britain less than thirty years to go from a socialized insurance market to a fully socialist healthcare system. The United States, being restive by nature, will probably move even faster.

Endgame

If we continue to work under the theory that Britain's past illuminates America's future, then it is worth noting, in brief, how the Lloyd George insurance system became the NHS that we know today.

The Lloyd George scheme, like ObamaCare, created perverse financial incentives that were ultimately unsustainable. In addition to buying off the insurance lobby, Lloyd George and the Liberals had to buy off the doctors, which they did by establishing a generous remuneration plan that kept them extraordinarily fat and happy; the volume of medical services rendered increased by 50 percent in the years following his insurance reforms, and doctors' fees increased by roughly the same amount, meaning that doctors' incomes rose sharply—doubling in poor areas. Later attempts under the NHS to rein in those expenses led to the catastrophic physician shortage experienced by Britain in the 1960s and 1970s, just as attempts to limit physicians' payments under Medicare and Medicaid in the United States have led to a critical shortage of practitioners willing to accept new patients under those programs.

The British friendly societies that were less successful in screening out high-risk subscribers soon found themselves in dire financial straits and resentful of their more successful competitors, creating a lobby for national action to produce a system that was more "fair"—meaning, of course, a system that would do more to guarantee their own profits and improve their position in the marketplace. Since medical services were "free" at the point of consumption, patients had no incentive to limit their use of healthcare services, and the addition of financial benefits—particularly disability payments that required a doctor's certificate—greatly increased the man-hours and administrative overhead necessary to maintain the system. Doctors responded by shunting as many of their patients as possible onto the dole and the charity hospitals. The radical difference in the quality of care provided to "private" patients—those paying their own expenses out of pocket—and to those in the national system led to social resentments that inevitably found expression in electoral politics. In other words, Britain found itself in precisely the position in which the United States is positioned to find itself in the next ten to twenty years.

"In the 1920s and 1930s, there were numerous recommendations to alter the national health insurance scheme," Professor Goodman writes. "They included recommendation to extend benefits to the dependents of the insured workers, and to expand the system to cover hospital treatment and other specialist care. Ultimately, these proposals were rejected in favor of a full-fledged, universal scheme of 'free' medical care. Many people saw reform of national health insurance as patchwork on a scheme that was fatally flawed in any event. Healthcare, they argued, should be available to *everyone* as a matter of 'right.' "[20]

The Lloyd George model turned out to be a transitional stage on the road to healthcare serfdom. ObamaCare will likely serve a similar purpose, as that is its intention. "I am a proponent of a single-payer universal healthcare program," then-Illinois state senator Obama said in 2003, back before he was politically required to pretend that he endorsed no such thing. "All of you know we might not get there immediately, because first we have to take back the White House, we have to take back the Senate, and we have to take back the House."[21]

Having done that in 2008, what comes next? In a 2007 interview, then-U.S. Senator Obama laid out the plan: "Let's say that I proposed a plan that moved to a single-payer system. Let's say Medicare plus. It would be, essentially, [that] everybody can buy into Medicare."[22] Allowing everybody to access Medicare is equivalent to what is known as the "public option"—creating a quasi-socialist system to run parallel to the existing system, and then using the coercive powers of the state to financially undermine what remains of the private system, leaving the public "option" the only option.

Senator Obama envisioned as much as far back as 2004, when he said, "At the federal level, what I'm looking at is a very specific proposal that would provide healthcare coverage for all children who need it all across the United States, would allow 55- to 64-year-olds to buy into the Medicare system. And I think that if we can start with children and those persons 55 to 64 that are most vulnerable, then we can start filling in those holes and ultimately I think, move in the direction of a universal healthcare plan."[23]

Democratic senator Barney Frank more succinctly described the strategy of using ObamaCare to establish the expanded federal role, supplementing it with a "public option," and then replacing the whole ugly tuna casserole of a system with an NHS-style full socialization: "We just don't have the votes for [single payer]. I wish we did. I think if we get a good public option, it could lead to single payer, and that's the best way to reach single payer. The best way we're going to get single payer—the only way—is to have a public option, and demonstrate its strength and power."[24]

It worked in Britain. It will work here.

In the course of lecturing a group of congressional Republicans about the wisdom of his healthcare proposal, President Obama said,

> If you were to listen to the debate—and, frankly, how some of you went after this bill—you'd think that this thing was some Bolshevik plot. That's how you guys presented it. . . . We've got to close the gap a little bit between the rhetoric and the reality. I'm not suggesting that we're going to agree on everything, whether it's on healthcare or energy or what have you, but if the way these issues are being presented by the Republicans is

that this is some wild-eyed plot to impose huge government in every aspect of our lives, what happens is you guys then don't have a lot of room to negotiate with me.[25]

But, of course, Obama's healthcare proposal, as articulated by the president himself and by his congressional colleagues, was anything but a Bolshevik plot. It was a David Lloyd George plot, a Wilson war-socialism program, an iteration of Bismarckian national socialism without the fancy uniform, braid, epaulettes, mustache, or Prussian accent. It is socialism in one sector, the fatal conceit of the best and the brightest, Chávez-ism without the red shirts and rousing party songs. It was and is a way station on the road to serfdom.

THE PRICE IS
METAPHYSICALLY RIGHT

"The attempt to reform the world socialistically might destroy civilization," Ludwig von Mises wrote. "It would never set up a successful socialist community."[1]

Mises never encountered the insightful social critic (better known as a guitar-picker) Guy Clark, who posited that there are precisely two commodities for which marketplace price signals cannot be generated: true love and homegrown tomatoes. Mr. Clark was half right about that, which is not bad when it comes to market predictions. It is really hard to find good tomatoes, and, if you want to see market failure in action, you can speed down the produce aisle at your local grocer's and have a gander at the mealy, tasteless wad of cellulosic pulp that Farmer Elmer is trying to pass off as a genuine tomato. While there has been some success in reviving such flavorful and fancifully named ancients of the tomato kingdom as the mortgage-lifter, the Cherokee purple, and the hillbilly, the overall failure of the marketplace to produce much fruit that could be dignified with the name "tomato" is one of the mysteries of capitalism.

Presumably, there is a way to blame Earl Butz or the factory-farm lobby (a.k.a. Big Elmer) for this, but we will leave that question, for the moment, to the historians and the Nixonologists.

Prices are, or should be, objects of awe and wonder, a mystery to be meditated upon. They are not mere intersections of supply and demand curves, the predictable $19.99 of late-night info-mercials; prices are the Paraclete of the market economy, the mystical intercessor between producers and consumers, performing miracles of information management and economic coordination that could not otherwise be accomplished. Prices are the epistemological movers and shakers of community life, transporting knowledge instantly and without friction, coordinating the actions of a shipyard in Virginia with those of a steel mill in China, directing global flows of capital, letting clueless executives in Atlanta know that New Coke is a fiasco.

That last bit of Cold War-era history is worth discussing: when it hit the market in 1985, New Coke was the most highly engineered, polished, researched, lovingly refined, focus-grouped, test-marketed product of its time. (Socialist governments aren't the only organizations whose planning efforts find themselves nullified by the market, which is to say, by reality.) Coca-Cola USA had everybody from food scientists to psychiatrists working on what they codenamed, in the military-industrial style, Project Kansas. All the best minds told them New Coke was going to be a smashing success.

Prices, however, said otherwise. While New Coke couldn't be given away, the price of Old Coke, if you could find it, skyrocketed. Consumers began to spend extraordinary sums of money—to pay very high prices— to import "The Real Thing" from overseas, and an organization calling itself "Old Cola Drinkers of America" was able to raise $120,000 to lobby Coca-Cola for a return to the original formula. So poorly regarded was the new product that, in some southern cities, revanchist cola conservatives paid full price for bottles of New Coke for the sole purpose of emptying them out in the streets as an act of protest. Sales tanked, orders nosedived, regional bottlers revolted. Prices were saying: all your best minds got it wrong. Coke's brain trust said "X," but prices said "Not X."

The price was right.

It took a little trauma to get there (Hail the Age of Reagan, when New Coke was our definition of an economic crisis!) but consumers prevailed, and New Coke followed socialism into the dustbin of history—for similar reasons, but with a lot less bloodshed. Coca-Cola USA had to bend to reality more quickly than the socialists did.

Prices are, among other things, a snapshot of the relationship between what producers are selling and what consumers want. That relationship, though intangible, is a reality, a reality as real as gravity or a skyscraper or a case of pancreatic cancer. To compare the contemporaneous declines of New Coke and Soviet socialism from 1985–91 is not to engage in frivolity.

As Hayek noted, the great problem facing central-planning regimes like that of the old Soviet Union is that there are no prices to facilitate communication between producers and consumers. The tales of Soviet-era production misalignments would be comical if they had not exacted such a high price in human blood. There would be huge surpluses of, say, pesticides (not to mention tanks and rockets and ideology) but acute shortages of sugar, flour, shoes, and other common items. Toilet paper was used as filler in sausages until the toilet paper itself went into short supply. Burglars would break into houses and steal everything but the money—there was no point in taking it, as there was little or nothing to buy.

For the Soviets, there were no real prices, so there was no feedback loop between producers and consumers. If we'd had that model for soft drinks, we'd still be drinking New Coke, and the cola executives in Atlanta would be strutting around in their nifty military uniforms, with epaulettes and braid, telling us to drink our New Coke and like it, because they had determined, *rationally*, that this is what we want. *It's scientific, damn it!*

A good rule of thumb: fear the man who says he will make things rational by ignoring reality—and ignoring prices is ignoring reality.

Once the powers-that-be in the socialist world were wielding calculators instead of AK-47s, this began to become apparent. In 1968, economist

Oldrich Kyn, who expressed considerable sympathy for the socialist system of the Soviet Union and for the socialist economies of Eastern Europe, nonetheless felt the need to broach the subject of pricing in a paper presented to a conference of the International Economic Association. In precise academic language, he reached the same conclusion that any number of anti-socialist economists had already come to—you aren't going to magic prices away:

> Until recently pricing was considered a secondary problem in a socialist economy. This was the result both of practices which had become established in the past, and of a set of generally-accepted theoretical postulates. Very little attention was paid to the theory of prices, the deficiency of which profoundly marked recent economic practice. This neglect of pricing was justified by the assumption that the central problem of the socialist economy was the assurance of planned proportions derived primarily from material balances and their disaggregation as directives for production enjoined upon individual plants. The role of prices was hence no more than as a subsidiary form of cost accounting; to make it independent and related to the market was in fact considered irreconcilable with the system of planning and central management.[2]

The major change in Marxist thinking came as the necessity of government forced socialists' focus away from moral theorizing and toward the realities of governance—or, as Professor Kyn puts it, by the "rapid infiltration of mathematics into Marxist economics." Like Mises before him, he came to the conclusion that prices hadn't been *planned* at all; they had merely been set, by fiat, in the absence of the sort of information that would be necessary to conduct actual planning. According to Kyn,

It followed that price problems were basic to socialism and could not be brushed aside as secondary.

... The idea of planning was erroneously presented as inseparable from the administrative determination of targets and of prices. In fact, there was no planning of prices, for they remained constant until glaringly proved incompatible with evolving economic conditions; sets of such prices were more random in their relative values than those formed on the market, for they were a compound of errors in computations, false appraisals of the situation, and lack of information and subjective criteria on the part of decision-makers. It seems entirely justified therefore to use 'central determination' rather than 'planning' of prices. It may be noted that such determination was in line with the view, then common, that the utmost centralization was to be imposed on decision-making in subordinate units, as the only way to coordinate development towards ends most beneficial to society. It was also thought that an increase in any retail price would negate the aim of raising the level of living under socialism; retail prices were regarded solely in the framework of the cost of living.[3]

In the market, prices go up and they go down. Under socialism, Professor Kyn discovered, that was not the case. In reality, the only direction prices were going to be allowed to move was downward—for political reasons, supply and demand be damned.

Indeed, a systematic deflation was seen as essential, because the Marxist labour theory of value implied that, during economic growth, a rise in labour productivity reduced the value of commodities: obviously, the reduction of the labour value of a commodity is inconsistent neither with stable prices nor with inflation. The same sort of over-simplification—in this case on the role of ownership in economic relations—made the planners indifferent on whether surplus product be realized on intermediate or on final products. It accrued to the state at either level and ease of administration favored a levy on final goods. With all this went an unreasoning repudiation of anything evolved by bourgeois economic theories such as market equilibrium, the theory of consumer's behaviour and the concepts of marginal utility and of the elasticity of demand. The incomprehensible rejection of mathematical methods, which, as can be seen today, are eminently applicable to pricing, had the same unfortunate results.

... An excessive centralization rendered a flexible price policy impracticable, for frequent adjustments of prices would have required a vast increase in the quantity of information processed at the center. Had the data been available, it would necessarily have enlarged inordinately the administrative apparatus. But information on changes of demand was not available and, given the priority allotted to industrialization, adjustments of the production pattern would not have been feasible. In this way a long-term disequilibrium on the market arose, a justification of which was sought in the theory that consumption demand had necessarily to exceed production under socialism.[4]

And thus did the socialists and the free-market men come to the same conclusion.

Unhappily, there are sectors of the American economy that are almost as lacking in meaningful prices as those old Soviet shops were. And where the epistemological labor performed by prices goes undone, you may be sure that dysfunction and unhappiness will follow. Most of the occasions that find us lacking good prices are the result of political manipulation of the economy—the allegedly rational government planner overruling prices—but not all of them are. Up until about fifteen years ago, for example, Nasdaq traders indulged a curious habit of quoting stock prices only in quarter-dollar amounts, even though the actual prices were expressed in amounts of one-eighth of a dollar. (This was back in the pre-decimal Dark Ages of the 1990s.) So a stock that might be offered at one and one-eighth dollars ($1.125) would end up being quoted on the market at one and a quarter ($1.25), increasing the traders' profits. It was a terrible system for everybody but the top dealers and, when the practice was exposed and discontinued, spreads on some high-volume stocks, like Microsoft, dropped by half.

But you don't have to go to Wall Street to find prices being hidden and distorted, with ugly consequences for consumers. One of the most bothersome examples is the woeful lack of price transparency in medical procedures in our already half-socialized, soon to be much-more-socialized, healthcare sector.

A few years ago, needing a medical procedure, I conducted an experiment, partly out of curiosity and partly out of dread of dealing with the insurance bureaucrats who are theoretically paid, by me, to provide me with an agreed-upon service, but who in fact earn their pay in no small part by scheming to undermine that agreement. I asked my doctor, "If my insurance will not pay for Procedure X, how much would it cost me to pay for it out of pocket?" Doc X looked at me skeptically, as though I had asked to borrow one of his Ferraris. "Just talk to Alice in our insurance office, and she'll sort out the insurance for you. You may have to jump through some hoops, but they'll cover it." Undeterred (actually, a bit deterred by the many photographs of Ferraris on his office wall), I pressed on: "But, say I didn't have insurance. What would it cost me?"

Doc X: "You have insurance."

Me: "Yes, but if I want to pay for it myself, how much?"

And so on.

He had to consult with his business manager. "We bill the insurance companies $25,000 for Procedure X. If you pay for it out of pocket, we charge $18,000." The fact that different parties are charged wildly different prices is one sign of a defective market.

Me: "So, is that $18,000 flat? Is there sales tax, or anything else?"

Doc X: "The $18,000 is my fee. There's the anesthesiologist, too, and the nurse, and the hospital will have charges, too. And . . . "

And, as it turns out, there was a whole battery of tests, screenings, pre-procedure procedures, etc., necessary before Procedure X.

"So, totaled up, the final bill looks like what?"

Doc X is one of the leading men in his field, a man of great learning, and wit, and rarified taste in fine automobiles. "I have no freaking idea," he said. "You should talk to Alice in insurance." I spent a few days making phone calls, talking to perplexed and befuddled healthcare providers who were absolutely nonplussed by the fact that I wanted to pay them rapidly depreciating American dollars to provide me with healthcare services. The best I could figure was somewhere between $25,000 and $250,000—which is to say, somewhere between a Honda Accord and a Ferrari F430.

So I talked to Alice in insurance. But even if you go through an insurer, it is well nigh impossible to find out in advance how much you will be charged for a particular procedure. Going into a doctor's office for some common blood-work, which was covered by my insurance, I tried, very diligently, to discover what I would be charged. "It depends," the receptionist told me. I had the numbers in front of me: my deductible was X, my co-pay was Y, etc. So, "What's the damage?" She: "I don't know." I called Alice in insurance. She didn't know.

Healthcare prices are a mishmash for lots of reasons, but one of the main ones is that the way we pay for healthcare—Provider A performs Service B for Consumer C and is paid by Insurer D—is an arrangement that gives A and D good incentives to obscure prices, so that C has no idea how good or how rotten a deal he is getting, while A and D attempt to game and swindle each other. Given the terrifying size of serious medical bills—my mother's last stay in the hospital billed out at $360,000 (that's a Ferrari Scaglietti for Doc X plus a BMW 5-Series for one of his kids)— Consumer C, quaking in his paper hospital slippers, no longer even asks, "What does Procedure X cost?" He only asks, "Does my insurance cover it?" No prices, no negotiation, no mystical coordination between producer and consumer—instead, maddening, expensive, and generally sneaky mediation by the insurer.

You can see the attraction of such an arrangement for the socialist central planner, who detects an open invitation to intervene.

Medicine is complicated. Then again, so are computers, but you can call Dell or Apple or Best Buy or whomever and ask, "What does Computer X cost?" and you will receive an answer. And then, when you get to the store—miracle of miracles!—*that will be the price*. Computers are damned complicated to make, with programmers in the United States and India collaborating with microchip fabricators in Taiwan, Dutch LED manufacturers, Irish customer-support agents, etc. Meanwhile, you can't get a doctor *or* an insurer to name a price to fix an ingrown toenail.

If I may make a populist-credibility-destroying admission, I live in New York City and I take yoga classes. Yoga is a super-competitive business in New York—there's big money in sweaty enlightenment. Signing up for a series of classes, I was surprised at the specificity of the prices and the number of options available: there's one rate for a one-off class, a discount for buying 10 classes at once, another for a month's or a year's worth of classes. You can elect to bring your own yoga mat or to rent one, or to buy your own but have the studio store and clean it for you for a fee. There is a menu of options for towels, lockers, etc.

Altogether, I counted nine major variables that could be combined in various iterations to determine the final cost of a yoga class. That means that there are 362,880 permutations of those nine factors. The yoga jock working the front desk at my studio does not, I would guess, enjoy quite as generous a neurological endowment as Doc X but, unlike Doc X, he could tell me what things would cost. He had the prices right there in front of him: magic! I suspect that healthcare would cost less, and that Americans would be much less anxious about it, if rotator-cuff surgeries were priced as transparently as yoga classes or computers or Oreo cookies.

But rather than bring price transparency to healthcare, we're going full-tilt boogie in the opposite direction, specifically by insisting that insurance companies be barred from putting real prices on pre-existing conditions. Set aside, if you can, all those images of poor little children with terrible diseases being chucked out into the Dickensian streets by mean old insurance executives in top hats and monocles, and think, for a second, about what *insurance* means, and what a *pre-existing condition* is.

Insurance is, basically, a bet: Insurer A calculates that the possibility of Problem B befalling Consumer C is X, and so A charges C Premium Z. Actuarially speaking, the number of people who will suffer Problem B is fairly predictable within a large pool of people, so Insurer A can figure out roughly what it will have to pay out every year for every 100,000 policies, and Premium Z will reflect that number. But *predictable* applies to things that happen *in the future*. Maybe 3 percent of those 100,000 people will need to see a cardiologist in a given year, but 100 percent of the people with Pre-Existing Condition X suffer from Pre-Existing Condition X. That's an existential fact. It's what *pre-existing* means.

Unless Governor Schwarzenegger manages to invent *Terminator* insurance, whereby Allstate agents travel back in time to insure you against problems you haven't developed yet, you cannot *insure* against something that *already has happened*, and to pretend otherwise dumps a whole metaphysical can of worms all over the insurance space-time continuum, landing us in an alternative universe where Insurance = Not Insurance.

You'd never take a bet that you knew you were going to lose, right? Insurance companies won't do that, either, unless they get paid to do so—

specifically, unless they are allowed to charge at least as much for covering Pre-Existing Condition X as it's going to cost them to treat Pre-Existing Condition X. Ignoring the reality of prices—waving the magic wand and saying, "There shall be no price put on pre-existing conditions," does not solve the problem. Healthcare costs money. The price is right, and you cannot politically engineer your way out of that reality, no matter how many diabetic toddlers you parade around on CNN.

Healthcare costs consume 17 percent of GDP and are growing at 10 percent a year; we spend about $7,000 per capita on it. Is there anything else you're spending seven grand a year on but can't get a price for? Yes, there is, now that you're heavily invested, through your government, in the financial-services industry, with a diverse portfolio of craptastic investments in mortgage-backed securities, wobbly insurance companies, zombie banks, etc. You'd think that Wall Street suits, of all people, would have been paying attention to prices. But they weren't. There were all sorts of pricing problems leading up to the financial crisis, the fundamental one being that the government wanted housing prices to keep going up but also wanted more and more people to buy houses, i.e. they wanted demand to rise with rising prices rather than to fall as prices went higher—which is to say, they wanted magical pixies to plant unicorn trees and fertilize them with fairy dust.

We could cloak the effects of rising house prices for a long time—about sixty years, as it turned out—through all sorts of schemes, including the mortgage-interest tax deduction, artificially low mortgage-interest rates, and Fannie Mae and Freddie Mac shenanigans. Mortgages, like all loans, entail risk, and risk has a price, too, but we managed to find a way around that, creating a federally chartered cartel of credit-rating agencies— Moody's, Standard & Poor, Fitch—that mindlessly applied the same formula over and over, slapping Triple-A ratings on securities. And it was the Triple-A rating, not the underlying security, that determined the price banks and other investors put on that risk.

The cartel was a favorite tool of such noted national socialist planners as Benito Mussolini and Adolf Hitler, who understood that fewer players in the marketplace meant higher profits (encouraging a level of moral and political elasticity on the part of the cartel bosses) and fewer entities over which to exercise brute-force control when necessary. (It was Caligula who once wished, "Oh, if only all Rome had but one neck"—that he might break it.) We used these cartels to inflate the price of houses, to artificially depress the price of mortgages, and to cloak the price of the risks attached to doing so.

Our central planners believed this would help those of modest means to save and acquire capital. (Never mind that the capital one acquires in a house—the savings—is the equity, and all of these programs encouraged first low-equity mortgages, then no-equity mortgages, and, finally, negative-equity mortgages.) But as even the Soviets found out, prices are not to be denied forever; the price of housing turned around, back down toward its normal, non-politically-adjusted level, taking the price of mortgage-backed securities with it, and sending the cost of borrowing, conversely, through the roof. Boom: financial meltdown. Turned out there was a lot of Triple-A toilet paper in our sausage.

The lesson: don't mess with prices!

So we messed with prices some more. Mark-to-market accounting, the accounting rule that says that banks and other financial institutions must value all the assets on their books at the most recent market price, decimated (and then some) the capital of our banks. Interesting thing about mark-to-market: it creates imaginary prices. If Security A sells at Price X, everybody who owns Security A has to write it down on his books to Price X—even if there is no way in tarnation he'd actually sell it at that price.

Think of it this way: for almost any asset, there will be times when distressed parties sell at a fire-sale price. A degenerate gambler may hock his wife's diamonds during a bad run in Vegas, but that does not mean that the folks at Tiffany's will immediately start selling the same jewelry at the price the pawnbroker paid. Mark-to-market essentially turned the structured-finance markets into a Quentin Tarantino Mexican standoff, with every bank holding a gun to every other bank's head. In that situation, there were no real market prices for lots of those mortgage-backed securities, because everybody was too terrified to buy or sell and establish a theoretical price that, because of accounting rules that do not reflect economic reality, would require them to rebalance their books, to catastrophic results.

Prices do their thing because of the nature of economic information. Information basically comes in two flavors. First, you've got your for-the-ages, centralized, Library of Alexandria–type information, your Big Truths that are relevant at all times for all men. These are things like scientific knowledge and works of history, scholarship, philosophy, the grammars and lexicons of ancient languages—you know: stuff practically nobody ever uses. Second, you have contingent, contextual information of the "Got milk?" variety.

"Got milk?" is an interesting question, as we discussed earlier, because the answer is likely to be different every time you ask. How much milk you and your family need on any given day is likely to vary wildly: if you're whipping up some home-made ice cream for a summertime party, you will probably buy more milk than you usually do. If your daughter goes vegan, you're buying less. Milk is complicated: survey the magnificence of the dairy aisle! You have nearly incalculable choice: 1 percent, 1.5 percent, 2 percent, skim, whole, organic, grass-fed, chocolate, strawberry, half-pints and pints and gallons. I have calculated that such is the complexity of the consumer milk market that the number of possible permutations of milk distributions among the 300 million consumers of the United States over the course of a year surpasses the number of seconds that have passed since the Big Bang. It's one of those numbers they don't even have a word for.

But milk prices in the United States are not set by the market—they are set by milk-pricing bureaucrats, partly in the employ of the U.S. government and partly in the employ of Big Bessy. Now, we know for a fact that, given the enormous number of possible distributions in the dairy market, the allegedly rational planners who set milk prices are not evaluating American milk consumption and production in their full glorious complexity—all the world's supergeniuses working together around the clock could not do that. So, how are they making their decisions?

Nobody really knows, but the Organization for Economic Cooperation and Development estimates that American families pay 26 percent more for milk than they would pay if they paid real prices, i.e. the prices set by a free market. Whoever's interest is being looked after, it isn't the interest of the guy on a tight budget staring down a dry bowl of Count Chocula. And as we continue to pretend there is another unseen economic reality beyond market prices when it comes to healthcare, banking, housing, labor, cotton, sugar, fuel-efficient Japanese cars, solar panels, and every other product with prices distorted by politics—whose interests do you imagine are being served? Yours, chump?

In healthcare, banking, education, and other critical areas, Uncle Sam is putting his big ugly federal boot squarely on the neck of prices, choking off the lifeblood that allows economies to act efficiently and rationally: not *perfectly* efficiently, not *perfectly* rationally—that's the stuff of theoretical models and utopian visions—but to make the best use of the best information we have.

Lowering healthcare costs will require consumers to comparison-shop between providers (insurers, doctors, hospitals, specialists) just as reforming Wall Street will require giving investors real prices for the risks they are bearing—and charging "too big to fail" institutions a real price for the subsidy they now collect from taxpayers. We cannot make intelligent reforms without real prices, because we are blind without them. But given that Washington has been setting the price of milk since 1930 and shows no sign of giving it up, the chances of their abandoning the Gospel of Scientific Socialist Central Planning, and taking up the Gospel of Price, are slim.

Let him with ears, hear.

ACKNOWLEDGMENTS

I am grateful to my friends and colleagues at *National Review*, especially to our editor, Rich Lowry, and our managing editor, Jason Lee Steorts, for their encouragement and criticism, and for allowing me the time to work on this book. My thanks to Sara Towne for her help preparing the manuscript. For their assistance and confidence at critical points over the years, I am particularly grateful to Eva Sorrells, Linda Stogner, Bill Kopf, Scott Stanford, Geoff Henley, Ron Gibson, Eddie the Bullet, the Suklikar family, and my family. I'd like to offer a particular word of acknowledgment to the U.S. government, the State of New York, and the City of New York, who among them will expropriate just about half of whatever proceeds are realized from this book, thereby inspiring the next one.

NOTES

Chapter 1

1. Weekly column by Hugo Chávez, www.Chavez.org.ve.

2. Ann Crittenden, "Growers' Power in Marketing Under Attack," *New York Times*, March 25, 1981, p. 1.

3. Doug Foster, "Forbidden Fruit," *Inquiry*, May 11, 1981, p. 23.

4. John Steinbeck, *The Grapes of Wrath* (New York: Penguin Books, 2002) 348.

5. *Dissent*, Winter 2010

6. Economists distinguish between public and non-public goods on two grounds, features known as *rivalry* and *excludability*. Public goods, under the economic definition, are goods which are non-rivalrous in their consumption and non-excludable in their distribution. If that sounds like academic gobbledygook, a couple of simple examples will make the distinction clear. A rivalrous good is one for which my consumption of one unit of the good leaves one unit less for your consumption. A mango is rivalrous in consumption: Every mango I eat is a mango you cannot eat. But some goods are non-rivalrous: a highway, for instance. If I drive down a mile of highway, that does not leave one less mile for you to drive down.

   But not all non-rivalrous goods are public goods. That highway, for instance, could be a private turnpike. That's where the second criterion, excludability, comes in. Excludable goods are those for which we can limit consumption to paying parties. Those mangos are excludable goods; if you don't pay me, you can't have any of my mangos. But some goods are non-excludable, for instance, a big fireworks display. You could sell tickets to a fireworks display, but people on the periphery would still be able to see the show. Public goods are those goods which are both non-rivalrous and non-excludable.

There are obvious examples of government action, such as national defense and law enforcement, that are classical public goods. But there also are less obvious examples, and it bears keeping in mind that useful public goods will vary from place to place. For instance, in New Delhi, there is a terrible problem with mosquitoes. Each year, hundreds of people die of dengue fever, and many others are sickened by mosquito-borne diseases. So the local authorities conduct mosquito-spraying campaigns at public expense. Mosquito-control is non-rivalrous (a mosquito that is dead to you also is dead to me) and non-excludable (you cannot arrange it so that mosquitoes only refrain from attacking paying parties) and therefore meets the definition of a public good. But a public good is not synonymous with "something that is good for the public at large." Mosquito-spraying in a place with no mosquito problem, for instance, would be a "public good" that is a waste of resources. Likewise, one might argue that there are significant public *benefits* from things like public schooling, government-subsidized health-care programs, and Amtrak, but those things, whether we like them or not, do not meet the technical definition of a public *good*.

7. Roger Kimball, "The Death of Socialsim," *The New Criterion*, April 2002; available at: http://www.newcriterion.com/articles.cfm/socialism-kimball-1985 [accessed October 21, 2010].

8. Zbigniew Brzezenski, *The Grand Failure* (New York: Scribner, 1989), 63.

9. Ludwig von Mises, *Socialism* (Ludwig von Mises Institute, 1981), 56.

Chapter 2

1. Absurdum, comment on "Communism vs. Capitalism," Convince Me: Start a Debate, comment posted Feb 2, 2007; available at: http://www.convinceme.net/coldebate/162/Capitalism-vs-Communism.html [accessed August 3, 2010].

2. yolei36, comment on "Communism vs. Capitalism," Convince Me: Start a Debate, comment posted Feb 2, 2007; available at: http://www.convinceme.net/coldebate/162/Capitalism-vs-Communism.html [accessed August 3, 2010].

3. mg41, comment on "Communism vs. Capitalism," Convince Me: Start a Debate, comment posted Feb 2, 2007; available at: http://www.convinceme.net/coldebate/162/Capitalism-vs-Communism.html [accessed August 3, 2010].

4. enricofrole, comment on "Communism vs. Capitalism," Convince Me: Start a Debate, comment posted Feb 2, 2007; available at: http://www.convinceme.net/coldebate/162/Capitalism-vs-Communism.html [accessed August 3, 2010].

5. Zbigniew Brzezenski, *The Grand Failure* (New York: Scribner, 1989), 212.

6. Karl Marx, *Capital*, ed. Friedrich Engels, trans. Samuel Moore and Edward Aveling (New York: Random House, 1906), 46.

7. Karl Marx, *The Poverty of Philosophy* (Chicago: Charles H. Kerr & Co., 1910), 56.

8. Adam Smith, *An Inquiry into the Nature and Causes of the Wealth of Nations,* Volume 1 (University of Lausanne, 1791), 45.

9. Karl Marx, *Capital*, ed. Friedrich Engels, trans. Samuel Moore and Edward Aveling (New York: Random House, 1906), 257.

10. Karl Marx, *"Theses on Feuerbach,"* trans. W. Lough, in *Marx/Engels Selected Works: Volume I* (Moscow, USSR: Progress Publishers, 1969), 15; available at: http://www.marxists.org/archive/marx/works/1845/theses/theses.htm [accessed August 5, 2010].

Chapter 3

1. Ludwig von Mises, *Socialism* (Ludwig von Mises Institute, 1981), 135–36.

2. Joseph Stalin, "Dialectical and Historical Materialism," in the Josef Stalin Internet Archive; available at:

http://www.marxists.org/reference/archive/stalin/works/1938/09.htm [accessed August 5, 2010].

3. Francis Spufford, *Red Plenty* (Faber & Faber, 2010).

4. Ludwig von Mises, *Interventionism, An Economic Analysis* (Foundation for Economic Education, 1998).

5. David Miller, "F.A. Hayek: Dogmatic Skeptic," *Dissent*, summer 1994.

Chapter 4

1. David Horowitz, "The Two Christophers," FrontPageMagazine, July 6, 2010; available at: http://frontpagemag.com/2010/07/06/the-two-christophers/ [accessed August 5, 2010].

2. Ibid.

3. Louis Uchitelle, "Paul Sweezey, 93, Marxist Publisher and Economist, Dies," *New York Times*, March 2, 2004.

4. Paul Sweezey and Leo Huberman, "Introduction to Socialism," *Monthly Review*; available at: http://www.skeptically.org/socialism/id18.html [accessed August 5, 2010].

5. Ibid.

6. Paul Sweezy and Leo Huberman, "Introduction to Socialism," *Monthly Review*, 1968.

7. Srinivas Murthy, *Mahatma Gandhi and Leo Tolstoy Letters* (Long Beach Publications: Long Beach, 1987), 189.

8. Sue, "Of Rural Welfare and Simplistic Living," A Schizoid Dream, August 16, 2005; available at: http://logicalschizoid.blogspot.com/2005/08/of-rural-welfare-and-simplistic-living.html [accessed August 10, 2010].

9. Mani Bhavan Gandhi Sangrahalaya, "Gandhi's 11 Vows," Mani Bhavan Gandhi Sangrahalaya: Mahatma Gandhi Information Website; available at: http://www.gandhi-manibhavan.org/gandhiphilosophy/philosophy_11vows.htm [accessed August 5, 2010].

10. Surur Hoda, "Schumacher on Gandhi," *Gandhi and the Contemporary World*, ed. Antony Copley and George Paxton (India: Indo-British Historical Society, 1997).

11. Gurcharan Das, "India: How a rich nation became poor and will become rich again," Gurcharan Das (Official Website), posted March 18, 2007; available at: http://gurcharandas.org/?page_id=70 [accessed August 5, 2010].

12. Milton Friedman, "Mahalanobis's Plan," *The Statesman*, November 26, 2006.

13. Jagdish N. Bhagwati, *India in Transition: Freeing the Economy*, 1993.

14. Ibid.

15. Gurcharan Das, "India: How a rich nation became poor and will become rich again," Gurcharan Das (Official Website), posted March 18, 2007; available at: http://gurcharandas.org/?page_id=70 [accessed August 5, 2010].

16. Ibid.

Chapter 5

1. John Fund, "Still the One," *The American*, published by the American Enterprise Institute, March/April 2007.

2. Sir Charles Phillip Haddon-Cave in "Intervention True to Guiding Policy," Joseph Yam, *South China Morning Post*, August 24, 1998.

3. "Old Deluder Act (1647)" in Records of the Governor and Company of the Massachusetts Bay in New England, 1853; available at: http://www.constitution.org/primarysources/deluder.html [accessed August 9, 2010].

4. Martin Luther, "Letter to the German Rulers, 1524" in *Education: Compulsory and Free*, Murray N. Rothbard (Auburn, Alabama: Ludwig von Mises Institute, 1999), 20.

5. Calvin Stowes in *Separating School & State: How to Liberate America's Families*, Sheldon Richman (Fairfax, Virginia: Future of Freedom Foundation, 1995), 46.

6. Barack Obama, "Prepared Remarks of President Barack Obama: Back to School Event," (remarks presented at Wakefield High School, Arlington, Virginia, September 8, 2009).

7. Nicweb, "Dear Repubs: Public Schools are Socialist . . . ," Daily Kos, posted September 6, 2009; available at: http://www.dailykos.com/story/2009/9/6/777995/-Dear-Repubs:-Public-Schools-Are-Socialist..- [accessed August 6, 2010].

8. Patrick Allitt, "What's All the Fuss?," *New York Times*, September 15, 2009.

9. Jerry Webster, Jerry Webster's Special Education Blog, September 18, 2010; available at: http://specialed.about.com/b/2010/09/18/give-socialism-a-chance.htm [accessed October 22, 2010].

10. "Capitalism vs. Socialism," Helium.net; available at: http://www.helium.com/debates/188058-capitalism-emsocialismem-which-prefer/side_by_side?page=10 [accessed October 22, 2010].

11. Murray Rothbard, *For a New Liberty: The Libertarian Manifesto* (Auburn, Alabama: Ludwig von Mises Institute, 2006), 160–61.

12. Newton Bateman in *For a New Liberty: The Libertarian Manifesto*, Murray Rothbard (Auburn, Alabama: Ludwig von Mises Institute, 2006), 153.

13. Ibid.

14. Robert Dale Owen in *Separating School & State: How to Liberate America's Families*, by Sheldon Richman (Fairfax, Virginia: Future of Freedom Foundation, 1995), 46.

15. William Seawell in *Separating School & State: How to Liberate America's Families*, by Sheldon Richman (Fairfax, Virginia: Future of Freedom Foundation, 1995), 51.

16. Ibid.

17. Daniel Henniner, "Failure Starts Young: School is for: a) diversity b) learning to read?" *Wall Street Journal*, January 24, 2003, Opinion Pages.

18. "D.C.'s Successful Voucher Program Deserves a Second Life," *Washington Post*, June 23, 2010.

Chapter 6

1. Paul Craig Roberts, "My Time with Soviet Economics," *The Independent Review*, v. VII, n. 2, Fall 2002, 259–64.

2. *Improving America's Schools: The Role of Incentives*, edited by Eric A. Hanushek and Dale W. Jorgenson. Board on Science, Technology, and Economic Policy, National Research Council, 1996.

3. Eric Hanushek, "Outcomes, Costs,and Incentives in Schools," *Improving America's Schools: The Role of Incentives, National Research Council* (Washington, D.C.: National Academy Press, 1996), 29–52.

Chapter 7

1. Hamish McRae, "The Most Successful Society on the Planet," *Independent*, September 20, 2006.

2. Poly Toynbee, "The Most Successful Society the World has Ever Known," *Guardian*, October 25, 2005.

3. "SWEDEN: Something Souring in Utopia," *Time*, July 19, 1976; available at: http://www.time.com/time/magazine/article/0,9171,914329-1,00.html [accessed August 10, 2010].

4. Jesse Larner, "Who's Afraid of Friedrich Hayek? The Obvious Truths and Mystical Fallacies of a Hero of the Right," *Dissent*, Winter 2008; available at: http://dissentmagazine.org/article/?article=992 [accessed August 9, 2010].

5. Ibid.

6. Ibid.

7. Milton Friedman in "Is Sweden a False Utopia?" Nima Sanandaji, *Newgeography*; available at: http://www.newgeography.com/content/001543-is-sweden-a-false-utopia [accessed August 9, 2010].

8. "Obama: No 'Easy Out' for Wall Street," Transcript: Terry Moran Interviews President Obama, *ABC News*, February 10, 2009; available at: http://abcnews.go.com/Politics/Business/story?id=6844330&page=1 [accessed August 9, 2010].

9. Christina Patterson, "The One Problem with this Lovely Swedish Utopia," *The Independent*, September 10, 2008; available at:

http://www.independent.co.uk/opinion/commentators/christina-patterson/christina-patterson-the-one-problem-with-this-lovely-swedish-utopia-924461.html [accessed August 9, 2010].

10. Johan Norberg, "Swedish Models," *The National Interest*, January 6, 2006; available at: http://www.nationalinterest.org/Article.aspx?id=11488 [accessed August 9, 2010].

11. Zbigniew Brzezenski, *The Grand Failure* (Scribner, 1989), 263–64.

12. Johan Norberg, "Swedish Models," *The National Interest*, January 6, 2006; available at: http://www.nationalinterest.org/Article.aspx?id=11488 [accessed August 9, 2010].

13. Tino Sanandaji, "David Brooks Uses Some of My Figures," Super-Economy: Kurdish-Swedish Perspectives on the American Economy, May 5, 2010; available at: http://super-economy.blogspot.com/2010/05/david-brooks-uses-some-of-my-figures.html [accessed August 10, 2010].

Chapter 8

1. Kim Jong Il, "On the Juche Idea," (treatise presented at the National Seminar on the Juche Idea held to mark the 70th birthday of the Great Leader Comrade Kim Il Sung, March 31, 1982); available at: http://www1.korea-np.co.jp/pk/062nd_issue/98092410.htm [accessed August 10, 2010].

2. Ibid.

3. *The Black Book of Communism*, Mark Kramer, ed. (Harvard University Press, 1999), 4.

4. Mitchell Lerner, "Making Sense of the 'Hermit Kingdom': North Korea in the Nuclear Age," *Origins*, December 2008 vol. 2 issue 3; available at: http://ehistory.osu.edu/osu/origins/article.cfm?articleid=21&articlepage=1&altcontent=no [accessed August 10, 2010].

5. Jim Kay in "Making Sense of the 'Hermit Kingdom': North Korea in the Nuclear Age," Mitchell Lerner, *Origins*, December 2008 vol. 2 issue 3; available at: http://ehistory.osu.edu/osu/origins/article.cfm?articleid=21&articlepage=1&altcontent=no [accessed August 10, 2010].

6. Kongdan Oh in "Understanding Kim Jong-il," Laura McClure, Salon.com, January 10, 2003; available at: http://dir.salon.com/news/feature/2003/01/10/korea/index.html [accessed August 10, 2010].

7. Anonymous in "Making Sense of the 'Hermit Kingdom': North Korea in the Nuclear Age," Mitchell Lerner, *Origins*, December 2008 vol. 2 issue 3; available at: http://ehistory.osu.edu/osu/origins/article.cfm?articleid=21&articlepage=1&altcontent=no [accessed August 10, 2010].

8. Owen Miller, "North Korea's Hidden History," *International Socialism*, February 3, 2006.

9. Juche Idea Study Group of England, "Juche Idea Study Group of England"; available at: http://www.korea-dpr.com/users/jisge/ [accessed October 26, 2010].

10. Joseph Stalin, "Dialectical and Historical Materialism," in the Josef Stalin Internet Archive; available at: http://www.marxists.org/reference/archive/stalin/works/1938/09.htm [accessed August 10, 2010].

11. Ibid.

12. Kim Jong Il, "On Some Problems of Education in the Jucha Idea," July 15, 1986; available at: http://ndfsk.dyndns.org/kuguk8/juche/06.html [accessed August 10, 2010].

Chapter 9

1. "Environmental Disaster or Communism There is No Third Way," *The Internationalists*, September 1, 2008; available at: http://www.leftcom.org/en/articles/2009-11-24/environmental-disaster-or-communism-there-is-no-third-way [accessed August 10, 2010].

2. Philippe Rekacewicz, "Environmental Disaster in Eastern Europe," *Le Monde diplomatique*, July 19, 2000; available at: http://mondediplo.com/2000/07/19envidisaster [accessed August 10, 2010].

3. Ibid.

4. Joseph W. Dellapenna, "Behind the Red Curtain: Environmental Concerns and the End of Communism" (Villanova University School of Law, 2010); available at: http://www.probeinternational.org/files/Behind%20the%20Red%20Curtain%20—%20Environmental%20Concerns%20and%20the%20End%20of%20Communism.pdf [available at October 26, 2010].

5. Eusebio Gonzalez in "Mexico's Giant Polluter: Will Privatization Force Premex to Clean Up Its Act?" Joel Simon, *Global Community Monitor*; available at: http://www.gcmonitor.org/article.php?id=391 [accessed August 10, 2010].

6. Betty Ferber in "Mexico's Giant Polluter: Will Privatization Force Premex to Clean Up Its Act?" Joel Simon, *Global Community Monitor*; available at: http://www.gcmonitor.org/article.php?id=391 [accessed August 10, 2010].

7. Joel Simon, "Mexico's Giant Polluter: Will Privatization Force Premex to Clean Up Its Act?" *Global Community Monitor*; available at: http://www.gcmonitor.org/article.php?id=391 [accessed August 10, 2010].

8. Chris Haslam, "Oil Prospecting in Gabon," *Wildlife Extra*, October 2006; available at: http://www.wildlifeextra.com/go/news/60 [accessed August 10, 2010].

9. Ibid.

10. Joseph W. Dellapenna, "Behind the Red Curtain: Environmental Concerns and the End of Communism," *Villanova University Legal Working Paper Series*, Working Paper 152; available at: http://law.bepress.com/villanovalwps/papers/art152/ [accessed October 26, 2010].

11. "Garbage islands threaten China's Three Gorges dam," Reuters; available at: http://www.reuters.com/article/idUSTRE6710SH20100802 [accessed October 26, 2010].

Chapter 10

1. Peter DeShazo, "Venezuela Forum: Conclusions and Future Implications: A Report of the CSIS Americas Program," April 2008.

2. Ludwig von Mises, *Socialism* (Ludwig von Mises Institute, 1981), 216.

3. Adolf Hitler in *The Duel: the Eighty-Day Struggle Between Churchill and Hitler*, John Lukacs (New Haven: Yale University Press, 1990), 223.

4. "Fidel: 'Cuban Model Doesn't Even Work For Us Anymore,'" *The Atlantic*; available at: http://www.theatlantic.com/international/archive/2010/09/fidel-cuban-model-doesnt-even-work-for-us-anymore/62602/ [accessed October 26, 2010].

5. John Lukacs, *The Duel: the Eighty-Day Struggle Between Churchill and Hitler* (New Haven: Yale University Press, 1990), 223.

6. Thor Halvorssen, "Behind Exhumation of Simon Bolívar is Hugo Chávez's Warped Obsession," *The Washington Post*, July 25, 2010.

7. Ibid.

8. Christopher Hitchens, "Hugo Boss: What I Learned About Hugo Chávez's Mental Health When I Visited Venezuela with Sean Penn," *Slate*, August 2, 2010; available at: http://www.slate.com/id/2262520 [accessed August 10, 2010].

9. John-Jacques Rousseau, *The Social Contract* (New York: Cosimo Classics, 2008), 14.

10. Ibid., 34.

11. Howard Wiarda, "Venezuela Alert: Understanding Chavez," *Hemisphere Focus*, September 18, 2001; available at: http://csis.org/files/media/csis/pubs/hf_v09_04.pdf [accessed November 11, 2010].

12. Ibid.

Chapter 11

1. *International Socialist Review* Issue 13, August-September 2000.

2. "Nationalism in the Soviet Union," Russian History Encyclopedia; available at: http://www.answers.com/topic/nationalism-in-the-soviet-union [accessed October 27, 2010].

3. Ibid.

4. Peter Hays Gries, "Nationalism, Indignation, and China's Japan Policy," *SAIS Review*, Vol. 25, No. 2, Summer–Fall 2005, pp. 105–14.

5. Faustino Ballvé, *Essentials of Economics*, Ludwig von Mises Institute, 2008.

6. Ibid.

7. *The Sunday Times* (London), April 31, 2009.

Chapter 12

1. "The Long Shadow of the Visible Hand," *Wall Street Journal*, May 22, 2010.

2. "Why Dilma Rousseff Is Still a Good Bet," *Foreign Policy*, October 19, 2010.

3. Jeff Merkley, "America Over a Barrel," Merkley for Senate.

4. Ibid.

5. Ibid., 2.

6. "Time to End Oil Dependence," *Energy Independence Now*, July 23, 2010.

7. Merkley, "America Over a Barrel," 2.

8. Ibid.

9. Ibid., 3.

10. Ibid., 4.

11. Ibid., 6, 7, 10.

12. "Time to End Oil Dependence," *Energy Independence Now*, July 23, 2010.

13. "America Is Addicted to Oil," www.pickensplan.com, 2010.

14. David Field, "On 40th birthday, interstates face expensive midlife crisis," *Insight on the News*; available at: http://findarticles.com/p/articles/mi_m1571/is_n28_v12/ai_18524905/ [accessed October 27, 2010].

15. Ibid.

Chapter 13

1. *Letters of Eugene V. Debs*, vol. 1, J. Robert Constantine, ed. (Urbana: University of Illinois Press, 1990), 82–83.

2. Michael Kazin, *Dissent*, Summer 2010.

3. "Is Dodd Bill Socialist? Don't Make Socialists Laugh," *The Nation*, July 12, 2010.

4. Robert Higgs, "How War Amplified Federal Power in the Twentieth Century," *The Freeman*, July 1, 1999.

5. Ibid.

6. Jonah Goldberg, *Liberal Fascism*, 107.

7. *Current History I: A Monthly Magazine of the New York Times*, Vol. III, 1916, p. 683.

8. Fred Siegel, "1919: Betrayal and the Birth of Modern Liberalism," *City Journal*, Nov 22, 2009; available at: http://www.city-journal.org/2009/eon1122fs.html [accessed October 27, 2010].

9. Bruce Caldwell, "Hayek and Socialism," *Journal of Economic Literature*, vol. 35, December 1997.

10. Ibid., 1856–90.

11. Margaret L. Coit, *Mr. Baruch* (Boston: Houghton Muffin Co., 1957), 219. As quoted in Murry Rothbard's "War Collectivism in World War I," from *A New History of Leviathan*, Ronald Radosh and Murray N. Rothbard, eds. (New York: E.P. Dutton & Co., 1972).

Chapter 14

1. Dan Jakopovich, "In the Belly of the Beast: Challenging U.S. Imperialism and the Politics of the Offensive," Committees of Correspondence for Democracy and Socialism, 2010.

2. Ibid.

3. Ibid.

4. Ibid.

5. Ibid.

6. Ibid.

7. Ryan O'Donnell, "ANSWER's Steering Committee," *FrontPage Magazine*, March 12, 2003.

8. Slavoj Žižek, "A Permanent Economic Emergency," *New Left Review*, July-Aug 2010.

9. Ibid.

10. Adam Shaw, "Obama's Socialism," *American Thinker*; available at: http://www.americanthinker.com/2010/02/obamas_socialism.html [accessed November 2, 2010].

11. Johnathan Derbyshire, "I am a Leninist. Lenin wasn't afraid to dirty his hands. If you can get power, grab it," *New Statesman*; available at: http://www.newstatesman.com/ideas/2009/11/381-382-interview-obama-theory [accessed November 2, 2010].

Chapter 15

1. Robin Blackburn, "Socialism and the Current Crisis," *Dissent*, Summer 2010; available at: http://www.dissentmagazine.org/article/? article=3263 [accessed November 3, 2010].

2. Transcript, *The Guardian*, September 10, 2009; available at: http://www.guardian.co.uk/world/2009/sep/10/barack-obama-healthcare-reform-speech-full-text [accessed November 3, 2010].

3. David Dranove, "The Accidental Socialists," *Code Red*, August 28, 2010.

4. Donald Berwick, "A Transatlantic Review of the NHS at 60," Physicians for a National Health Program; available at: http://www.pnhp.org/news/2010/may/a-transatlantic-review-of-the-nhs-at-60 [accessed November 3, 2010].

5. "Barrasso slams Berwick appointment: Obama 'intentionally' misled," *Washington Examiner*, July 7, 2010; available at: http://www.washingtonexaminer.com/opinion/blogs/beltway-confidential/barrasso-slams-berwick-appointment-obama-intentionally-misled-97977404.html [accessed November 3, 2010].

6. "Confirmation fight on Health Chief," *New York Times*, June 21, 2010; available at: http://www.nytimes.com/2010/06/22/health/policy/22medicare.html [accessed November 3, 2010].

7. "Obama's Nominee to Run Medicare: 'Please Don't Put Your Faith in Market Forces,'" CNS News, May 24, 2010; available at: http://www.cnsnews.com/news/article/66553 [accessed November 3, 2010].

8. Sen. Jon Kyl, "No Chance to Question Donald Berwick's Dangerous Views," Heartland Institute, September 2010.

9. Philip Klein, "Obama's Rationing Man," *American Spectator*, May 13, 2010; available at: http://spectator.org/archives/2010/05/13/obamas-rationing-man/print [accessed November 3, 2010].

10. "Will Donald Berwick Ration Healthcare? Conservatives Pounce on Obama Appointee," CBS News; available at: http://www.cbsnews.com/8301-504763_162-20009880-10391704.html [accessed November 3, 2010].

11. "Confirmation fight on Health Chief," *New York Times*, June 21, 2010; available at: http://www.nytimes.com/2010/06/22/health/ policy/22medicare.html [accessed November 3, 2010].

12. "Health Patients suffer from NHS rationing," BBC News, January 7, 1999; available at: http://news.bbc.co.uk/2/hi/health/249938.stm [accessed November 3, 2010].

13. Ibid.

14. Ibid.

15. Chapter 13 of "Report of the Committee of Inquiry into Allegations of Ill-Treatment of Patients and other irregularities at the Ely Hospital, Cardiff," Socialist Health Association; available at: http://www.sochealth. co.uk/history/Ely13.htm [accessed November 3, 2010].

16. Michael Cooper, "Rationing Health Care," p. 87. As cited by John Goodman in *National Health Care in Great Britain: Lessons for the U.S.A.* (Fisher Institute Publications, 1980).

17. John Goodman, Ibid.

18. Interview published by NHS in July 2008.

19. "Does Preventive Care Save Money? Health Economics and the Presidential Candidates," *New England Journal of Medicine*; available at: http://www.nejm.org/doi/full/10.1056/NEJMp0708558 [November 3, 2010].

20. John Goodman, *National Health Care in Great Britain: Lessons for the U.S.A.* (Fisher Institute Publications, 1980).

21. Video available at: http://www.youtube.com/watch?v=fpAyan1fXCE [accessed November 3, 2010].

22. Video, Breitbart TV; available at: http://www.breitbart.tv/exposed-expanding-medicare-has-been-obamas-plan-to-get-to-single-payer-all-along/ [accessed November 3, 2010].

23. Audio, Breitbart TV; available at: http://www.breitbart.tv/exposed-expanding-medicare-has-been-obamas-plan-to-get-to-single-payer-all-along/ [accessed November 3, 2010].

24. "Transcript: Rangel and Demint" on "FNS," FoxNews.com; available at: http://www.foxnews.com/story/0,2933,536263,00.html [accessed November 3, 2010].

25. Transcript, "Obama speaks at House Republican retreat in Baltimore," *Washington Post*, http://projects.washingtonpost.com/obama-speeches/speech/173/ [accessed November 10, 2010].

Epilogue

1. Ludwig von Mises, *Socialism* (Ludwig von Mises Institute, 1981), 137.

2. O. Kyn, "The Role of Prices in a Socialist Economy," in M. C. Kaser ed., *Economic Development for Eastern Europe* (Macmillan, 1968).

3. Ibid.

4. Ibid.

INDEX